God and Israel

God and Israel

Providence and Purpose in Romans 9–11

Todd D. Still
Editor

BAYLOR UNIVERSITY PRESS

Waco, Texas 76798

Cover Design by Cindy Dunne
Cover image: Eighth-century mosaic of St. Paul the Apostle; a feature of the papal Lateran Palace, now on display in the Vatican Museums, Rome.

This book has been cataloged by the Library of Congress
with the ISBN 978-1-4813-0702-4.

Printed in the United States of America on acid-free paper with a minimum of 30 percent post-consumer waste recycled content.

Contents

Preface

Todd D. Still

It is hard to believe that roughly three years have now passed since Beverly Roberts Gaventa, Bruce W. Longenecker, and I sat over salads, sandwiches, and sodas at Newk's Eatery in Waco to begin brainstorming about the possibility of hosting a New Testament colloquy at Baylor. At that point in time, Beverly had just joined the Baylor University religion faculty as a distinguished professor, and the three of us were eager to begin collaborating together. (Bruce had come to Baylor five years earlier, and I five years earlier still.)

Unsurprisingly, it took three Pauline scholars very little time to gravitate toward a symposium topic related to Paul. As to why Romans 9–11, there appears, at least in retrospect, to have been three main reasons: (1) We had all been working on Romans off and on in recent years. (Given that Beverly is writing a commentary on Romans for the New Testament Library, her work on Romans has been more on than off!) (2) While still on faculty at Princeton Theological Seminary, Beverly had coordinated a conference on Romans 5–8 held in May 2012 in conjunction with that venerable institution's bicentennial. (As it happens, Baylor University Press published the plenary papers read at the aforementioned conference in 2013 under the title *Apocalyptic Paul: Cosmos and Anthropos in Romans 5–8*.) (3) Not only did investigation into Romans 9–11 follow nicely and naturally from that event, but it is also a passage that requires and repays careful, ongoing inquiry. Indeed, ever since Phoebe (presumably) read and sought to explicate Romans to groups of believers scattered over the epicenter of the Empire, recipients and interpreters alike have puzzled over and been perplexed by a passage where the apostle agonizes and anguishes over God's purposes for God's people.

Fortunately, we three did not have to go hunting for funding for the gathering. Rather, due to the magnanimity of the Drumwright family and friends, we were able to program and conduct the colloquy under the auspices of the Minette and Huber Lelland Drumwright Jr. Colloquium on New Testament Studies. The primary challenge before Beverly, Bruce, and me, then, was to enlist New Testament colleagues to prepare and offer addresses for that occasion. Thankfully, Simon Gathercole, Ann Jervis, Jonathan Linebaugh, Davina Lopez, Ross Wagner, and Michael Wolter graciously accepted our invitation and agreed to treat certain aspects of Romans 9–11. What one finds here, then, is not a verse-by-verse treatment of those chapters. Instead, one discovers within this book's covers exploratory and explanatory probes into various texts and topics contained in the rich depths that are Romans 9–11.

Were it not for the effort of the contributors to turn papers into chapters and for the willingness of Carey C. Newman and Baylor University Press to publish these essays, it is possible that their impact would have been confined to the audiences that were fortunate to hear them initially presented at Baylor University's George W. Truett Theological Seminary in late November 2014. Thankfully, the salient insights of six leading Pauline scholars into Romans 9–11 are now available to all who would dare to think with Paul about the unsearchable judgments and untraceable ways of a God from whom, through whom, and unto whom are all things (Rom 11:33-36).

1
Promise and Purpose in Romans 9:1-13
Toward Understanding Paul's View of Time

L. Ann Jervis

In what follows I ask a question of Paul for which he offers neither a direct answer nor explicit discourse: what is the apostle's conception of time?[1] Despite the necessity—shared by all Pauline interpreters—of working with hints rather than clear evidence, this is a question that begs to be asked for at least two reasons: First, interpreters of Paul are heavily invested in the apostle's view of time. Second, there is currently a stalemate in Pauline scholarship between the salvation historical and apocalyptic interpretative frameworks. I will begin by examining the first reason, and will then move on to the second.

Scholars with salvation historical or apocalyptic convictions about Paul, in particular, interpret certain passages in relation to their views concerning Paul's conception of time.[2] Salvation historical interpreters regard Paul's conception of time as linear: Time moves forward under

[1] The critiques and observations of four generous and wise readers have strengthened this chapter. I record their names here not as a claim that they endorse my work in its entirety, but out of my immense gratitude. Thanks are due to my colleagues in New Testament Studies, Prof. Ross Wagner and Prof. Jonathan Linebaugh; to my colleague at the University of Toronto, Prof. David Townsend; and to Andy Witt, a doctoral student in Bible at Wycliffe College, University of Toronto.

[2] For a fine analysis of the difference that views about time make for interpretation, see D. Harink, "Time and Politics in Four Commentaries on Romans," in *Paul, Philosophy and the Theopolitical Vision*, ed. Douglas Harink (Eugene, Ore.: Cascade, 2010), 282–312.

the direction of God. Time, understood as human history, is progressing ahead in divinely ordained stages.[3]

The apocalyptic reading claims that Paul is convinced, in the words of one of the most generative of current apocalyptic interpreters M. de Boer, that "believers . . . live at the juncture of the ages where the forces of the new age . . . are in an ongoing struggle with the forces of the old age."[4] In this view, Paul adapted Jewish apocalyptic eschatology in light of Christ. And believers in Christ know that "the future has invaded the present."[5] Apocalyptic interpreters claim, then, that Paul conceived of the present time as having been invaded by the future time,[6] and so, as it is often said, time is now "already/not yet."[7] As de Boer describes, there is "tension between an 'already' (God has already acted apocalyptically to liberate human beings from enslaving powers) and a 'still more' (God has not yet

[3] N. T. Wright describes this idea in terms of chapters. "It is not simply that Paul alludes to a number of well-known narratives . . . Paul's whole point is precisely that with the coming, the death and the resurrection of Jesus the Messiah a *new chapter* has opened within the story in which he had believed himself to be living. . . . [T]he great stories of Abraham, of Exodus, of David . . . , and of exile and restoration . . . create not merely a rich narrative backcloth . . . but . . . a single narrative *line*, containing typological recapitulations but not reducible to them, in which Paul believed that he and his contemporaries were living" (*Paul: In Fresh Perspective* [Minneapolis: Fortress, 2005], 9; emphasis added). For Wright's more detailed presentation, see *Paul and the Faithfulness of God*, 2 vols. (Minneapolis: Fortress, 2013), 1:456–537.

[4] M. de Boer, *Galatians: A Commentary* (Louisville, Ky.: Westminster John Knox, 2011), 34.

[5] de Boer, *Galatians*, 389.

[6] The image of invasion is found particularly in the works of J. L. Martyn and de Boer. In Martyn's case this is due to a particular translation of *apocalyptô* (which he reads in the context of verbs that he translates as "to come on the scene" and "to send into the scene" [Martyn, *Galatians* (New York: Doubleday, 1997), 99]). In addition, both Martyn and de Boer think that Paul was influenced by what de Boer categorizes as "Jewish cosmological apocalyptic eschatology." This is a kind of eschatology that expects "the powers of the new age (God and those whom he delegates, such as the Messiah) [to] . . . invade the orb of the powers on earth below" (de Boer, *Galatians*, 34). B. R. Gaventa implies the idea of invasion in her presentation of cosmic battle imagery in Paul: "God wages war against anti-God powers" ("The Cosmic Power of Sin in Paul's Letter to the Romans: Toward a Widescreen Version," *Int* 58, no. 3 [2004]: 229–40, 236).

[7] Salvation historical interpreters also use this description (e.g., J. D. G. Dunn, *The Theology of Paul the Apostle* [Grand Rapids: Eerdmans, 1998], 466), although rather than speaking of an invasion of the new age they speak in terms of a process (461).

finished the job)."[8] This tension will end when what is now only inaugurated is all that remains. Apocalyptic interpreters typically speak of what has been inaugurated but not completed as the future, new age[9] or the new creation.[10]

Moreover, the apocalyptic reading connects space and time: the two ages are both "temporal categories" and "spatial categories."[11] Thanks to de Boer,[12] Pauline apocalyptic interpreters typically understand the two ages in light of Jewish cosmological apocalyptic eschatology in which "the two ages are not simply, or even primarily, temporal categories, referring to two successive, discontinuous periods of world history ('ages'): they are also spatial categories, referring to two spheres or orbs of power, both of which claim sovereignty over the world."[13] The two ages (the present age and the future/new age/new creation) are structured by different powers: this age by anti-god powers[14] and the age to come by God. These two interpretative frameworks about Paul's view of time deeply affect interpretation of his letters.[15]

[8] de Boer, *Galatians*, 34.

[9] de Boer works with "the future" (*Galatians*, 389) and the "new age," which he also refers to as the kingdom of God (34).

[10] Martyn, *Galatians*, and *Theological Issues in the Letters of Paul* (Edinburgh: T&T Clark, 1997), e.g., 120.

[11] de Boer, *Galatians*, 33.

[12] M. de Boer, "Paul and Jewish Apocalyptic Eschatology," in *Apocalyptic and the New Testament: Essays in Honor of J. Louis Martyn*, ed. J. Marcus and M. L. Soards (Sheffield: JSOT, 1989), 169–90.

[13] de Boer, *Galatians*, 33.

[14] B. Gaventa regularly uses this term to describe the powers of this age; e.g., "Interpreting the Death of Jesus Apocalyptically," in *Jesus and Paul Reconnected: Fresh Pathways in an Old Debate*, ed. T. D. Still (Grand Rapids: Eerdmans, 2007), 125–45, 136.

[15] Of course, there are other important frameworks for understanding Paul's view of time and consequently his meaning in particular passages. Another framework is what Harink helpfully calls "gospel time in secular history" ("Time and Politics," 285). Harink uses for his example R. Jewett's Hermeneia commentary on Romans, which seeks to understand the entire letter in its first century context (285–89). R. Jewett's assumption is that Paul thought of time the same way his Greco-Roman contemporaries did (*Romans*, Hermeneia [Minneapolis: Fortress, 2007]). H. D. Betz' Hermeneia commentary on Galatians [Minneapolis: Fortress, 1989] could be adduced as another example of working entirely with historical time. Consequently, Betz' interpretation of, for instance, the phrase "the present evil age" (Gal 1:4) is significantly different from that of Martyn or de Boer.

The second pressing reason for interrogating Paul's view of time follows from the first: the current stalemate in Pauline scholarship between the salvation historical and apocalyptic interpretative frameworks. It seems the right moment to raise the question again. I will now speak to Paul's use of the concepts of promise and God's purpose of election in Romans 9:1-13 in hopes of offering some fresh suggestions about how Paul might have thought about time.[16]

Briefly, let me emphasize that I am exploring what *Paul* might have thought about time. Before engaging with my investigation, then, it may be necessary for my readers to identify their assumptions about what time may or may not be—assumptions based on education in physics or philosophy, based on ordinary experience of time, or based on theological convictions such as are evidenced in the salvation historical and apocalyptic interpretations.

Promise, But Not Fulfillment

In what follows we will see that Paul refers to promise/s without, as one would expect, also referring to fulfillment of the promise/s. I will suggest that this says something about Paul's view of time. Paul thinks of God's promise/s chiefly in the context not of the human linear experience of time, but rather in the context of the life of God—God's time.

Promise in Romans 9:4-13. One of the curiosities, among many, of Romans 9–11 is that though Paul affirms that the promises belong to the Israelites (οἵτινές εἰσιν Ἰσραηλῖται, ὧν . . . αἱ ἐπαγγελίαι, 9:4), he does not speak of those promises being fulfilled. Given Paul's aim in these chapters, this seems curious indeed.

In Romans 9–11 Paul ponders the mysterious state of affairs in which God's people have not accepted the one the apostle believes is their Messiah. Given this, we might then rightly expect that after Paul's statement, the promises belong to the Israelites that in service of this argument he would introduce also the idea of fulfillment. Yet Paul's discourse—which climaxes in the claim that God has not rejected God's people (11:1) and that all Israel will be saved (11:26)—is not

[16] This chapter is part of my larger ongoing investigation of Paul's view of time. As such I hope it makes a small contribution to a large question. If space allowed, I would have at least here also discussed Paul's use of Scripture in Romans 9–11, since for interpreters that issue is so entwined with the matter of Paul's use of promise. Here I can merely summarize what I have found in my work so far on that topic, which I do in the next footnote.

structured by a promise-fulfillment scheme.[17] Paul claims that the

[17] As mentioned in the previous footnote, the matter of Paul's use of Scripture in these chapters is interpretatively connected to the matter of how he uses promise. Here I summarize my current understanding of Paul's use of Scripture in Romans 9–11.

Paul does not state that the Scripture he works with is fulfilled. In Romans 9–11 Paul's allusion to or citation of Scripture is not used in a promise-fulfillment pattern. Rather, Paul uses Scripture in order to state who God is; to give a glimpse into the realm of God's life, of God's mind. Scripture is a window into God's purpose. It helps Paul to communicate the significance of what he thinks God is demonstrating about Godself. It is not a collection of promises awaiting fulfillment.

This is nowhere clearer than in the curiosity of 10:6, where "the righteousness of faith" speaks Scripture. It is the righteousness of faith that speaks Deuteronomy's "do not say in your heart 'who will ascend into heaven?' or 'who will descend into the abyss?'" Early on in Romans Paul made it plain that the righteousness of faith has always been God's intention with God's people. The righteousness of faith is, then, one way to speak of God's intention; the righteousness of faith is consonant with God's mind. When the righteousness of faith speaks Scripture it speaks Scripture as Godself. Scripture speaks God's mind.

At 9:17 Paul writes that Scripture says to Pharaoh, "I have raised you up for the very purpose of showing my power in you." Scripture articulates God's purpose. When Paul speaks in 11:25 and 26 about the mystery that a hardening has come on a part of Israel until the fullness of the Gentiles comes in and thus all Israel will be saved, he says not that this fulfills Scripture, but that this is "just as it is written" (11:26). Paul's Isaiah citations are not fulfilled but rather provide words to describe what Paul sees as God's purpose. It is clear to interpreters that at 11:26-27 Paul uses Scripture to declare the certainty of his conviction concerning the salvation of all Israel. But the basis of Paul's certainty is not his hope of Scripture's *fulfillment*—he does not say that. He simply says that these events are "just as it is written." Scripture enunciates God's purpose. Paul believes these events are God's intention, as Scripture says. Scripture is not awaiting fulfillment; rather, Scripture gives words to what is.

Paul's statement that Isaiah προείρηκεν (9:29) is regularly translated as predicted or prophesied. The word simply means "said before" (interestingly, this is how the KJV translates it). Like the word προεπηγγείλατο (Rom 1:2), προείρηκεν indicates prior knowledge of an event. Given that the event is sourced in God, it is knowledge of an event that *is*. (Later in the text of this chapter, I will make the case for this reading of προεπηγγείλατο.)

The νῦν καιρός manifests phenomena the existence of which are sourced in God's purpose. So, for instance, the remnant (11:5) is because it is according to God's election of grace (11:5). The remnant is not, as R. Jewett for instance would have it, a typological fulfillment (*Romans*, 658). Paul says nothing about fulfillment. The οὕτως οὖν at the beginning of 11:5 indicates that the current remnant is in line with God's reply to Elijah that he has kept for himself seven thousand men who have not bent their knee to Baal (11:4). Both the remnant in Elijah's time and the present remnant exist because God determined they would.

promises *belong* to Israel, but he does not say that they are fulfilled. (Neither does he say that Scripture is fulfilled.) I suggest that this curious fact may indicate something of Paul's view of time.

A promise-fulfillment scheme (such as is found so plenteously in, for instance, the Gospels of Matthew and Luke, and even John, as well as in Acts) relies on a linear conception of time—an event happens following another event (the fulfillment after the promise). So, for instance, in the Gospel of Matthew when Jesus sends his disciples to find an ass and a colt in preparation for his entry into Jerusalem, Matthew writes, "This happened in order that the word of the prophet might be fulfilled [πληρωθῇ], saying, 'Tell the daughter of Zion, Behold, your king is coming to you, humble, and mounted on an ass, and on a colt, the foal of an ass'" (Matt 21:4-5).[18]

Promise-fulfillment, which is fundamental to the salvation historical interpretative framework, works with a conception of time as an entity that moves linearly forward, in this case from potential to actuality (from the promise of something that is not yet, to the coming into existence of what is promised).

In Romans 9–11, however, Paul does not speak of the promises that belong to the Israelites as being *fulfilled* by God's action in Christ. Neither at 9:4, nor elsewhere in chapters 9–11, or indeed the rest of

---

Scripture is not awaiting fulfillment but rather is a voice for God's intention. Scripture is a way that God communicates and a way to communicate about God. At 11:34 Paul uses Scripture—"who has known the mind of the Lord or who has been his counsellor?" (Isa 40:13, with a slight difference in word order)—to corroborate his own thoughts about how unsearchable are God's judgments and how unfathomable are God's ways (11:33).

I wonder if my fine colleague Ross Wagner and I do not find partial agreement when, for instance, he states, concerning Isa 53:1 in Rom l:16, that "it is not simply that Isaiah long ago predicted something that is now fulfilled in Paul's ministry. Rather, Isaiah remains a living voice for Paul, one who speaks alongside the apostle as an authoritative witness to the gospel" (*Heralds of the Good News: Isaiah and Paul in Concert in the Letter to the Romans*, NovTSup 101 [Leiden: Brill, 2002], 179–80; see also 257). If I am correct that Wagner claims that Paul uses Scripture as both: (1) witness to the fulfillment that has occurred in the gospel and Paul's ministry; and (2) a living voice that helps Paul communicate his understanding, then, in regard to Wagner's second claim, I venture that we might agree somewhat (although, see my caveat in a note below).

[18] Scripture translations are the author's.

Romans, does Paul connect the promise with fulfillment.[19] Paul says simply that the promises *belong* to the Israelites, along with other divinely given attributes, including "the Messiah according to the flesh"—which Messiah, it should be noted, Paul does not describe as the fulfillment of the promises (9:5). The promises belong to the Israelites, along with gifts from God that, as Paul will affirm, are permanent—"the gifts and the call of God are irrevocable" (11:29). The promises are an aspect of the identity of the Israelites, but Paul does not claim that they need to be or are being fulfilled. This raises the question of whether Paul thought of the promises in a context other than a promise-fulfillment scheme.

At Romans 9:8-9 we again see this use of the concept of promise. Paul does not speak of the children of the promise as a fulfillment. The promise in the phrase "the children of the promise" is, rather, contextually equated with "the word of God" (9:6). This is made clear when at 9:9 Paul combines "the word" with "promise"—"the word of promise." Promise here appears, then, not with the idea of fulfillment but with the concept of "word": ἐπαγγελίας γὰρ ὁ λόγος οὗτος.

Paul frames 9:6-13 with his assertion of the certainty of ὁ λόγος τοῦ θεοῦ. Using the perfect tense, Paul affirms that the word of God has not failed (9:6). That is, the word of God is continually certain. The "word of God" at Romans 9:6 presumably does not stray far from the meaning it has in 2 Corinthians 4:2, where it is equivalent to "the truth," and so an entity that lacks no completion.

In context Paul's use of the phrase "word of promise" at 9:9 suggests that he is seeking to view the promise from *God's* perspective. While from human perspective the promise might be described as fulfilled (Sarah gives birth to Isaac), fulfillment is not where Paul puts his attention. Paul focuses rather on the promise as "the word," presumably God's word. It is the promise in and of itself, an entity that is an aspect of the certainty of God's word and the continuance of God's purpose of election (9:11), to which Paul attends. Paul is, I submit, thinking of the promise from God's, and not from a human, perspective. The promise *is*, and it is certain in and of itself. And so the children of the promise (9:8; spoken of not as a fulfillment) are evidence of

[19] Contra J. A. Fitzmyer, whose stated salvation historical framework shapes his claim that Paul "found the promises (9:4) . . . have been realized in the death and resurrection of Jesus Christ." Fitzmyer sees a comparison here to the Lukan Paul in Acts 13:32-33—a passage that speaks explicitly about the fulfillment of the promises (*Romans*, AB 33 [New York: Doubleday, 1993], 233).

God's unfailing word and abiding purpose. The promise itself, then, is not an entity of potential, but an one of actuality. Promise here might be understood as an abiding vow, such as one makes in a marriage ceremony. The promise/vow is foundational: it is enough in itself (as long as the one who made the promise does not break it).

As mentioned, a promise-fulfillment scheme fits an understanding of time as an entity that moves from what is not to what is, and so is linear. In the context of fulfillment, a promise is a pledge to be fulfilled at a moment down the line—it signifies potential. In a promise-fulfillment scheme, a promise looks ahead to its completion at the moment when it is fulfilled.

Paul's use of promise here, however, teases our minds to ponder whether the apostle is thinking of the promises not as awaiting completion, but as already sufficient and complete—and so to imagine that Paul conceived of time in a manner other than the linear progression that a promise-fulfillment format assumes.

Promise Elsewhere in Romans. Let us take a necessarily brief look at what Paul says elsewhere in Romans about promise.

> (1) Rom 4:13-20: For the promise to Abraham and his seed . . . is not through law but through righteousness of faith. For if those who are of the law are heirs . . . the promise is nullified. . . . On account of this it is from faith, in order that it might be according to grace, in order that the promise might be confirmed/firm [εἰς τὸ εἶναι βεβαίαν τὴν ἐπαγγελίαν] for all the seed. . . . Yet, with respect to the promise of God he . . . grew strong in faith.

Paul's claim that the promise to Abraham and his descendants is "through righteousness of faith" (4:13) declares that this promise is to be believed in. For Paul, God's promise must be understood as being entirely in God's hands, an entity that is to be believed; it is to be recognized as a gift ("according to grace"), and so not something on which humans have any purchase, particularly not through obedience to the law (4:13). The appropriate response to God's promise is to know that it is certain—that it is confirmed—for all of Abraham's descendants (4:16).[20]

[20] Understanding βεβαίαν with the accusative, which has the fundamental sense of "confirm, establish" (see 1 Cor 1:6, 8; Col 2:7), as firm, permanent, reliable, certain. See also L. Keck, who translates it as "firm, reliable, valid" and writes that to translate it as "'guaranteed' is excessive" (*Romans*, ANTC [Nashville: Abingdon, 2005], 127).

At Romans 4:13-16 Paul's point is that the promise is certain, not that it will be seen to be certain once it is fulfilled. It is certain now. This, I venture, is why Paul does not couple promise with fulfillment. Fulfillment indicates that something has come about that was not before, whereas confirmation indicates that something is and is being attested to. There is a distinct absence of a sense of future in Paul's use of promise here—the focus is on promise as the solid ground that can be trusted.

The sense of promise here is that it is complete in itself (without fulfillment). This accounts for Paul's pronouncement that it could be nullified (κατήργηται, 4:14)—not if it were unfulfilled, but if it were misunderstood. The promise would be made ineffective as promise if it were the case that Abraham and his seed were inheritors of the world ἐκ νόμου—on the basis of law (4:14). Abraham's response of continuously strengthening faith is the right response to the promise (4:20). The promise is and is to be trusted in.

> (2) Romans 15:8-9: For I tell you, Christ has become a servant of the circumcision on behalf of the truthfulness of God in order to confirm the promises and [a servant] with respect to the Gentiles on behalf of the mercy [of God] [in order] to glorify God.[21]

The notoriously difficult grammatical and semantic tangle of Romans 15:8-9 cannot nearly be unraveled here. Nevertheless, with a focus on Paul's use of promise and what that might tell us about how he conceived of time, I offer the following.

The subject of Romans 15:7-12 is Christ, and, I contend, the subject is Christ in his life with God rather than Christ in his human life. In essence, Paul is seeking to present the divine Christ's vantage point in these verses. (Interestingly, L. Keck, who understands Christ to be the one praying the Psalms in 15:9-11, claims something similar: Romans 15:9-11 presents "the pre-existent Christ's declaring in advance the purpose of his impending incarnation."[22])

R. Wagner's insight that Christ is the "subject" of the infinitive δοξάσαι (Rom 15:9)[23] clarifies Paul's focus. As Wagner puts it,

[21] Following Keck's translation (*Romans*, 355).

[22] L. Keck, "Christology, Soteriology, and the Praise of God," in *The Conversation Continues: Studies in Paul and John in Honor of J. Louis Martyn*, ed. R. T. Fortna and B. R. Gaventa (Nashville: Abingdon, 1990), 85–97, 93.

[23] R. Wagner, "The Christ, Servant of Jew and Gentile: A Fresh Approach to Romans 15:8-9," *JBL* 116, no. 3 (1997): 473–85, 482.

in 15:7b-11 "Christ is the main actor."[24] I contend that the apostle's reference to Christ's glorifying God on behalf of God's mercy does not correspond to an occasion that took place when Christ was in human form. Rather, here Paul is speaking about Christ glorifying God in Christ's life with God.[25] Here, as almost everywhere, Paul is not speaking of Christ's earthly ministry.[26] Christ's welcome of the Gentiles for the glory of God (15:7) refers not to some event in Christ's ministry in Galilee, but to Christ doing so in the mode in which Paul normally contemplates him. When Paul presents Christ praying the Psalms in 15:9 and 11[27]—Psalms that dramatize Christ's welcome of the Gentiles—this is not a reference to a moment in Christ's ministry on earth. Paul is imagining Christ in the divine life glorifying God by praying the Psalms,[28] thereby initiating and encouraging praise of God among the Gentiles.[29]

Along with L. Keck, I hear Paul to be presenting Christ also as the subject of v. 10—it is Christ who speaks the words of Deuteronomy.[30] Again, this reference is not to Christ's historical ministry but to his life with God.[31] Christ is welcoming the Gentiles in the context of the divine life.

With this interpretative context, the reference to the promises of the fathers (v. 8) fits awkwardly in a promise-fulfillment pattern,

[24] Wagner, "The Christ, Servant of Jew and Gentile," 484.

[25] Wagner does not ponder this particular question.

[26] Paul, of course, rarely speaks of Christ's earthly life. Rather, it is normally the risen Christ—and on occasion the preexistent Christ (e.g., Phil 2:6, 1 Cor 8:6)—about whom the apostle writes.

[27] Accepted by, among others, C. E. B. Cranfield, *A Critical and Exegetical Commentary on the Epistle to the Romans*, 2 vols., ICC (Edinburgh: T&T Clark, 1979), 2:745; Keck, "Christology, Soteriology, and the Praise of God"; and R. B. Hays, "Christ Prays the Psalms: Paul's Use of an Early Christian Exegetical Convention," in *The Future of Christology: Essays in Honor of Leander E. Keck*, ed. A. J. Malherbe and W. A. Meeks (Minneapolis: Fortress, 1993): 122–36.

[28] Keck hears the preexistent Christ. Hays hears here the risen Christ in an "eschatological congregation composed of Gentiles and Jews." See Keck, "Christology, Soteriology, and the Praise of God," 93; Hays, "Christ Prays the Psalms," 123.

[29] An underlying purpose of this presentation of Christ's leading the Gentiles' praise is, of course, to authorize Paul's Gentile mission. Paul presents his ministry to the Gentiles as endorsed by Christ who lives with God.

[30] Keck, *Romans*, 356.

[31] In his commentary, Keck ponders whether this is Christ speaking before his incarnation or after his resurrection.

since the focus of 15:7-12 is not on Christ's earthly life (and so not on the human linear experience of time for which promise-fulfillment is appropriate). Paul is not drawing attention to the promises having been fulfilled in the human experience. While the idea of Christ becoming a servant of the circumcised may include reference to the human life of Jesus, the "promises of the fathers" and the subsequent Scriptures that Christ speaks are embedded in a much larger narrative than Christ's earthly life as the fulfillment of Israel's messianic hopes. "The promises of the fathers" are surrounded by, even subsumed by, Paul's pondering not Christ's earthly life, but Christ's life with God. Paul here, as elsewhere, is seeking to peer into the life of God.

The implicit narrative of Romans 15:8-9 shares features similar to the explicit narrative of Philippians 2:6-11. As in the Philippian passage, so here Paul contemplates Christ's life with God prior to Christ taking the form of a servant and being found in human form (cf. Phil 2:7). I take γεγενῆσθαι (Rom 15:8) to indicate what Paul states directly in the letter's opening narrative: that Christ is God's Son who was born (τοῦ γενομένου, cf. Rom 1:3). The word γεγενῆσθαι implies that prior to his becoming a servant Christ lived in another mode/form. In Romans 15, rather than focusing on Christ's death and exaltation (cf. Phil 2:8-9) being what follows from Christ becoming a servant, Paul highlights other consequences of Christ's becoming a servant.[32] In Romans 15 Paul emphasizes that Christ becoming a servant of the circumcision was on behalf of God's faithfulness to Israel;[33] and that Christ did this (note Paul's focus on *Christ's* action) in order to confirm the promises of the fathers.

Let us pause to note that there is the closest of connections between the promises and the truth of God. In distinction from Paul's mention of God's mercy with respect to the Gentiles[34] (which is not coupled with anything else), God's faithfulness to Israel is joined to God's promises to the fathers. God's special relationship with Israel

[32] The particular shaping of the implied narrative of Rom 15:8-9 is doubtless due to Paul's specific concerns for the Roman congregations.

[33] T. Donaldson, among others, rightly interprets ἀληθείας θεοῦ as God's faithfulness to Israel (*Paul and the Gentiles: Remapping the Apostle's Convictional World* [Minneapolis: Fortress, 1997], 99).

[34] It is to be noted that Wagner convincingly untangles the "syntactical mare's nest" (474) of 15:8-9 by reading the accusative τὰ ἔθνη as an accusative of respect standing parallel to περιτομῆς. The meaning is: Christ became a servant . . . with respect to the Gentiles ("The Christ, Servant of Jew and Gentile," 482).

is evident because of the promises. The promises are an extension of God's faithfulness to Israel, as if they are the umbilical cord between God's truth and God's chosen people. The promises join God's people to God's faithfulness.

As noted, moreover, the promises in 15:8 are not framed by Christ's earthly life—or indeed by the human horizon. Paul does not follow reference to the promises with presentation of evidence in the human temporal experience as, for instance, do Matthew and John.[35] While the Isaianic messianic prophecy in v. 12, like Paul's reference to Christ becoming a servant to the circumcised, includes Christ's earthly life, it is not contextualized in Christ's human life. In Romans 15:12 Isaiah speaks alongside Christ—the speaker of the previous three scriptural citations. (Note that Paul uses the same words to introduce the Isaiah quote used in v. 10, a verse in which Christ is the speaker.) In v. 12 Isaiah is not speaking out of the past, but alongside the living Christ. It is Isaiah, a "living voice,"[36] who speaks alongside Christ in describing God's purpose.

If Paul's focus were on the human experience of linear time he would surely say that this purpose has been fulfilled—Christ, the root of Jesse, has risen[37] and rules the Gentiles by virtue of being Lord. However, Paul does *not* say that this Scripture has been fulfilled. Paul hears this Scripture being spoken by Isaiah in order to give voice to God's promises to the fathers. Paul's focus is not on the promises from the human vantage point, but from God's—as indicated by it being Christ in his divine life speaking Scripture. When Isaiah speaks, it is Scripture speaking God's mind and will. It is Scripture not as a promise in need of fulfillment, but as promise as part of God's life; promise as always and already present.

Paul, then, presents the promises in 15:8 primarily in the environment not of human temporality but of the life of God. While Paul nods to the earthly life of Christ in v. 8, his chief focus is on Christ's life in God's life. From the point of view of human experience, the promises are fulfilled—as if they were not complete until Christ came as a servant of the circumcised. However, this is not Paul's emphasis.

35 E.g., Matt 21:4; John 12:38.

36 This is Wagner's term, although he uses it in a different way (Isaiah speaking alongside Paul, rather than alongside Christ) and for a different purpose (*Heralds of the Good News*, 180).

37 Wagner notes the "delicious double-entendre" present in the word ὁ ἀνιστάμενος (*Heralds of the Good News*, 319).

It is the vantage point of Christ in his life with God that Paul presents throughout this passage.

From the divine Christ's point of view the promises are not fulfilled, but rather Christ, in his life with God, confirms them (note in this regard that it is Christ who is the subject of the εἰς τό clause). It was because of the promises that Christ became a servant to the circumcised. The promises are fundamental to God's relationship to Israel, and Christ's intent in becoming a servant of the circumcised was to confirm them[38]—which is at once to confirm God's faithfulness to Israel. The promises are, for Christ, part of his life with God; they are a feature of God's truthfulness to Israel that Christ knows in his divine life. Like God's faithfulness, the promises need no fulfillment—they need only to be confirmed. As an aspect of God's faithfulness with Israel, they *are*. And so Christ confirms them.

From the perspective of God's life with which Christ lives, the purpose of Christ's becoming a servant of the circumcised on behalf of the truth of God is not to fulfill the promises but to confirm them. Paul thinks of the promises in a wider horizon than the human experience of linear time.

> (3) <u>Romans 1:2</u>: . . . which he announced in advance [προεπηγγείλατο] through his prophets in the holy writings.

Paul's opening declaration that the gospel of God was προεπηγγείλατο (1:2), normally translated as "promised beforehand," is typically interpreted to imply that God's promise, made by means of God's prophets in the holy writings (1:1-2), was *fulfilled* in the life, death, and resurrection of Jesus Christ.[39] However, this rare word, which hardly appears prior to the NT and occurs elsewhere in the NT only in 2 Corinthians 9:5, may also be translated as "had notice before." (This is how the KJV renders it at 2 Cor 9:5.) Given that even in Romans 1:1-2, which is surely a most fitting place, Paul does not use the word "fulfill" (and, as mentioned, that there is no place in Romans where the promises are said to be fulfilled), let us play with the meaning "had notice before." When προεπηγγείλατο is translated this way, the emphasis is on God's prophets in the holy Scriptures having prior knowledge of the Christ event. They knew about it and

[38] εἰς τό can indicate purpose or result. I take here the former meaning.

[39] E.g., Cranfield, *Romans*, 1:55. Fitzmyer speaks of the promises being "realized" (*Romans*, 233).

gave notice of it before it occurred in human history. Presumably Paul thought that what the prophets knew about came from God; what they announced came from God. Paul's choice of the aorist middle word προεπαγγέλλω calls attention to the subject of the verb's involvement in the action. The prophets' announcement is in essence God's action.[40] As such, the event, sourced in the eternal God, *is*. The linear sequence of events—God's Son was born of the seed of David, designated son of God in power, etc.—is not fulfillment of a promise in the sense that these events were only potential prior to their occurrence in human history. Indeed, to humans these events appear sequential: from the human perspective, they were not and then they are; and they are announced prior to occurring in the human linear experience of time. Yet, what is announced *is* already, for it is knowledge that is of God.[41]

Summary. Paul certainly describes the *human* experience of God's promise/s as moving from what is not, to what is—time as linear.[42] Paul writes that the word of promise is that God will do something "about that time" (9:9). The event that occurs κατὰ τὸν καιρὸν τοῦτον is, however, not the realization of something that was not before it

[40] J. D. G. Dunn (*Romans*, 2 vols., WBC 38 [Dallas: Word, 1988], 1:10; and Jewett, *Romans*, 103, make a similar point about the semantic significance of the aorist middle here. The emphasis on God is evident also in the pronoun αὐτοῦ (διὰ τῶν προφητῶν αὐτοῦ)—the referent of which is God.

[41] I suggest that in Rom 1:1-2 Paul is thinking in a manner similar to how he does in Rom 3:21, where he writes that the righteousness of God has been manifested and that that manifestation was witnessed to by the Law and the Prophets. The manifestation of God's righteousness is revelation of something eternal. Within four verses of his announcement of the revelation of God's righteousness and declaration that the gospel is the power of God (Rom 1:16-17), Paul refers to God's *eternal* power and deity (1:20). Presumably, Paul understood God's righteousness also to be eternal: the manifestation of God's righteousness to which the Law and the Prophets witness is witness to what is eternal. This may be why at 3:21-26 Paul does not use the concept of fulfillment—he does not state that the righteousness of God is the fulfillment of the Law and the Prophets. For fulfillment conveys the idea of something not being and then coming into being.

[42] It will be noted that I refer to the "human linear experience of time." I do this for three primary reasons: (a) to distinguish the human linear temporal experience from other experiences people have of time; (b) because I am at an exploratory stage in regard to whether Paul thinks there is an entity we might call "human time" (perhaps he thinks there is only one time and that humans have a particular experience of it); and (c) because when Paul does refer to time as humans experience it he presents it as linear/sequential.

is experienced.[43] When Abraham and Sarah have a son it is not the *fulfillment* of a promise, but it is the *word of promise* (9:9). Human experience of God's promise is that it is realized at a moment in *our* future.[44] Yet, Paul does not indicate that the promise itself is in need of realization or fulfillment. Rather, God's promise is a certain foundation from which events in human history occur. Paul's use of promise/s but not fulfillment suggests that, while he acknowledges the human linear experience of time, he is primarily contextualizing promise/s in another temporal mode—what I will call God's time.

God's Time

Speaking of God's time is, of course, to go against the grain of much of Western theological and philosophical thought. The Christian tradition has typically understood God to live in eternity—eternity being understood as timelessness. That is, eternity (God's mode of existence) is, in Kierkegaard's famously generative words cited at the beginning of K. Barth's 1932 Romans commentary, in "infinite qualitative distinction" from time.[45] The classic understanding of the difference between the two is that time involves change and movement and, relatedly, it has tenses—past, present, and future. Eternity, on the other hand is, in Augustine's words, "without change."[46] God lives not in time but in eternity.

Let us, however, notice that though it is clear that Paul understood God to be eternal (Rom 1:20), the apostle never uses the adjective *eternal* in a way that indicates that he thought it signified timelessness. In fact, the occurrence that gives the clearest hint as to how the apostle understood "eternal" signals that he thought of it as simply a lot of time. When in 2 Corinthians 4:18 Paul uses the neuter plural adjective αἰώνια, he juxtaposes it with the neuter plural adjective πρόσκαιρα,

[43] Of course, Isaac was not in human linear time prior to his birth to Sarah. Yet, from the perspective of God, Isaac already was. Psalm 139 expresses this understanding of the relationship between human life and its time, and God's time. See esp. Ps 139:16.

[44] At Rom 4:21 Paul writes that Abraham was fully convinced that the one who promised was able also to do (what was promised). From Abraham's perspective, there is a distinction between a promise and its being "done."

[45] K. Barth, *The Epistle to the Romans*, trans. from the 6th ed. by E. C. Hoskyns (Oxford: Oxford University Press, 1933), 10.

[46] Augustine, who thought God lived in eternity (*Confessions* XI.1), put it this way: the eternal God is "eternally without change" (*Confessions* XI.28).

which means "temporary" or "transitory." On the one hand, there are things that last only for a short while (πρόσκαιρα); and on the other hand, there are things that are eternal (αἰώνια)—that last forever. The distinction is one of quantity, not quality.

Likewise, in regard to the concept of eternity, the apostle does not define or use it in a manner that would suggest that he thought eternity was timeless, or that it was infinitely, qualitatively different from time. And, it is to be noticed that, unlike one of his most famous interpreters, Paul does not juxtapose eternity and time, that is, put them in opposition.[47] In fact, while Paul refers to eternity in several places, as we shall see, he does so in a way that indicates he thought there was a relationship between eternity and the human experience of time—and so, I will suggest, that both are temporal modes.

Despite being at odds with standard notions of the meaning of "eternal" and "eternity," I invite consideration that Paul may have thought of the eternal God living eternal *time*. This is not an invitation to think, à la O. Cullmann, that Paul thought that God lives unending linear time.[48] Indeed, one of the rare places where Paul speaks of aspects of time in relation to God would suggest that the apostle was not at all conceptually constrained by only the human (linear) experience of temporality.

At the end of Romans 8 Paul describes the trustworthiness and strength of God's love in Christ Jesus by claiming that neither time's finitude (death) nor time's presence (life), nor the things of the present time (ἐνεστῶτα) nor the things of the future (μέλλοντα) are capable of separating us from the love of God in Christ Jesus. On the understanding that "the love of God which is in Christ Jesus" (Rom

[47] While Barth relies on this distinction in his Romans commentary, in *CD* he does speak of "God's time" (e.g., II.1, ¶31, ¶613).

[48] O. Cullmann famously argued that, for early Christianity, eternity (which he understood to be designated by the term "aeon") "carried a time meaning" (*Christ and Time: The Primitive Christian Conception of Time and History*, trans. F. V. Filson [Philadelphia: Westminster, 1950], 47). Moreover, eternity moves endlessly backward and forward in a linear fashion. Eternity is time "in its entire unending extension, which is unlimited in both the backward and the forward direction" (48). According to Cullmann, "primitive Christians" had a "simple rectilinear conception of unending time" (49). It is to be noted that in this work (unlike in *Salvation in History*) Cullmann does not study Paul independently and synthesizes various NT writers on the matter of time.

J. Barr equally famously criticized Cullmann for his interpretation of "aeon" (*Biblical Words for Time*, 2nd rev. ed. [London: SCM Press, 1969], esp. 71–85).

8:39) is central to Godself, here we have Paul imagining God encountering and conquering the features of time that can threaten humans.[49] God does not maintain loving connection with humans by destroying time, for humans continue to live temporal existences while being connected to God's love. God can be trusted to deal with frightening features of time, while leaving humans living time, presumably because God transcends and is not bound by the human experience of time. Whatever existence Paul imagines the eternal God to live, it is, then, not the same as or the same shape as the human experience of linear time. I offer the idea that Paul conceives of God's eternal existence as temporal—a kind of time (eternity) that is not only forever, but simply is.

In regard to this last thought, which I have already introduced in the discussion of Paul's use of promise (and will further discuss in the following section on God's purpose), it may seem a matter of semantics or an error to propose both that Paul thought of God living eternal *time* and that he understood eternal time not as linear, but as time that simply *is*. If eternal time simply is—if it is tenseless, without past, present, and future—is it right to call it "time"? I suggest that it is only wrong if our definition of time is limited to the human experience. I offer the idea that Paul—as he did with so much else[50]—reconceptualized the meaning of time.[51]

The apostle considered (perhaps due to his central conviction that he lived "in Christ") that he could peer beyond and outside of the human horizon. Paul in Christ sees time as an entity not limited to the human experience.[52] I note here, as I will repeat below: Paul does not say that time will end. While an entity that simply continuously is may not be the human experience of time, this does not mean that it is not time. Perhaps, for Paul, such "is-ness" truly is time.

[49] Note that the features of time Paul mentions are contextualized among things that are powerful and threatening, such as angels, principalities, and powers.

[50] For instance, if we accept the subjective genitive reading of *pistis Christou*, the meaning of faith moves beyond trust in another to sharing another's faith.

[51] U. Schnelle also recognizes that Paul's view of time is without precedent, due to "the uniquely new aspects of the event" that shaped it (*Apostle Paul: His Life and Theology*, trans. M. E. Boring [Grand Rapids: Baker, 2005], 593).

[52] Schnelle's claim that for Paul "all time has the quality of the time of God" (*Apostle Paul*, 593) echoes some of what I hear in Paul. Where I differ from Schnelle is that the slice of Paul I study in this chapter indicates that for Paul the quality of God's time was available prior to Christ's death and resurrection.

Paul may have understood the eternal God to live eternal *time* (although not linear time). The apostle presents a relationship between God's eternal existence and human temporality; he conceives of God interacting with the human experience of time. I take this to indicate that the apostle did not consider the eternal God to live timelessness, or a mode completely other than time. Rather, I suggest that Paul's presentation of the interlacing of God's existence with human life indicates that he considered these to be two relatable modes of time. There is for Paul a temporal mode that is all the time there is (eternity) and a temporal mode that is limited (human temporal experience).

Eternal Time

Paul thought of God's eternal existence as eternal time. As is clear from Romans 9:1-13, Paul was convinced that God interacts with humans in the course of their temporal experience. I take this to mean that Paul thought God's eternal existence was not entirely other and separate from time.

Of course, God's eternal existence is entirely distinct in that, as far as the evidence allows us to propose, Paul thought God created the kind of time that humans experience.[53] For Paul, the distinction between Creator and created is a clear and vast one. This is nowhere clearer than at Romans 11:33-36. However, recognizing that Paul believed in a fundamental distinction between God and all that God created (including time as humans know it) does not mean that the apostle also thought that God's existence is atemporal. It means only that whatever temporality God lives transcends, exceeds, and in some way includes the time that God created for humans to live in.

As I hope to demonstrate, it is most straightforward to account for the (unfortunately) slight evidence we have by interpreting Paul to conceive of God living eternal time rather than eternal non-time or eternal timelessness. Again, I am not suggesting that Paul thought of eternal time as simply an extension of the human linear experience of time.

Perhaps Paul would put it this way: God's time is all the time there is—what humans experience is a portion and a particular experience of time. It is, then, not that *created* time is all the time there is. Rather, time as humans know it is a sliver of a much vaster entity—God's time.

[53] Romans 8:38-39 speaks of aspects of time as among what is created.

One of the most telling indications of this is that Paul does not say that time will end. Among the key passages used as evidence for the very widespread perception that Paul believes that time will end is 1 Corinthians 7:29. Here Paul famously describes the present (ἐστίν) as ὁ καιρός that has contracted or compressed (συνεσταλμένος).[54] The compression of ὁ καιρός may describe—and let it be said that no scholar, least of all me, can be conclusive about what Paul's *hapax* expression means[55]—not the length of time but the quality of time. A compressed or contracted or compact time may indicate not a shortened time but a time of clarity.[56]

As a warrant for why marriage and mourning and rejoicing and commerce are not the fundamentals of life, and as an explanation for why the most fundamental feature of believers' lives is their call to be with God (1 Cor 7:24), Paul says that the time is compressed, drawn together, compacted, by which he may legitimately be taken to mean that matters are clarified. Just as when things or ideas are drawn together or compressed so they may be seen more clearly, we may fittingly hear Paul to be saying that the time has been drawn together, compressed, and so it may be seen more clearly. While I am not sure G. Agamben's explanation of Paul's words as operational time or messianic time—a time in which we can grasp time and accomplish

[54] "Compressed" is one of the options G. Fee offers for translation (*The First Epistle to the Corinthians*, NICNT [Grand Rapids: Eerdmans, 1987], 338)—although, in distinction from me, he understands this in the context of a salvation historical framework.

[55] BDG: "It is not certain whether Paul has a divine act of shortening in mind (J. Weiss) or whether there is no reference intended to a time that was originally longer" (613).

[56] The widespread eschatological interpretation of this passage is often bolstered by a certain reading of τὴν ἐνεστῶσαν ἀνάγκην (v. 26), understood to refer to intensified suffering expected before the Messiah arrives. Whether or not we translate ἐνεστῶσαν as "present" or "impending," it is entirely unclear what Paul means by ἀνάγκην. (Some have suggested he is referring to a grain shortage in Corinth.) If Paul is referring to "the distress" in a manner comparable to the "messianic woes," this would be the only place he does so. Elsewhere Paul refers to his apostolic sufferings as ἀνάγκην (1 Thess 3:7), but he does not say that those sufferings are signs of the Day of the Lord. The referent for "the distress," or "necessity" (cf. translation of the same word in 1 Cor 7:37) is too unclear to place much interpretative weight on it.

it[57]—completely explains Paul here, I agree with Agamben that Paul is saying something primarily about how believers may now perceive time.

Paul may be justifying his advice about social and sexual relations not on the basis not that time will shortly end—note he does *not* say it will end—but on the basis that because time has been drawn together, things are clearer. Due to the compression of time, believers can perceive more clearly that the fundamental relationship is being with God on the basis of their call (1 Cor 7:24).

Paul also explains why marriage and mourning, etc., are not fundamental by saying that the form of the world passes them by (παράγει). *Paragô* is in the present tense. The form of the world is now passing by. My translation of 7:31b—"for the form of the world passes you by"—understands παράγει to be, not pass *away*, but pass *by*.[58] I include the object "you"—passes *you* by—because I suggest Paul is here referring to the same idea as in Romans 8:1-13. In Romans 8 Paul describes two different realities—one, the flesh, in which those in Christ do not need to live, and which they can let go of, and the other, the Spirit. There is a similar thought at the end of Galatians where Paul claims that the cosmos has been crucified to him and he to the cosmos (Gal 6:14), and in his exhortation to the Romans to consider themselves dead to sin and living to God in Christ Jesus (Rom 6:11). Likewise, in 1 Corinthians 7:31b Paul may be heard to be saying that the form of the world, which must include the matters about which Paul has just spoken (namely, social and sexual relations), can pass by those in Christ.[59] They do not need to hold on to these things, because the most fundamental reality for them is being with God.[60] This can be clear to them because they live in *hô kairôs* that is compressed.

While, of course, Paul expects the return of Christ, and the Day of "our Lord Jesus Christ,"[61] which in 1 Corinthians 1:8 he calls the *telos*,

[57] G. Agamben, *The Time That Remains: A Commentary on the Letter to the Romans*, trans. Patricia Dailey (Stanford, Calif.: Stanford University Press, 2005), 72.

[58] BDG notes examples of this verb being used to indicate that a god passes by, or that someone passes along the lake (613).

[59] Interestingly, Fee says something comparable about this verse: "the form of this world is already passing away (v. 31). Christians do not thereby abandon the world; they are simply not to let this age dictate their present existence" (*1 Corinthians*, 330).

[60] To be called by God means to be παρὰ θεῷ (1 Cor 7:24).

[61] When Paul speaks of the day of Christ he describes it as the moment of completion (Phil 1:6) and of judgment (1 Cor 1:8; 3:13, 4:5; 2 Cor 1:14; Phil 1:10; 1 Thess 2:9, 3:13, 5:23). Christ's return from heaven is the advent of the resurrection for

he does not refer to that day as the end of *time*. First Corinthians 15 has the fullest description of Paul's vision for what occurs at the *telos*. The final scene is God being all in all (1 Cor 15:28). Paul does not indicate that this entails the end of time. Paul never refers to the *last* day.

I cannot find Paul saying that time will end. What Paul does say is that death will end: the last enemy to be destroyed will be death (1 Cor 15:26). Unless we want to argue that Paul thought that death is a defining feature of time—that is, that there cannot be time without death—it oversteps the evidence to say that Paul thinks that time will end. Perhaps, in fact, Paul might consider that time is among death's enemies and that when death is ultimately defeated, time is freed.[62]

I now return to explaining my reasons for suggesting that Paul thought of God living eternal time. These reasons involve Paul's references to eternal life and to eternity. Paul appears to assume an interaction between God's eternal existence and the human experience of time. I interpret the apostle to conceive of this interaction as one between two temporal modes.

Eternal Life. Paul uses the term "eternal life" five times in the undisputed letters.[63] Eternal life is a gift of God. God gives eternal life (Rom 2:7) and does so by means of Jesus Christ (Rom 5:21; 6:23) and the Spirit (Gal 6:8). Those who are set free from sin are liberated in order to serve God, which results in eternal life (Rom 6:22). Presumably, just as Paul thought of righteousness as the gift of an aspect of Godself, so he thought the gift of eternal life is the gift of an aspect of Godself. When God, by means of Christ and the Spirit, gives eternal life, God gives the life that God lives.

---

believers (1 Thess 4:16) and will mean believers' deliverance (1 Cor 5:5; 1 Thess 1:10). Note: 2 Cor 1:13, which some versions translate as "I hope you will understand until the end" (NASB), is better translated as "I hope you will understand fully" (see V. Furnish, *II Corinthians*, AB 32A [New York: Doubleday, 1984], 128).

[62] It might be argued that Paul is best read as equating the beginning of history, understood as the beginning of time, with the entry of sin and death into the world "through one man" (Rom 5:12). Consequently, when sin and death are annihilated at Christ's return, this would correspond to the end of history—the end of time. However, that would mean that Paul thought that Adam was not living in time before he was surrounded by sin and death (or that sin and death and Adam all came at once and so Adam never was without sin). Who is to know what Paul might mean in this regard in this famous passage? In my view, Rom 5 does not give us enough information to decide either way.

[63] The occurrences in Rom 16:25 and 26 are not taken into account because of the question of whether these verses are original.

The gift of eternal life is not only something to which humans may look forward; it may also be lived in the course of their linear experience of time. Those who have been liberated from sin through Jesus Christ know that they will share eternal life with God (Rom 6:22); and eternal life is not only the future for such persons, it is also their present life. Those who are "in Christ Jesus" are at once in eternal life (6:23).[64] Paul, then, conceives of humans living eternal life in conjunction with their linear experience of time. For Paul, eternal life appears to bear some relationship to time as humans experience it.

Paul's idea that those in Christ Jesus presently live eternal life (interpreted here as the life that God lives) has significant consequences for understanding what he means by eternal. If Paul thought of eternal life as timeless, it is difficult to perceive how he would have thought it could be lived in conjunction with the human experience of time. One might rather expect that, if Paul thought that eternal life (God's life) is timeless, the apostle would teach those who are in Christ Jesus (and living eternal life) to anticipate that their normal lives would occasionally be interrupted or intercepted by timeless moments.[65] That is, that when eternal life happens, humans would be translated from the temporal to something entirely other. Paul, however, does not describe those who are in Christ Jesus experiencing tension between a linear experience of time and living eternal life.[66]

Paul appears to conceive of a porousness between eternal life and the human sequential experience of time—they can be lived together.[67] I propose that the apostle may have thought that the reason humans can live eternal life while living the human linear experience of time is that he did not conceive of the two modes being at odds with each other, but rather as different manifestations of one entity. In this regard, it is to be noted that Paul never juxtaposes eternal life

[64] Cf. Rom 5:21, which may also refer to presently living eternal life. (So also de Boer, *Galatians*, 389.)

[65] Paul's description of the experience of "a man in Christ" (typically interpreted to be self-referential) who was caught up to the third heaven (2 Cor 12:2-6) does not indicate timelessness in paradise. On the basis of the longstanding assumption that change requires time and is impossible with timelessness (cf. Augustine's definition of changelessness, *Confessions* XI.28), the fact that Paul hears something new—words too wonderful to tell—suggests that he did not perceive his experience in paradise to be in timelessness.

[66] This is not to say that there is no struggle with sin for those living "in Christ Jesus," that is, living in eternal life.

[67] Again, this not to say that Paul thought that eternal life is linear.

and time. According to the apostle it is death (not time) that is the opposite of eternal life (Rom 5:21).[68]

Eternity. Paul's references to eternity occur when he is expressing the extent of human devotion to God.[69] Paul offers no thought on eternity as a separate concept. What he says about eternity is found in his doxologies. As a human glorifying (Rom 11:36, 14:26; Gal 1:5; Phil 4:20) or blessing (Rom 1:25, 9:5; 1 Cor 11:31) God or Christ, Paul prays that such glory and blessing would continue forever—into eternity. Paul's focus when he speaks of eternity is on the intensity of his devotion to God (and on encouraging this devotion in his hearers). In the midst of the human linear experience of time, Paul expresses his love of God by hoping for God's glory and blessing to be forever. Paul's devotional expressions indicate that he thinks it possible to imagine such devotion continuing forever. This imagination, it should be noted, takes place while living the human linear experience of time.

There is, then, for Paul permeability between humans' experience of time and eternity, without the human linear experience in any way defining eternity. Rather, in Paul's doxological statements, he is peering from human life into the greatness of God's life. From the human vantage point, he believes he is able to conceive of God's forever life.

The most that might be said is that Paul thinks it is possible while living a human life to hope for things like God's glory to continue forever. Time and eternity have a relationship. I suggest that Paul supposed eternity to be a temporal mode that embraces (while transcending) the human linear temporal mode.

I now proceed to explore Paul's use of the concept of God's purpose, which, like the apostle's use of promise, suggests that he thought of God's eternal time as time that simply *is*.

"In Order That God's Purpose of Election Might Remain"

The phrase "word of promise" at 9:9 is, as mentioned, semantically contextualized by the phrase "word of God" (9:6)[70] and by the clause "in order that God's purpose of election might remain" (9:11). The word of promise is a word of God. God's word of promise to Abraham is

[68] As I read Rom 5:21, eternal life and death are opposites, as are grace and sin.

[69] Paul's expressions for eternity are εἰς τοὺς αἰῶνας, εἰς τὸν αἰῶνα, or εἰς τοὺς αἰῶνας τῶν αἰώνων, terms he uses only with reference to God and Christ (2 Cor 9:9 uses εἰς τὸν αἰῶνα with reference to God's righteousness).

[70] So Fitzmyer, *Romans*, 559.

a word of God that has not failed and serves the continuance of God's purpose of election. Paul uses both God's announcement to Abraham and the news to Rebecca while she was pregnant with Jacob and Esau that the elder would serve the younger (9:10-13) as examples of God's word not having failed and so as events the aim of which was "ἵνα ἡ κατ' ἐκλογὴν πρόθεσις τοῦ θεοῦ μένῃ" (9:11).

The remaining/continuance (μένῃ) of God's purpose of election is often understood in the framework of a linear understanding of time. With human experience of time as the standard, God's purpose for humanity is typically comprehended as continuing from one divinely ordained historical event to the next. Paul, according to many of his interpreters, sees God's purpose as sequential.[71]

This may be right in regard to how Paul understands *humankind* experiencing God's purpose. The word of promise is that at a certain time after the word is given God will return and Sarah will have a son. From the perspective of human life, God's purpose occurs in linear time, and when it does the continuance (μένῃ) of God's purpose is evidenced. However, Paul also hints that, while he conceives of the word of promise from the vantage point of humankind, he is also seeking to peer into God's life.

The word of God has not failed, and the events that serve God's abiding purpose of election come about because of that word (of promise). Given that Paul thought of God as eternal, Paul surely thought that God's purpose of election was eternal as well. (He says this in a different manner when he states that the call of God is irrevocable [11:29].) Another way Paul might have expressed 9:11 is that God's purpose *is*. God's purpose manifests itself in human history, but it resides in God's life and so in God's time—life/time that is eternal.

God's purpose/resolve remaining suggests a kind of time that is, not a kind of time that progresses. Particular events that God initiates

[71] N. T. Wright may serve as representative of this view, although his presentation is more complicated than most. Wright writes that the "point of Romans 9 and 10" is the "central affirmation that there is indeed a *single divine plan* to which God has been faithful" (*Paul and the Faithfulness of God*, 499; emphasis in original). Wright speaks of Paul having a narrative substructure to his worldview (537). Paul thinks in terms of a grand narrative (a framing story) with an overarching plot in which are nested three other stories and several subplots (486–537). The concept of narrative as Wright uses it indicates sequential divinely ordained events. Paul works with "a single summary story from Adam to the Messiah, and on to the 'life of the age to come'" (531).

in human history do not correlate to new moments in God's time. God's purpose μένει.

I submit that Paul's description of God's purpose in Romans 9:9-13 evidences his assumption that, in addition to humans experiencing linear time, there is opportunity for them to know the time of God's existence—time that simply, continuously *is*.

All the Time There Is

I have proposed that Paul conceived of the promises of God and God's purpose as residing fundamentally in God's time. They are. And, as humans are aware of the God's promises and purpose, so they experience God's time in conjunction with their normal experience of time.

Paul's use of promise and his presentation of God's purpose of election suggest that while it is beyond dispute that the apostle conceived of the human experience of time in a linear fashion (as we see for instance at 9:9), he was also aware of another temporal mode. I have suggested that Paul may have conceived of this other temporal mode—God's time—to be all the time there is. Human linear experience of time is a particular quantity and experience of God's time. I have offered the suggestion that Paul thought there were two relatable temporal modes that in essence are two manifestations of one entity—God's time.

If my reading has merit, it calls into question the adequacy of the salvation historical viewpoint. In regard to the question of Paul's understanding of time, the interpretative framework of salvation history focuses on God's use of human history/time. It understands Paul to think that created time is all the time there is; and that God, who does not live time, directs human history/time and will at some point bring time to an end.[72] While Paul includes the human linear experi-

[72] For instance, O. Cullmann, working specifically on Paul, contrasts existing "in time" with "the consummation," that is, the general resurrection that Paul believes will come at "the end" (*Salvation in History*, trans. S. G. Sowers [New York: Harper & Row, 1967], 268). Within the salvation historical approach N. T. Wright may be an outlier in this regard. If I am reading him correctly, Wright's claim that for Paul the Day of the Lord is not the end of the world (*Paul: In Fresh Perspective*, 141) and Wright's focus on the renewal of creation that has begun now in the new age suggests that Wright thinks that for the apostle time (presumably time appropriate to the new creation) continues after the parousia. Wright's musing on the "new *sort* of time" that has come with Jesus the Messiah indicates that Wright equates the new creation (which will presumably continue forever) with a kind of time (*Paul and the Faithfulness of God*, 1:558; emphasis in original).

ence of time in his vision, he has, I propose, a much wider horizon than simply human history: Paul thinks that God's time is all the time there is and that the human linear experience is a particular quantity and quality of God's time. What will end is not time but the limited human experience of it.

On the other hand, my proposal could be heard as compatible with the apocalyptic reading of Paul. In the view of apocalyptic interpreters, Paul is aware of two ages/two temporal epochs, and he believes that the new age/the future/the new creation has invaded time (the present age).

While in the foregoing I argue that Paul conceived of two temporal modes and that in the midst of our normal experience of time humans can experience a mode that is of God, my suggestion differs from the apocalyptic reading in regard to the identity of one of these modes, and, consequently, the relationship between these modalities.

In Romans 9:1-13, where Paul is not overtly contemplating the "juncture of the new creation and the evil age"[73] but rather Israel—before Christ's death and resurrection—experiencing God's promises and purpose, the apostle presupposes a kind of time that he does not attach to conversation about the new creation. Paul assumes a time that for him may be more fundamental than the new creation/new age: God's time.[74] These verses suggest that Paul believed that humans (even those who lived before Christ's death and resurrection) can, in our sequential temporal existence, know God's eternal time. This sheds light on the nature of human linear time—it is not all the time there is.

In the apocalyptic reading the relationship between the new creation and human history is oppositional—the new creation invades. What we see in passages such as Romans 9:1-13,[75] which do not address the new creation explicitly, is rather Paul's conception of a porousness between human history and God's time.

The peculiarities of Romans 9:1-13 entreat us to consider that the apostle's view of time may exceed both the comforting logic of the salvation historical approach and the striking power of the apocalyptic rendering.

[73] Martyn, *Galatians*, 102.

[74] My musings here invite discussion about the distinction (if any) between the new creation and God's eternal life/time. Did Paul assume that the new creation is shaped by and lived in God's time, but that it is not identical with God's forever time or were the two ideas synonymous for Paul?

[75] And elsewhere, as I have indicated in this chapter.

2
"It Is Not as Though the Word of God Has Failed"

God's Faithfulness and God's Free Sovereignty in Romans 9:6-29

Michael Wolter

I

The beginning of Romans 9:6-29 is formulated in the negative: "It is not as though the word of God has failed" (v. 6a). This reminds of the several fictive dialogues that occur a number of times in Romans:[1] in them Paul formulates a rhetorical question and rejects the implied proposition by μὴ γένοιτο ("absolutely not!"). In this respect Romans 9:6a is a shortcut of a fictive dialogue, as possibly, "What shall we say then? That the word of God has failed? Absolutely not!" Instead of using this form of argument Paul jumps directly into the problem he is worried about.[2] The rhetorical questions just mentioned and the statement in Romans 9:6a have in common that the misunderstandings that they reject emerge from what Paul in each case has said immediately before.[3] Therefore, our first question has to be: what in what Paul has written before Romans 9:6a could have led to the conclusion that "the word of God has failed"? Of course, the answer to this question is to be found in vv. 1-5. However, this text must be read carefully; two aspects are important.

1 Cf. 3:3-4, 5-6; 3:31; 6:1-2, 15; 7:7, 13; 9:14; 11:1, 11.

2 Cf. also E. Brandenburger, "Paulinische Schriftauslegung in der Kontroverse um das Verheißungswort Gottes (Röm 9)," *ZThK* 82 (1985): 1–47, 10; Klaus Haacker, *Der Brief des Paulus an die Römer*, 4th ed., THKNT 6 (Leipzig: Evangelische Verlagsanstalt, 2012), 229.

3 This holds especially for Rom 3:31 after vv. 27-30, for 6:1 after 5:21, and for 6:15 after v. 14.

1. The theological problem, with which Paul grapples in 9:1-5, is perceptible in vv. 3-5. He first states that his "siblings and brothers according to the flesh" (v. 3), that is, the non-Christian majority of Israel, is "banned . . . away from Christ" (ἀνάθεμα . . . ἀπὸ τοῦ Χριστοῦ), which means that they are presently alienated from salvation. In vv. 4-5b he confronts this situation with a catalogue of distinctions that God has bestowed on his people, in order thereby to indicate Israel's election from among the nations.[4] That the focus is on Israel's present situation and not on their future is recognizable by the perfect form of the verb ἐκπέπτωκεν. Paul here is not yet concerned about the future fate of the non-Christian majority of Israel.[5] This perspective does not come into view until 11:11.

From this follows that the starting point of Paul's argument is not the tension between Israel's election and unbelief, as it is argued occasionally.[6] In Romans 9:1-5 Israel's unbelief does not yet play any role.[7] Paul is rather concerned with Israel's discrepancy in status: how can Israel's present situation of misery be theologically reconciled with their election?

It is remarkable that the proposition that the non-Christian part of Israel is in a situation of misery or perdition is not explicitly expressed on the surface of the text. Instead, Paul disguises this matter of fact in clothes that make it virtually unrecognizable: The text begins with a ceremonious oath (v. 1), which is followed by the sworn statement (v. 2). Paul writes that he feels "great sorrow and unceasing distress." The basis for this remains unmentioned; we can deduce it only from v. 3: Paul prays that he could take on himself the curse of exclusion from Christ in the place and for the sake of (ὑπέρ) his Jewish compatriots. Since this prayer cannot be fulfilled, vv. 1-3 achieve the

4 Correspondingly Paul here also no longer speaks of "Jews" as in 1:16; 2:9, 10, 17, 28, 29; 3:1, 9, 29; 9:24; 10:12, but of "Israelites."

5 Pace Ulrich Wilckens, *Der Brief an die Römer*, 3 vols., EKKNT 6 (Zürich: Benziger Verlag, 1978–1982), 2:191; James D. G. Dunn, *Romans*, 2 vols., WBC 38 (Dallas: Word, 1988), 2:539.

6 Cf., e.g., Wilckens, *Brief an die Römer* 2:186; Hans Hübner, *Gottes Ich und Israel: Zum Schriftgebrauch des Paulus in Römer 9–11*, FRLANT 136 (Göttingen: Vandenhoeck & Ruprecht, 1984), 15; Dunn, *Romans*, 2:530; Michael Cranford, "Election and Ethnicity: Paul's View of Israel in Romans 9.1-13," *JSNT* 50 (1993): 27–41, 32; Dieter Sänger, *Die Verkündigung des Gekreuzigten und Israel*, WUNT 75 (Tübingen: Mohr Siebeck, 1994), 152–54.

7 Cf. also Lloyd Gaston, "Israel's Enemies in Pauline Theology," *NTS* 28 (1982): 400–423, 411.

character of a lament about Israel's disastrous fate. In vv. 1-3 Paul makes not Israel but himself and his mental state the subject matter of his account. It is only behind this rhetorical disguise that the actual topic can be discovered. The intention of Paul's hiding the statement about Israel's misery under two layers of rhetorical disguise—an oath first and then a lament—is at hand: he avoids formulating his proposition as a factual claim, because such a claim would always be questionable and open to denial.[8]

2. The second aspect of this text, and one that deserves close attention, concerns the role of God within the drama of Israel. Although apart from v. 5 God is not present on the surface of the text, he is implicitly there, to wit, in v. 3 and v. 4.

In v. 3 God can be recognized in the expression τοῦ Χριστοῦ, because immediately before, in 8:39, Paul has stated that it is "Christ Jesus, our Lord," in *whom* the love of God has become manifest and accessible. Insofar as we may take as given that Paul at the beginning of chapter 9 still knew what he had written at the end of chapter 8, his words in 9:3 imply the proposition that his "siblings and brothers according to the flesh" in that they are "banned away from Christ" are also "banned away from" the love of God.[9]

On the other hand, we may also take as given that Paul still knew his Bible and that he therefore also knew that it was nothing but God's love that motivated God to choose Israel from among the nations: "It was not because you are the largest of all nations that YHWH set his heart on you and chose you, for you are really the smallest of all nations. It was because YHWH loved you," as one can read in Deuteronomy 7:7-8a. Similar texts are evidenced in many other places of the

[8] That the unfulfillable prayer in v. 3 implies the proposition that unbelieving Israel is indeed "banned away from Christ" and thereby distanced from God is indicated by the preposition ὑπέρ (cf. BDAG 838–39 [s.v. ὑπέρ 1.c]); see also H. Räisänen, "Römer 9–11: Analyse eines geistigen Ringens," *ANRW* 2.25.4 (1987): 2891–939, 2896–97; Cranford, "Election," 28, rightly criticizing J. D. G. Dunn's view, according to whom this understanding "is more than open to question" (*Romans*, 2:525).

[9] Therefore, when M. Theobald boils down Paul's argument to the key sentence "Separated from *Christ*, allied with *God*!," thereby detaching God from "Christ," he downplays the sharpness of the tension in Paul's view on Israel (Theobald, "Unterschiedliche Gottesbilder in Röm 9–11?" in *The Letter to the Romans*, ed. U. Schnelle, BETL 226 [Leuven: Uitgeverij Peeters, 2009], 135–77, 151). For Paul, being "separated from Christ" always also includes separation from God.

Old Testament.[10] It is precisely this tension that is verbalized in the catalogue of distinctions that Paul enumerates in v. 4. In them God is also present, since not only is he the one who had made the "Israelites" to become "Israelites" and the one who adopted them as children (υἱοθεσία), but he has also made them participate in his "glory" (δόξα), has made the "covenants" (διαθῆκαι) with them, has granted them the law (νομοθεσία), the "service" (λατρεία), and the "promises" (ἐπαγγελίαι).

If we take these two lines together, the shape of the problem becomes visible. It differs slightly from the usual determination of the question from which Paul proceeds in 9:6-29: he is concerned with the question whether or not there is a contradictory tension in the actions of God: has his activity in the Christ-event made his election of Israel invalid, or can both actions be theologically associated with each other?

II

Let us start with some remarks on three linguistic details—the reference of ὁ λόγος τοῦ θεοῦ (v. 6a), the meaning of γάρ (v. 6b), and the structure of vv. 6b-7a.

1. The introductory statement οὐχ οἷον δὲ ὅτι ἐκπέπτωκεν ὁ λόγος τοῦ θεοῦ in v. 6a reflects a biblical expression that is attested mainly in the Deuteronomistic literature. Here it is often said of God's word that it has not failed (*lo'-nāfal dābar*; Josh 21:45; 23:14; 1 Sam 3:19; 1 Kgs 8:56; 2 Kgs 10:10; cf. also Tob 14:4a). The positive equivalent is the assertion that God's word "stands forever" (*jaqūm lecōlām*; Isa 40:8; cf. also Ps 119:89; Hag 2:5). Therefore, ὁ λόγος τοῦ θεοῦ in v. 6a is neither simply an umbrella term for the list of distinctions that God bestowed on his people according to v. 4,[11] nor semantically isotopic with the λόγια τοῦ θεοῦ of Romans 3:2.[12] It also does not denote

[10] Cf., e.g., Deut 23:6; 2 Chr 20:7 LXX; Ps 60:7 = 108:7; 127:2; Isa 5:7 LXX; 44:2 LXX; Hos 3:1; 11:1; 14:5; Pss Sol 18:3; Jub. 1:25; 4 Esd. 6:58; m. Avoth 3:14: "Beloved is Israel in that they are called sons of the place (i.e., of God)." Cf. also Rom 11:28.

[11] Cf. Gaston, "Israel's Enemies," 413; Douglas J. Moo, *The Epistle to the Romans*, NIC (Grand Rapids: Eerdmans, 1996), 572f; Haacker, *Brief des Paulus an die Römer*, 229.

[12] Cf., e.g., Wolfgang Kraus, *Das Volk Gottes: Zur Grundlegung der Ekklesiologie bei Paulus*, WUNT 85 (Tübingen: Mohr Siebeck, 1996), 298 n. 174; Beverly Roberts Gaventa, "On the Calling-Into-Being of Israel: Romans 9:6-29," in *Between Gospel and*

the gospel as elsewhere in the Pauline writings.[13] Rather, it has to be understood as a generic expression making comprehensive reference to any assurance and promise whatsoever God has made on behalf of Israel. What Paul is claiming here is that Israel's present misery does not have an effect on God, because it does not mean that one single word of God has become inefficacious.

2. γάρ in v. 6b should not be understood anaphorically as referring to what precedes and giving a rationale for the statement formulated in v. 6a. Under the presupposition that "the word of God" refers to God's promise to Israel, it would be absurd to argue that "God's word has not failed 'because' or 'for' not all those who belong to Israel are Israel."[14] Therefore, γάρ has a cataphoric reference. Its meaning is attested in BDAG as "expressing continuation or connection" and translated by "indeed" or "to be sure."[15] Thus, the γάρ-sentence in v. 6b does not give an explanation but expresses something like a restriction or a relativization to the statement formulated in v. 6a.

3. As to the structure of vv. 6b-7a, the context requires a chiastic reading of Paul's statement. Verse 8 evidences that in v. 7 τέκνα has to be taken as the broader category, whereas σπέρμα is the more restrictive one.[16] From this follows that πάντες τέκνα at the end of v. 7a parallels πάντες οἱ ἐξ Ἰσραήλ at the beginning of v. 6b.

Election: Explorations in the Interpretation of Romans 9–11, ed. Florian Wilk and Ross Wagner, WUNT 257 (Tübingen: Mohr Siebeck, 2010), 255–69, 258.

13 This identification is advocated by Erhard Güttgemanns, "Heilsgeschichte bei Paulus oder Dynamik des Evangeliums? Zur strukturellen Relevanz von Röm 9–11 für die Theologie des Römerbriefs," in *Studia Linguistica Neotestamentica*, BEvT 60 (Munich: Chr. Kaiser Verlag, 1973), 34–58, 40; Roy D. Kotansky, "A Note on Romans 9:6: *ho logos tou theou* as the Proclamation of the Gospel," *StBT* 7 (1977): 24–30; Paul-Gerhard Klumbies, "Israels Vorzüge und das Evangelium von der Gottesgerechtigkeit in Römer 9–11," *WuD.NF* 18 (1985): 135–57, 141–42; Robert Jewett, *Romans*, Hermeneia (Minneapolis: Fortress, 2007), 574.

14 For this translation, cf. below n. 17.

15 BDAG 152 (s.v. γάρ 4: "where more recent users of the texts . . . would often prefer to see it replaced by δέ") with reference to Rom 2:25; 4:3-9; 5:7; 12:3; 14:5 and to Trypho Gramm., Fragm. 54: γάρ . . . εἶς οὖν ἐστιν ἀντὶ τοῦ δέ ("γάρ . . . is one and the same thing as δέ").

16 Those who interpret σπέρμα in v. 7a as the wider category and τέκνα as the more restricted one are scarcely right; cf., e.g., Brendan Byrne, *"Sons of God"—"Seeds of Abraham": A Study of the Idea of the Sonship of God of All Christians in Paul against the Jewish Background*, AnBib 83 (Rome: Editrice Pontificio Istituto Biblico, 1979), 130–31; Folker Siegert, *Argumentation bei Paulus, gezeigt an Röm 9–11*, WUNT

"Israel" cannot refer to Jacob here, as many assume,[17] because in formulations with "οἱ ἐκ/ἐξ + proper name" the proper name never denotes the progenitor from whom the so-designated people descend. Instead, it refers mostly to cities and territories (cf. 1 Esd 5:18-21; Jdt 15:5; 1 Macc 6:49; 9:36; Oba 9). First Esdras 9:37 corresponds closest to the Pauline expression: "The priests and the Levites and οἱ ἐκ τοῦ Ἰσραήλ. . . ." Thus, οἱ ἐκ Ἰσραήλ in Romans 9:6b does not designate descent but affiliation.[18] Therefore, this expression is semantically akin to οἱ ἐκ τοῦ λαοῦ, what 1 Esdras 5:45, the parallel to 1 Esdras 9:37, has instead of the expression attested there, οἱ ἐκ τοῦ Ἰσραήλ (cf. also 1 Esd 1:13; Jdt 11:13). Formulations in the Septuagint that have ἐξ Ἰσραήλ as a prepositional attribute denoting the belonging of individuals or groups to Israel point in the same direction (2 Sam 19:23: οὐ θανατωθήσεταί τις ἀνὴρ ἐξ Ἰσραήλ; cf. also 6:1; 1 Chr 19:10; 1 Macc 1:30; 6:21; 7:5; 10:61; Esd 2:59).[19]

The grammatically incoherent repetition of πάντες in v. 7 (πάντες is masculine, whereas τέκνα is neuter)[20] makes this correspondence especially obvious. Accordingly, the predicate nominative Ἰσραήλ at the end of v. 6b corresponds to the predicate nominative σπέρμα, which in v. 7a is in the first position. Thus, vv. 6b and 7a exhibit a chiastic structure:[21]

---

34 (Tübingen: Mohr Siebeck, 1985), 125; Heinrich Schlier, *Der Römerbrief*, 2nd ed., HThKNT 6 (Freiburg: Herder, 1977), 290; Ernst Käsemann, *Commentary on Romans*, trans. G. W. Bromiley (Grand Rapids: Eerdmans, 1980), 262; Leon Morris, *The Epistle to the Romans* (Grand Rapids: Eerdmans, 1988), 353; Joseph A. Fitzmyer, *Romans*, AB 33 (New York: Doubleday, 1993), 560.

17 Cf., e.g., Adolf Schlatter, *Gottes Gerechtigkeit: Ein Kommentar zum Römerbrief* (Stuttgart: Calwer Vereinsbuchhandlung, 1935), 297; Otto Michel, *Der Brief an die Römer*, 5th ed., KEK 4 (Göttingen: Vandenhoeck & Ruprecht, 1978), 300; Haacker, *Brief des Paulus an die Römer*, 230; Filippo Belli, *Argumentation and the Use of Scripture in Romans 9–11*, AnBib 183 (Rome: Gregorian & Biblical Press, 2010), 74.

18 Cf. also BDAG 235 (s.v. ἐκ 3.d).

19 Jewett, *Romans*, 574 n. 41, mentions twenty-eight Septuagint occurrences of ἐξ Ἰσραήλ, though most of them are not adnominal phrases as in Rom 9:6b, but adverbial phrases. This important difference ought not be overlooked.

20 πάντες is not conceived of as an attribute adjective to τέκνα (this is the misunderstanding of Belli, *Argumentation*, 76 n. 61), but τέκνα is something like an elliptical relative clause that serves as an apposition modifying πάντες: "all (those who are) children."

21 Cf. also Jack Khalil, "Translating Rom 9:7a: For an Accurate Understanding of a Difficult Verse," in Schnelle, *Letter to the Romans*, 691–97, 693–95.

6b οὐ γὰρ
(a) πάντες οἱ ἐξ Ἰσραήλ
(b) οὗτοι Ἰσραήλ
7a οὐδ᾽ ὅτι εἰσὶν
(b) σπέρμα Ἀβραάμ
(a) πάντες τέκνα

From this follows that the negation in v. 6b does not negate the expression οὗτοι Ἰσραήλ, as John Piper and others have advocated,[22] but is ambiguous: if we take v. 6b as such, the negation refers only to πάντες οἱ ἐξ Ἰσραήλ. It follows the same syntactic pattern as Matt 7:21 ("Not everyone [οὐ πᾶς] who says to me, 'Lord, Lord!,' will enter the kingdom of heaven").[23] If we read it together with v. 7a, it refers to the entire statement, as Beverly Roberts Gaventa has argued: "For it is not the case that all those who are from Israel . . . , these people are . . . Israel."[24] Correspondingly, v. 7a is introduced by the negation οὐδέ, which according to BDAG "joins negative sentences or clauses to others of the same kind."[25] οὐδ᾽ ὅτι at the beginning of v. 7a corresponds to οὐ (v. 6b)[26] and not to οὐχ οἷον δὲ ὅτι at the beginning of v. 6a, as some assume.[27]

[22] So, e.g., John Piper, *The Justification of God: An Exegetical Study of Romans 9:1-23* (Grand Rapids: Baker, 1983), 48; Moo, *Epistle to the Romans*, 573; Thomas R. Schreiner, *Romans*, BECNT (Grand Rapids: Baker, 1998), 493; Florian Wilk, *Die Bedeutung des Jesajabuches für Paulus*, FRLANT 179 (Göttingen: Vandenhoeck & Ruprecht, 1998), 313; Richard Bell, *The Irrevocable Call of God: An Inquiry into Paul's Theology of Israel*, WUNT 184 (Tübingen: Mohr Siebeck, 2005), 210; Brisio J. Oropeza, "Paul and Theodicy: Intertextual Thoughts on God's Justice and Faithfulness to Israel in Romans 9–11," *NTS* 53 (2007): 57–80, 61. Brian J. Abasciano, *Paul's Use of the Old Testament in Romans 9.1-9: An Intertextual and Theological Exegesis*, LNTS 301 (London: T&T Clark, 2005), 183–89, has criticized this interpretation with convincing arguments; cf. also Jewett, *Romans*, 574.

[23] Cf. also Aristoteles, *Eth. Eud.* 1248a13: οὐ πάντες οἱ δοκοῦντες εὐτυχεῖν διὰ τύχην κατορθοῦσιν ("not all those who seem fortunate succeed because of fortune"); Galenus, In Hippocrat. aphor. comm. vii, ed. Kühn XVIIb, 540,1: οὐ πάντες οἱ ἐκλυόμενοι ἐξαίφνης τελευτῶσιν ("not all those who lose weight die suddenly").

[24] Cf. Gaventa, "On the Calling-Into-Being," 259.

[25] BDAG s.v. οὐδέ 1 (p. 591).

[26] Cf. also C. E. B. Cranfield, *A Critical and Exegetical Commentary on the Epistle to the Romans*, 2 vols., ICC (Edinburgh: T&T Clark, 1979), 2:473–74.

[27] Cf., e.g., Dunn, *Romans*, 2:540; Haacker, *Brief des Paulus an die Römer*, 231.

III

In the third section I examine the two arguments from Scripture with the help of which Paul tries to corroborate the restriction formulated in v. 6b.

Verses 7-9: Abraham's "Children" and His "Seed." In v. 7a the plural τέκνα should be taken seriously. Paul not only is talking here about the opposition between Isaac and Ishmael as in Galatians 4:21-31, but takes all sons of Abraham into account, including the six sons of Ketura (cf. Gen 25:1-4). It is they and Ishmael whom he calls τέκνα τῆς σαρκός because they were begotten and conceived in the natural way, that is, as it has ever been usual among human beings. On the contrary, this was not the case with Isaac. The reason for his exceptional status is well known. Since both Abraham and Sara were already beyond procreational age, Isaac could not have been conceived κατὰ σάρκα but only δι' ἐπαγγελίας, as Paul had argued in Galatians 4:23. In Romans 9:8 he uses the same distinction that he evidently takes up from Galatians 4. The distinction between Isaac and the other seven children of Abraham consisted in that only Isaac came into being by God's intervention and not in the way usual among human beings. God did not reject the other seven, but he simply did not originate them.[28] Abraham does not determines the identity of his children, but only God does. Being Abraham's "child" does not make a human being Abraham's "seed," because only those children of Abraham who are in that sense τέκνα τοῦ θεοῦ as they had been originated by God's intervention are reckoned as "seed." Perhaps we could invoke Philo's explanation of Gen 16:1 in QG 3.18:

> A barren woman has been made the mother of Isaac "in order that conception and birth might be not so much the result of the union with a man as through God's providence. For if a barren woman gives birth, then this was not by way of generation but the work of God's power."

The ἐπαγγελία in v. 8 must not be confused with the ἐπαγγελία mentioned in Romans 4:13-14, 16, 20: here, in Romans 4, Paul explicitly refers either to the promise that Abraham and his seed will inherit the land in Genesis 12:7; 13:15, 17; 15:7f.18; 17:8 (Rom 4:13-14, 16) or to the promise of the vast multitude of Abraham's offspring in Genesis 15:5 (Rom 4:20). Instead, according to Romans 9:9, it is a quotation

[28] Cf. also Gaventa, "On the Calling-Into-Being," 260.

put together from Genesis 18:10 and 18:14 that Paul identifies as the promise that has made Abraham's τέκνα to be his σπέρμα: "At this time I will come, and Sarah will have a son." Therefore, although Isaac is only one and Paul in v. 8 speaks of the "children of God" and the "children of promise" in the plural, his perspective at this point of his argument does not yet go beyond the Abraham narrative as if he already had in view the calling of the Gentiles to be God's people referred to in vv. 24-26,[29] or all those who believe in Christ.[30]

Verses 10-13: Jacob and Esau. This situation is quite different from that of Abraham and his offspring. Here it has to do not only with just one mother instead of three, but also with one and the same way and situation of conception. In distinction from vv. 7-9 the two sons of Isaac were both "children of the flesh" because they were begotten in the natural way by one and the same man—by "our father Isaac." God and his word of promise were completely absent from the origin of both. This difference is emphasized by ἐξ ἑνός in v. 10. Beyond that, both sons were even begotten in one and the same moment, which can be concluded from their being twins. All this means that in this case the difference between the two children is not rooted in the difference of their genealogy. Here Paul does not argue against corporeal descent as he did in vv. 7-9. Therefore, it is not possible to construct two typologically parallel lines consisting of οἱ ἐξ Ἰσραήλ, τέκνα τῆς σαρκός, and Esau on one side and Ἰσραήλ, τέκνα τῆς ἐπαγγελίας, and Jacob on the other.

A further difference can be seen in Paul's characterization of the action of God. Whereas in vv. 7-9 he left Abraham's children who were not σπέρμα because they were "children of the flesh" simply unmentioned, in vv. 10-13 Paul explicitly emphasizes that in this case God's election is accompanied by rejection, when in v. 13 he quotes Malachi 1:2-3: "Yet I loved Jacob, but hated Esau." Also, by the quote of Genesis 25:23 in v. 12b, he leads his readers to understand that God's election created a winner and a loser: "The older will serve the younger." However, this has only illustrative purposes and does not constitute the essence of God's election. The essence is identified in v. 11: God's election is always and only God's antecedent *action* and

[29] So Wilk, *Bedeutung*, 120 n. 7; Gerhard Sass, *Leben aus den Verheißungen: Traditionsgeschichtliche und biblisch-theologische Untersuchungen zur Rede von Gottes Verheißungen im Frühjudentum und beim Apostel Paulus*, FRLANT 165 (Göttingen: Vandenhoeck & Ruprecht, 1995), 435–36.

[30] So Abasciano, *Paul's Use*, 195.

never *re-action*. When Paul indicates that God elected and rejected before both children had the opportunity to differ in terms of behavior, he depicts God's election against a sapiential background. He characterizes the essence of God's election and rejection by underlining that it was not the nexus of conduct and consequences as it is well known from sapiential teaching by which God's decision was determined. Rather, there is no other criterion for the election other than "God's prior decision" (v. 11: his πρόθεσις). There is not only no indication that Paul indirectly speaks here "against those who attempt righteousness through the works of the law rather than faith,"[31] but this interpretation is explicitly disproved by the final clause in v. 11b in which Paul explains that election and rejection is always only God's sovereign action.[32]

Both sections of Paul's argument have in common that it is solely the sovereign initiative of God who decides about who is in and who is out. This leads us to another insight: neither when God distinguished between Isaac and Abraham's "children of the flesh" nor when he discriminated between Jacob and Esau, he differentiated *within* Israel.[33] Both stories to which Paul here refers narrate actions of God, which have the result that only the favored side—Isaac and Jacob—is Israel whereas the others—the sons of Hagar and Ketura and Esau—are definitely *not*. In this sense the two examples from the history of Israel's forebears are only formally compatible with the concept of Israel that stands behind the distinction between οἱ ἐξ 'Ισραήλ and 'Ισραήλ in v. 6b and between the υἱοὶ 'Ισραήλ and the ὑπόλειμμα in v. 27.

[31] This is the opinion of Oropeza, "Paul and Theodicy," 63, who clearly misses the point of argument (cf. the critique of this interpretation by Moo, *Epistle to the Romans*, 583).

[32] The closest parallel to the concept expressed in 9:11b is probably attested in Isa 14:24 LXX: τάδε λέγει κύριος σαβαωθ ὃν τρόπον εἴρηκα οὕτως ἔσται καὶ ὃν τρόπον βεβούλευμαι οὕτως μενεῖ ("Thus says the Lord of hosts: 'As I have spoken so shall it be, and as I have planned, so will it happen'"). μένειν here means that God's "prior decision" will be realized without any change.

[33] Cf. also Susan Grove Eastman, "Israel and the Mercy of God: A Re-reading of Galatians 6:16 and Romans 9–11," *NTS* 56 (2010): 367–95, 377 n. 34. This is overlooked by many; cf., e.g., William S. Campbell, "The Freedom and Faithfulness of God in Relation to Israel," *JSNT* 13 (1981): 27–45, 29; Michael Theobald, "Kirche und Israel nach Röm 9–11," in *Studien zum Römerbrief*, WUNT 136 (Tübingen: Mohr Siebeck, 2001), 324–49, 333. On the other hand, this does not of course imply that according to Paul's view the other children of Abraham "became the progenitors of the Gentiles" (Eastman, "Israel and the Mercy of God," 377 n. 34).

In vv. 7-9 and 10-13 Paul demonstrates from Scripture that God has not differentiated *within* Israel, but has determined who is Israel and who is *not*.

IV

In v. 14 Paul picks up a possible misinterpretation of the account of God's actions given in vv. 7-13.[34] With the rhetorical question, "What then shall we say? Is there injustice with God?" a new section begins that stretches to v. 26. I include also vv. 24-26 in this section because by means of the relative pronoun οὕς (v. 24) the following is connected to the preceding words about the "vessels of mercy" (v. 23).

1. The coherence of this section is determined by three linguistic items:

- first by the cascading linkage of the words ἔλεος/ἐλεεῖν (vv. 15, 16, 18, 23), θέλειν (vv. 18, 22), and σκεῦος (vv. 21, 22, 23);
- second by terms denoting God's sovereignty: δύναμις/δυνατός (vv. 17, 22), βούλημα (v. 19), ἐξουσία (v. 21), and θέλειν (vv. 18, 22);
- and third and mainly by the antithetical oppositions that run throughout the entire section thereby describing and characterizing God's actions: "Moses" (v. 15) and "Pharaoh" (v. 17), ἐλεεῖν and σκληρύνειν (v. 18), τιμή and ἀτιμία (v. 21), εἰς ἀπώλειαν and εἰς δόξαν (vv. 22/23), and finally σκεύη ὀργῆς and σκεύη ἐλέους (vv. 22/23).

2. A different usage of Scripture in vv. 15-17 indicates that the new section varies from the preceding one. It is not only so that in vv. 15 and 17 the historical sequence is not carried forward—Moses and Pharaoh appear in reversed order—but the character of God's actions to which Paul now refers is completely different: God does not separate brothers from each other but demonstrates that he treats human beings contrastively, to wit, as he "wills," as it is said in v. 18 where Paul summarizes vv. 15-17. A further difference can be seen in the fact that different from vv. 7-13 God's actions do not aim to determine the status of human beings as it was the case with the sons of Abraham and Isaac, but Paul makes them aim to God himself: for no other reason has God "raised up" Pharaoh, than "to show my power

[34] Cf. already Rom 3:3-4, 5-6, 31; 6:1-2, 15; 7:7, 13; and thereafter 11:1, 11.

through you that my name may be proclaimed throughout the earth."[35] The question for Israel has virtually disappeared from Paul's argument. This complies with the fact that the only connection between the two pairs of scriptural references is not Israel, but solely God himself. This is perceptible in the only resumption from vv. 7-13 in vv. 14-26: that God chose Jacob and rejected Esau without them "having done anything, good or bad" (μηδὲ πραξάντων τι ἀγαθὸν ἢ φαῦλον,[36] v. 11a), that is, "not from works" (οὐκ ἐξ ἔργων, v. 12a)[37] corresponds to "it is not up to a person's will or exertion" (οὐ τοῦ θέλοντος οὐδὲ τοῦ τρέχοντος, v. 16), and also what follows in v. 11b ("in order that God's elective purpose should stand") and v. 12 ("from the one who calls") finds its counterpart in the almost tautological formulation in v. 16: to whom God shows mercy is only "up to the mercy-showing God" (τοῦ ἐλεῶντος θεοῦ).

Oddly enough, herewith Paul repeats exactly the same principle that, albeit mistakenly, had earned God the reproach that there is "injustice with God" if his treatment of human beings entirely disregards their behavior. Paul answers a rhetorical question that implies a reproach by simply repeating the matter of fact against which the reproach is directed!

3. Paul can argue that way because he does not discuss the question at the level of the substantial subject matter denoted by the rhetorical question in v. 14b ("Is there injustice with God?"). Instead, in v. 20, Paul moves to a superior level and principally denies the legitimacy of asking God reproaching questions: "O human being (ὦ ἄνθρωπε)—who are you (σὺ τίς εἶ) indeed that you talk back to God (ἀνταποκρινόμενος τῷ θεῷ)?"

This kind of rhetorical question in which a human τίς is confronted with God is very well known from other texts. Not very much

35 Paul here alludes to Exod 4:21; 7:3, 22; 8:15; 9:12, 35; 10:1, 20, 27; 11:10; 13:15; 14:4, 8, 17.

36 Here we have to do with an incomplete *genitivus absolutus*; to γεννηθέντων and πραξάντων has to be added αὐτῶν; cf. BDF §423.

37 Exegetes should be reluctant to discover here Paul's doctrine of justification (cf., e.g., Brandenburger, "Paulinische Schriftauslegung," 34–35; see also above with n. 31). Against this speaks that not only that any talk of "justice" and "faith" is missing, but also that ἐξ ἔργων in v. 12a does not refer to the "works of the law" (ἔργα νόμου). Thus, the center of the semantic field of Paul's justification discourse is absent here (cf. Michael Wolter, *Paul: An Outline of His Theology* (Waco, Tex.: Baylor University Press, 2015).

later, at the end of ch. 11, Paul will repeat exactly this same structure in a hymn celebrating God's wisdom unknown to human beings (11:33-35):

> [33]Oh the depth of the wealth and of the wisdom and of the knowledge of
> *God* (θεοῦ)!
> How unsearchable are his judgments and inscrutable his ways!
> [34]For *who* (τίς) has known thinking of the *Lord* (κυρίου)?
> Or *who* (τίς) has been *his* (αὐτοῦ) counselor?
> [35]Or *who* (τίς) has brought a contribution to *him* (αὐτῷ),
> to have to be compensated in return?

All three questions expect the answer "No one!" and they are intended to demonstrate the impossibility of human beings to understand God's decisions and judgments. The argumentative force of those questions is based on common knowledge: that there is a categorical distinction between God and human beings and that the border between them can never be transgressed. That means: asking God reproaching questions and thus "talking back to God" (Rom 9:20) is the same as if human beings claim to "know thinking of the Lord" or to "have been his counselor" or to have "brought a contribution to him in order to be recompensated" (11:33-35). It is altogether impossible because in each case human beings are trying to cross an uncrossable border.

A further parallel can be found in Romans 8:31b-34a:

> [31b]If *God* (θεός) is for us, *who* (τίς) is against us?
> . . .
> [33a]*Who* (τίς) will bring a charge against *God's* (θεοῦ) elect?
> [33b]*God* (θεός) is the one who justifies! [34a]*Who* (τίς) is there to condemn?[38]

All these juxtapositions have their closest parallels in the Old Testament. Let me bring in only three representative examples, the content of which comes close to Romans 9:19-20:

> The *Lord* has said to him, "Curse David." *Who* (*mī*) then shall say, "Why have you done so?" (2 Sam 16:10)

> For the *Lord of hosts* has purposed. *Who* (*mī*) will annul it? (Isa 14:27)

> *I* work. *Who* (*mī*) can turn it back? (Isa 43:13)[39]

[38] In 8:34b-35a the line of thought is continued christologically: "*Christ (Jesus)* is the one who died. . . . *Who* will separate us from the love of Christ?"

[39] Cf. also Num 24:23; 1 Sam 2:25; 6:20; Ps 60:8 LXX; 89:9; 113:5; Eccl 7:13; Job 9:12; 11:10; 34:29ab; 36:22-23; Wis 9:13; 12:12-13; Sir 18:5; Isa 50:8-9; Amos 3:8; Joel 2:11.

In all cases the rhetorical questions indicate that there is no being and no power that is able to oppose God. And what comes still closer to the topic of Romans 9:14-26, the reproach against God of being unjust (v. 14), is in the book of Job: Job's accusation against God and God's second speech from the whirlwind in Job 40:6–41:26. By his very first words God repels Job's demand for a courtroom confrontation (Job 40:7-9):

> 7Gird up your loins, like a man. I will question you, and you tell me the answers.
> 8Will *you* really challenge *my* justice?
> Will *you* declare *me* guilty that *you* may be in the right?
> 9Have *you* an arm like *God's*?
> Can *you* thunder with a voice like *his*?

We have here not only the same rhetorical questions as in Romans 9:20, but also an analogous confrontation: the juxtaposition of a human being and God in Romans 9:20 corresponds in Job 40:7-9 to the confrontation between the "you" of Job and the "I" of God that brings to Job's mind that—to say it with the words of Romans 9:20—"God is God, and he is a human being who has not the right to talk back to God." Just as in the book of Job Paul appeals to God's omnipotence, and just as in Job the question for God's justice in Romans 9:14 does not receive an answer but is simply rebuked. God is not merely a functionary who has to execute the nexus of conduct and consequences, but he is God Almighty who has the right to act as he wills without being compelled to give an account to anybody.[40]

4. By alluding to Isaiah 29:16, Paul parallels the relationship between human beings and God to the relationships first between the "molder" (ὁ πλάσας) and that "what is molded" (τὸ πλάσμα; v. 20b) and then (in v. 21) between the "potter" (ὁ κεραμεύς) and the "vessels" (τὰ σκεύη) that are produced by him. In contrast to vv. 7-18 Paul here does not argue with recourse to the history of Israel's forebears, but he confronts the creature with his creator.[41] This linguistic usage goes back to Genesis 2:7 where it is said that God "molded (ἔπλασεν) the man out of the dust from the ground." Since the Hebrew equivalent of the verb is *jāśar*, which not only describes the work of the "potter," but stands also always behind the Greek word κεραμεύς, the connection between Romans 9:20 and v. 21 becomes evident. As an

40 Cf. also Brandenburger, "Paulinische Schriftauslegung," 11.
41 Cf. again Brandenburger, "Paulinische Schriftauslegung," 11.

example, I invoke Jeremiah 18:6, which also comes very close to the use of this imagery in Romans 9:21:

> "House of Israel, can I not do to you as this potter (LXX: κεραμεύς) does?"—declaration of the Lord. "Just like clay in the potter's (LXX: τοῦ κεραμέως) hand, so are you in my hand, house of Israel." (Jer 18:6)

In the context of Romans 9:14-26 the intention of this imagery is solely focused on the illustration of the relationship between God and human beings.[42] Paul wants to qualify God with regard to his absolute sovereignty and his right to arbitrariness. Therefore, we are well advised to resist the temptation of an allegorical identification of the vessels of honor and dishonor mentioned in v. 21b-c.[43] Paul's argument remains purely metaphorical, and everybody can understand its direction without postulating a specific reference of this imagery outside the text. Instead, the antithetical juxtaposition of the two kinds of vessels serves the intention to illustrate God's power to do this and the very opposite in equal measure. The interaction between this imagery and the words denoting God's power—i.e., δύναμις (v. 17c), θέλειν (vv. 18a.b.22a), βούλημα (v. 19c), ἐξουσία (v. 21a), δυνατόν (v. 22b)—prompts the conclusion that it is not God's faithfulness to his promises given to Israel that is in the focus of Paul's argument, but God's free sovereignty, because God is absolutely free to act as he wills.

Even in vv. 22-23 where Paul transfers the metaphorical imagery from the relationship between the potter and the pots to the relationship between God and human beings, he identifies neither the σκεύη ὀργῆς "made ready for destruction" nor the σκεύη ἐλέους "prepared beforehand for glory" with specific groups of human beings. Instead, the different kinds of "vessels" illustrate in an ideal-typical way the same contrastive treatment of human beings as in Romans 2:6-11, the description of God's righteous judgment. And just the same as in this text the character of God's judgment is illustrated by the different fates of distinct *types* of human beings. In Romans 9:22-23 Paul is not interested in the human beings and in the question of who has to expect "wrath" and who "glory," but what is at issue is only God and

[42] Cf. also Isa 45:9; 64:7; Jer 19:10-11; Sir 33(36):13: "Like clay of a potter (πηλὸς κεραμέως) [is] in his hands, to be molded according to his pleasure, so are human beings in the hands of their Maker, to be assigned according to his decision."

[43] Cf. also Jewett, *Romans*, 594–95.

the principles of his action. This is discernible from the two intentional clauses in v. 22b (θέλων . . . ἐνδείξασθαι τὴν ὀργὴν καὶ γνωρίσαι τὸ δυνατὸν αὐτοῦ) and in v. 23b (ἵνα γνωρίσῃ τὸν πλοῦτον τῆς δόξης αὐτοῦ). According to these two explanations, the only underlying principle of God's different treatment of the two kinds of vessels is to demonstrate that he is the Almighty God. There is no indication that Paul here identifies the "vessels of wrath" with the non-Christian Jews and the "vessels of mercy" with the Christians, as it is often assumed.[44]

In vv. 22-23 two clauses of the sentence have been dropped elliptically:[45]

Syntactic level

(a) Protasis: εἰ δὲ
(c) **θέλων**
(b) *ὁ θεὸς*
(c) **ἐνδείξασθαι τὴν ὀργὴν καὶ γνωρίσαι τὸ δυνατὸν αὐτοῦ**
(b) *ἤνεγκεν ἐν πολλῇ μακροθυμίᾳ σκεύη ὀργῆς*
(d) κατηρτισμένα εἰς ἀπώλειαν,
(b) *καὶ*
(c) **ἵνα γνωρίσῃ τὸν πλοῦτον τῆς δόξης αὐτοῦ ἐπὶ σκεύη ἐλέους**
(d) ἃ προητοίμασεν εἰς δόξαν
(b) *???????????????????????????*
(a) Apodosis: ??????????????????????????????

There is not only on level (a) the *apodosis* of the conditional clause missing, but also on level (b) the continuation of the ἤνεγκεν . . . καί clause. The missing *apodosis* on level (a) can perhaps be filled in with words taken from v. 20a: "If God . . . endured . . . and . . . , 'which human being could talk back to him?' "[46]

The two missing clauses have been replaced by another thought that was caused by the talk of σκεύη ἐλέους ἃ προητοίμασεν εἰς δόξαν (v. 23) and plugged in by vv. 24-26: a diverting excursus on the status of the Christian "we" called by God from among Jews and Gentiles.

But what about Israel?

[44] E.g., by Wilckens, *Brief an die Römer*, 2:203; Moo, *Epistle to the Romans*, 609; Jewett, *Romans*, 597.

[45] This speaks against the proposal of R. Wagner, *Heralds of the Good News: Isaiah and Paul in Concert in the Letter to the Romans*, NovTSup 101 (Leiden: Brill, 2002), 76–77, to fill in the missing *apodosis* with thoughts taken from Rom 11:11-16, 25-32.

[46] In favor of this addition can be adduced that in 8:31 the same syntactic and semantic structure is attested: "If God (εἰ ὁ θεός) is for us, who (τίς) can be against us?"

V

1. The original question whether or not Israel's election has been made invalid has entirely passed from view in Paul's argument after v. 13. However, it has not passed out of his mind. This results from the formulation ὑπὲρ τοῦ 'Ισραήλ in v. 27a. By the explicit indication that "Israel" is the subject matter of the quotations from Hosea 2:1, Isaiah 10:22-23, and Isaiah 1:9 following in vv. 27b-29, Paul not only highlights the beginning of a new section in the text,[47] but also resumes the initial question of the entire section. An additional connection with the beginning in Romans 9:6-7 can be seen in the resumption of the words λόγος and σπέρμα from these verses in the quotations of Isaiah 10:22-23 and Isaiah 1:9 in vv. 27-28 and v. 29.

Whether the expression ὑπὲρ τοῦ 'Ισραήλ has to be translated by "*concerning* Israel" or "*on behalf of* Israel" is neither decidable[48] nor important for the understanding of the quotations from Hosea 2:1, Isaiah 10:22-23, and Isaiah 1:9 following in vv. 27b-29. This is so because "Israel" here does not refer to non-Christian Judaism as in Romans 9:31; 10:19, 21 and as we understand this term today. Instead "Israel" here encompasses as in Romans 11:25, 26, and possibly also in 11:7 both non-Christian Jews and Christian Jews.[49] However, the quotations point into two different directions:[50]

(1) In Isaiah 10:22-23 (quoted in vv. 27b-28) the "numerical disparity"[51] between "the sand of the sea" (ἡ ἄμμος τῆς θαλάσσης) and "the remnant" (τὸ ὑπόλειμμα) reproduces the difference between πάντες οἱ ἐξ 'Ισραήλ and (οὗτοι) 'Ισραήλ in 9:6b.[52]

[47] This is not sufficiently taken into consideration by N. T. Wright, *Paul and the Faithfulness of God*, 2 vols. (Minneapolis: Fortress, 2013), 2:1193–94, who therefore mistakenly constructs a continuity between Rom 9:24-26 and 9:27-29 and parallels it with 10:20 and 10:21; cf. also n. 54.

[48] Cf. Wagner, *Heralds of the Good News*, 93.

[49] Yet a different meaning is attested in Rom 11:2; 2 Cor 3:7, 13: "Israel" here designates the people of God of the time of Elijah or Moses.

[50] Cf. already Michel, *Brief an die Römer*, 318; Moo, *Epistle to the Romans*, 615; Wagner, *Heralds of the Good News*, 94.

[51] Wagner, *Heralds of the Good News*, 107.

[52] This has been overlooked by John Paul Heil, "From Remnant to Seed of Hope for Israel: Romans 9:27-29," in *CBQ* 64 (2002): 703–20, who tries to understand Rom 9:27b "as an eventual conditional sentence expressing the hope" that, because the sons of nonbelieving Israel "will be as numerous as the sand of the sea, then surely at least a remnant of this great number will be saved in the future" (708, cf. also already Richard B. Hays, *Echoes of Scripture in the Letters of Paul* [New Haven, Conn.: Yale

Therefore, together with ὑπόλειμμα an unambiguous "only" cannot but be overheard. The fulfillment of God's promises to Israel goes hand in hand with a decimation of Israel to a remnant. Therefore, although the quotation of Isaiah 10:22-23 in Romans 9:27b-28 is of course not "an announcement of condemnation on Israel,"[53] Paul makes it declare that presently the vast majority of Israel is "out" and only a remnant is "in." This "remnant"-Israel is the Christian Jews.[54]

(2) The quotation of Isaiah 1:9 in v. 29 points into the opposite direction: here the "remnant" is called "seed." The reference is of course the same: the Jewish Christians. The connection between the two is signaled by ἐγκατέλιπεν (v. 29b), which is taken from the same root as ὑπόλειμμα. The first-plural forms ἡμῖν, ἐγενήθημεν, and ὡμοιώθημεν refer to Israel as God's chosen people, and it is the "remnant"/"seed" that marks the difference between Israel on the one side and Sodom and Gomorrah on the other. It is by this quotation that Paul elucidates the thesis of v. 6a, that the word of God has not fallen away.

From this follows that both quotations can be read as chiastic resumptions of 9:6b (by Isa 10:22-23 in v. 27b-28) and of v. 6a (by Isa 1:9 in v. 29). Accordingly, Paul's argument becomes clear: it is only they, the Christian Jews, who stand in continuity with Israel's election and in whom the promise to Israel's fathers remains alive. God's word has not "fallen away," and Israel has not become like Sodom and Gomorrah, only because there is this Jewish Christian "remnant." This is so because it is this Jewish Christian "remnant" in whom the manifestations of God's love in the Christ-event (9:3) and in Israel's election (9:4) overlap and in whom the tension between these manifestations is resolved.

2. On the other hand, there is no use denying that Paul has not at all resolved the problem that formed the starting point of his argument. He has simply bypassed it. The main question remains open:

University Press, 1989], 68). Beyond that, this interpretation contradicts straightaway what Paul will write in Rom 11:11-32.

[53] Wagner, *Heralds of the Good News*, 107.

[54] And definitely not the Gentile Christians and Jewish Christians, as it was advocated in earlier scholarship (e.g., Schlier, *Römerbrief*, 303: "the true Israel in the Ekklesia") and was recently proposed again by Eastman, "Israel and the Mercy of God," 367–68, and Wright, *Paul and the Faithfulness of God*, 2:1193–94. Therefore, it is also not possible to say that "Israel as a whole" has rejected the Messiah (Wright, *Paul and the Faithfulness of God*, 2:1193).

what about Paul's "siblings and brothers according to the flesh" (v. 3), the οἱ ἐξ 'Ισραήλ who have not accepted the gospel of Christ and therefore, by having been "banned away from Christ," have fallen away from the sphere of God's salvation?

Paul will not come back to this question until the beginning of chapter 11, where he asks rhetorically whether God has rejected his people (v. 1a). However, here also his answer does not go beyond what he has written in 9:27-29. By pointing to himself as a Christian Jew ("I too am an Israelite, a descendant of Abraham, of the tribe of Benjamin"; 11:1c) he denies this assumption categorically: μὴ γένοιτο (v. 1b). Thus, here also he plays the Jewish-Christian card. Because there are Jewish Christians, one cannot say that God has rejected Israel.

In the following section he makes reference to the time of Elijah, and by quoting 1 Kings 19:10, 18, he parallels the present division within Israel with the division at the time of Elijah when God had "left" only "seven thousand" of his people "who [had] not bowed the knee to Baal" (Rom 11:4). The seven thousand set apart from the majority of Israel in Elijah's time correlate with the "remnant (λεῖμμα)[55] chosen by grace at the present time" (v. 5). In v. 7 Paul calls them "the elect" (ἡ ἐκλογή), whereas the non-Christian majority simply are "the rest" (οἱ λοιποί). It is obvious that also in this section Paul does not come one step closer to a solution of the original problem. The continuity of Israel's election is still perceptible only in the Jewish Christian "elect" as he calls them in 11:7. Thus, at the end of 11:10 the question "what about the unbelieving majority of Israel?" is still unanswered, and the tension between the manifestations of God's love in the Christ-event and in the election of Israel, which Paul described at the beginning of ch. 9, is still unresolved.

3. This changes in 11:11a, when Paul directs his eyes to the future and asks whether unbelieving Israel's present situation of misery is definitive and final: "Have they stumbled so that they go under?"

The answer that Paul himself gives is again unmistakable: μὴ γένοιτο (v. 11b). Israel's present situation of being "banned away from Christ" (9:3) is only a temporary phase in their history. And here also he brings the relationship between the Christian Jews and the unbelieving majority of Israel into play—albeit with an important difference: in distinction from the texts discussed so far Paul here does not

[55] Here, the use of this term is probably unleashed by ὑπελείφθην and κατέλιπον in the Old Testament quotations in vv. 3 and 4.

separate the Christian Jews as "remnant" or "elect" from the unbelieving majority of Israel as he did in 9:6, 27-29 and in 11:7-10. Instead, he argues from the solidarity of Jewish Christians and non-Christian Israel. In v. 16 at least, the metaphor of the "first fruits" and the "lump" refers allegorically to the relationship between the Christian Jews and the unbelieving majority of Israel.[56] Paul here alludes to Numbers 15:20-21, according to which a first part of the bread batter shall be offered as a sacrifice. He relates this procedure to the significance of the Christian Jews for all Israel: the sanctity of the Christian Jews guarantees the sanctity of Israel as a whole—including also its presently unbelieving majority. Paul here proceeds from the indivisibility of Israel, and with this he places the accent differently from what he has said in 9:27-29. On the other hand, in 9:6-29 and 11:16 there is also a continuity in Paul's argument: according to 9:27-29 the Christian Jews guarantee that the word of God has not fallen away, although unbelieving Israel is "banned away from Christ" (9:3). According to 11:16 they guarantee that there will be a positive outcome also for the non-Christian majority of Israel because the whole of Israel's sanctity is vouched for by the sanctity of the Jewish Christians.

4. As far as God is concerned, the course of Paul's argument meanders heavily through the landscape of Romans 9–11. The starting point is the ostensible *tension* within God and his activities in the Christ-event and in the election of Israel (9:3-4). In 9:6 Paul transforms his description into the question of the *reliability* of the word of God. In 9:14 this question is replaced by rhetorically casting doubt on God's *justice*, which is in turn immediately repelled by reference to God's *omnipotence* and *absolute sovereignty* (vv. 15-26). When at the end of this section Paul eventually answers the initial question by bringing the Christian Jews into play, he simply detours around the original problem. The readers have to wait until the end of ch. 11. Only then does Paul comes back to the opening question, and by doing so he

[56] ἀπαρχή here refers neither to Jews and Gentiles (so Dunn, *Romans*, 2:659) nor to the patriarchs (so Wilckens, *Brief an die Römer*, 2:246; Dieter Zeller, *Der Brief an die Römer*, RNT (Regensburg: Friedrich Pustet, 1985), 196; Moo, *Epistle to the Romans*, 699). Against the latter identification speaks Paul's argument in 9:6-29, especially in vv. 7-13, which has made a connection between the patriarchs and non-Christian Israel questionable. A reference to Jewish Christians is advocated by Hans Lietzmann, *An die Römer*, 3rd ed., HNT 8 (Tübingen: Mohr Siebeck, 1928), 104; Charles Kingsley Barrett, *The Epistle to the Romans*, BNTC 6 (Grand Rapids: Baker, 2011), 200; Cranfield, *Epistle to the Romans*, 2:564; Fitzmyer, *Romans*, 614.

points to the *irrevocability* of God's "gracious gift and calling" (11:29). This ascertainment however does not result from Paul's course of argument in the preceding sections, but is a mere proposition. Therefore, it is not surprising that at the very end of the entire section, in 11:33-36, Paul touches down at a confession of God's *incomprehensibility*. It is only this essential characteristic of God that makes it possible for Paul to reconcile the assurance of God's faithfulness and the awareness of God's absolute sovereignty, and it is only this feature—God's incomprehensibility—that makes Paul's argument in Romans 9–11 theologically halfway coherent.

3
Grafting Rhetoric
Myth and Methodological Multivalence in Romans 11

Davina C. Lopez

> Paul is essentially first and foremost a hero of religion. The theological element in him is secondary. Naiveté in him is stronger than reflection; mysticism stronger than dogmatism; Christ means more to him than Christology, God more than the doctrine of God. He is far more a man of prayer, a witness, a confessor and a prophet, than a learned exegete and close thinking scholastic.
>
> —Adolf Deissmann[1]

> When the architects of our republic wrote the magnificent words of the Constitution and the Declaration of Independence, they were signing a promissory note to which every American was to fall heir. This note was a promise that all men, yes, black men as well as white men, would be guaranteed the "unalienable Rights" of "Life, Liberty and the pursuit of Happiness."
>
> —Martin Luther King Jr.[2]

Debates about what should be primary and secondary as far as Paul is concerned—religion or theology, naiveté or reflection, mysticism or dogmatism, and so on—have long been a prominent characteristic of Pauline studies. Regardless of what kind of person we think Paul was, at the center of these debates, in some respect, lies concerns

[1] Adolf Deissmann, *Paul, A Study in Social and Religious History*, trans. William E. Wilson (London: Hodder & Stoughton, 1926), 6.

[2] Martin Luther King Jr., "I Have a Dream (28 August 1963)," *American Rhetoric: Top 100 Speeches*, http://www.americanrhetoric.com/speeches/mlkihaveadream.htm (accessed 3 July 2015).

about Pauline intentionality. What, we Paul scholars ask, did Paul intend? How far into the mind of the apostle can we, in fact, see, and with how much certainty? In this chapter I move beyond questions about what we can know about Pauline intentions and move toward questions about what, and how, we might know something about what I call the Pauline imagination. That is, I articulate a series of questions about Paul's rhetoric, his rhetorical choices, and their possible resonances among the recipients of Romans. To do so, I will briefly investigate the mytho-historical dimensions of Paul's immediate ideological context: the Roman Empire. Specifically, I will explore how attending to the broad and interrelated mythological, metaphorical, and rhetorical contexts of Paul's letter might provide some different interpretive options for engaging Paul's rhetoric *in* the letter, as well as subsequent rhetoric *about* the letter. Herein I will examine the visual narrative program of a single monument—the Ara Pacis Augustae—believed to be contemporaneous with Paul's letter and his addressees in the city of Rome. I will use this monument as a possible *comparandum* for Paul's own mytho-historical discourse in Romans 9–11. While the methodological and interpretive potential at the intersection of ancient monuments and Pauline literature is vast and understudied, for the purposes of this chapter I am most interested in how reading an ancient monument such as the Ara Pacis alongside Romans might illuminate a most "thorny" example of what I would call mytho-historical imagery in Pauline literature: the "olive tree" allegory about the historical and contemporary relationship of Jews and Gentiles in Romans 11:11-24.

Paul and Romans between Theology, Politics, Myth, and History

Asking the questions proposed above, however, is no easy task. For those interpreters interested in history of religions as a productive approach to and method for studying the New Testament and early Christian literature, Paul's work can provide a major stumbling block of sorts because of the theological "flavor" of the texts, their presence and status in a canon of Scriptures, and their subsequent deployment as windows onto an earlier time in the history of Christianity. To be fair, in my view it is not so much Paul himself who presents a stumbling block, but rather the vast reservoir of New Testament scholars who have interpreted his writings, particularly over the past two centuries or so, who have focused on Romans as Paul's theological "crowning achievement." It is often assumed to be self-evident and natural in contemporary interpretation that Romans represents Pauline theology at its most coherent and finest, or constitutes what Krister Stendahl called a "final account" of Pauline themes such as justification by faith, the relationship of Jews to "Gentiles," and an overall plan for salvation in a world of sin.[3] Since Paul has been utilized as a *resource* for dogmatics, he must be considered to be a natural *source* for dogmatics. Classicists and ancient historians have also tended to maintain a division between "their" material and "our" material, further occluding interpretive options. Dynamics such as these have made it difficult to see Paul as part of a broader conversation about religion and culture in antiquity and today.

Admittedly, part of the methodological conundrum with regard to Pauline studies has been the practice of "historical criticism" itself, as scholars set about to enact an approach to biblical texts that would take seriously historical contingency and sociocultural frameworks in the production and transmission of ancient sacred texts. Naturally, the major clash between so-called radical historical critics and the ecclesial establishments focused largely on the issue of historical contingency versus theological transcendence, as well as whether the two were ever reconcilable. It was not, as is often suggested, simply that historical critics sought to interpret the text freely, objectively, and scientifically, apart from intervention by church authorities or circumscription by dogmatic theologians.[4] Rather, more basically, historical criticism, in its initial impetus, was a methodology committed to understanding the transcendent and universal language and concepts deployed by early Christians and reflected in the New Testament texts as contingent human expressions, that is, located in space and time, related to their environment, and therefore subject to change and adaptation. Maintaining that all texts are human products and are historically located—especially when the discourses embedded in

[3] Krister Stendahl, *Final Account: Paul's Letter to the Romans* (Minneapolis: Fortress, 1995).

[4] For a brief assessment of this legacy, see Gerd Lüdemann, "The Relationship of Biblical Studies to the History of Religions School, with Reference to the Scientific Study of Religion," *Toronto Journal of Theology* 24, no. 2 (2008): 171–81. Lüdemann is clear that theology as such is not, and has never quite been, the issue; rather, it is the assumption that theology must always be circumscribed by the questions posed by ecclesial hierarchies that is to be questioned by "scientific" approaches to the study of religion.

and around those texts would maintain otherwise—is a hallmark of the historical study of religious rhetoric and practices that historical criticism took up with regard to biblical texts and traditions. And it is precisely at this juncture of the transcendent and the contingent that so many problems exist in the interpretation of New Testament texts,[5] and probably nowhere is this clearer than in the study of Pauline texts and theology.

Given such a methodological context as I have described above, it is relatively easy to see how the Letter to the Romans can be configured and reified as Paul's "crowning achievement," promulgating clearly (if we can ever really use the term "clearly" with respect to Paul!) the underpinning theological affirmations regarding Jews and "Gentiles" and their interrelationship in light of the coming of Jesus, the Christ. Herein it has been incredibly challenging for New Testament scholars on two fronts. First, it has become nearly impossible to maintain fully the historical-critical line on the contingency of the Pauline language that bears so much transcendent theological weight. The influence and reception of Romans have been simply too great in the history of Christian theology, particularly its Protestant varieties, to make it readily accessible as a contingent religious expression without also, at the same time, giving credence to its transcendent conceptions and enduring legacies.[6] Second, given the high stakes involved in the theology of Romans overall, *and particularly in interpreting Romans 9–11*, it has become exceedingly difficult for scholars of Pauline literature to avoid argumentative strategies wherein we provide (c)overt theological renderings of Paul's arguments, offering only a proverbial tip of the hat to its historical, social, political, and rhetorical contexts and agendas. Despite the frequent claims that scholarship is proceeding along the lines of historically contextualizing Paul's arguments in Romans, what we see more often is the theological commitments that shape the way such contextualization takes place and on what terms. This is completely understandable, of course, since key concepts of Christian identity for a good many centuries have rested on specific

[5] For discussion of these issues, see Todd Penner and Davina C. Lopez, *De-introducing the New Testament: Texts, Worlds, Methods, Stories* (Hoboken, N.J.: Wiley-Blackwell, 2015), esp. 71–118.

[6] For an engagement of the interpretation and reception of Romans across time and in different cultural settings, see the volumes in the "Romans through History and Culture," project edited by Daniel Patte, Eugene TeSelle, et al. (London: Bloomsbury, 2002–).

understandings of Romans, and perhaps especially on the "climax" of Paul's theological program thought to be presented in Romans 9–11.

Over the past several decades, a major concern for some scholars in Pauline studies is how we might move beyond some of the constraints presented by theology in particular and perhaps raise broader questions about the social and religious patterns that might help us understand Paul's writings in a more contextual and perhaps even more complex manner. To be sure, there is much richness to be found in what we might identify as a predominantly theological interpretation of Paul's life, work, and legacies. However, insofar as "theology" is taken as a naturally given lens through which to see the whole of Paul's life and work, and the configuration of that category never clearly defined except in opposition to other categories of analysis such as "politics" or "religion," then this significant category is worth interrogating for its own historical contingency and ideological contours. In my view, every study of the New Testament in its connection to the ancient world on its terms is ultimately also about the kind of relationship we want to cultivate with that world and these texts on our terms. Thus, in order to highlight and take responsibility for those terms, I am interested in what is thought to be self-evident and beyond question as a matter of course in Pauline studies, as that which has the effect of hiding the human hands at work in these and all of "our" material. This includes the categories of theology, religion, and politics alike. In recent interpretation, two major trajectories have attempted to wrestle with the humanity of Paul's life, letters, and legacies: the "New Perspective" on Paul, which takes Paul's Jewishness, and Jewishness generally, seriously; and a range of studies connected by I would call "empire-critical" approaches, which to take the Roman Empire seriously as the world to and out of which Paul responds through his letters. Each of these is worth discussing briefly in turn.

Judaism and Empire in Context

E. P. Sanders' seminal work in Pauline studies, *Paul and Palestinian Judaism*, sought to move beyond theology as the primary lens through which Pauline studies might be conducted. This major work, often considered to be one of the earlier resources for the so-called New Perspective on Paul,[7] is subtitled *A Comparison of Patterns of Religion*.

[7] I mention the New Perspective here because in my view no development in Pauline studies during the past century has been as critical and fruitful as the call to rethink the apostle's relationship with Judaism, as well as to develop methods by which

In this landmark study, Sanders traced a persistent pattern of misrepresentation of ancient Judaism in the history of New Testament scholarship from Ferdinand Weber to Rudolf Bultmann. Although some correctives had been attempted along the way, Sanders argued, much of the view on ancient Judaism, including Judaism's appearances in Pauline literature, was in fact circumscribed and determined by Christian theological concerns. In other words, the Judaism characterized by "works-righteousness" that Paul appears to "reject" in his letters was found to be wholly "rejectable" by scholars, in part because of the way Paul's rejection had been taken at face value and as foundational to Christian theologizing and identity formation on the "faith" side of a "works-faith" semantic opposition. In seeking to provide a methodological corrective to this pervasive misrepresentation and misunderstanding, Sanders attempted to move the conversation from theology to what he called "religion," rereading the primary sources and attempting to articulate what makes Judaism work as a religious system. To this end he asked not only what one must believe, but also what one must do, to attain entry and belonging in religious communities such as those thought to belong to Judaism in the first century C.E.

The post-Sanders shift from a "works-righteousness" to "covenantal nomism" in Pauline studies and the study of ancient Judaism has been significant, with the latter term subject to much debate. In a 2008 essay outlining his intellectual biography, Sanders relates how he came to undertake such a massive project published some thirty years earlier.[8] The path to completion had many twists and turns, and,

scholars might do that. For an overview of the issues at stake therein, see Magnus Zetterholm, *Approaches to Paul: A Student's Guide* (Minneapolis: Fortress, 2008); Kent Yinger, *The New Perspective on Paul: An Introduction* (Eugene, Ore.: Wipf & Stock, 2011); and Stephen Westerholm, *Perspectives Old and New on Paul: The "Lutheran" Paul and His Critics* (Grand Rapids: Eerdmans, 2003). Also see John Gager's recent study, in which he presents a slightly different approach to the question of Paul and Judaism, asking what difference it makes now to rethink Paul's anti-Jewish legacy: *Who Made Christianity? The Jewish Lives of the Apostle Paul*, American Lectures on the History of Religions (New York: Columbia University Press, 2015).

8 Sanders relates that the three main concerns with which he entered his doctoral program have animated his entire career: that religion is not just about theology, and that New Testament scholars have paid too much attention to the latter rather than the former; that knowing about one religion is not enough, and thus comparison is essential to the study of religion; and that New Testament scholars ought to study Judaism (and on its own terms). See E. P. Sanders, "Comparing Christianity and

perhaps surprisingly, began in part with his interest in Erwin Goodenough's interpretation of Philo's mystical Judaism.[9] As part of his own response to Goodenough's conception of Judaism and Jewishness, Sanders relates how he slowly moved into the rabbinic materials, worked through those, and then turned to the Qumran and the Jewish pseudepigraphical texts. Only later, after abandoning Philo, did Sanders turn to Paul. In other words, as odd as it may seem for a book that has profoundly shaped the direction of Pauline studies in the present, finding a way to understand Paul was not the initial impetus behind the questions driving the research. Rather, Sanders had become interested in the legacy of German presentations of rabbinic Judaism and rabbinic Jewish thought. Sanders determined that examining the original rabbinic sources rather than reading secondary interpretations of them made all of the difference in terms of formulating a conception of rabbinic Judaism that was not focused on legalistic renderings of its core religious language. By including Paul as an "add-on" of sorts, rather than as the architectural principle guiding his analysis, Sanders offered a breakthrough moment in Pauline studies. And he did so by presenting Paul as one Jewish strand of religious expression alongside others, not allowing Pauline theology—or, more precisely, the theology that shapes Pauline studies—to guide the framework and *telos* of the analysis. In the end, Paul looked surprisingly (to many scholars) Jewish and fit rather comfortably within his ambient Jewish environment. And the later rabbinic tradition did not look all that out of place next to Paul either. To be sure, Paul had certain commitments regarding how to gain access to the "in-group," particularly his thematic focus on "faith in Christ," but his overall pattern of religion, at its core, was rather similar. Subsequent scholarship on Paul would either agree or disagree with the specifics of Sanders' work, but interpreters would need to wrestle with how to negotiate Paul, Jewishness, and Paul's Jewishness in ways that were less informed by Christian theological assumptions. And since Sanders, proponents of the New Perspective have largely appropriated the comparative question toward understanding Pauline theology in less expansively comparative ways.

Judaism: An Academic Autobiography," in *Redefining First-Century Jewish and Christian Identities: Essays in Honor of Ed Parish Sanders*, ed. Fabian E. Udoh, with Susannah Heschel, Mark Chancey, and Gregory Tatum, Christianity and Judaism in Antiquity (South Bend, Ind.: University of Notre Dame Press, 2008), 11–41.

9 Sanders, "Comparing Christianity and Judaism," 19–22.

Another recent interpretive pattern of interest, exemplified by the work of scholars such as Dieter Georgi, Richard Horsley, and John Dominic Crossan, claims to read Pauline literature in light of political issues, and addresses the question of how, or to what degree, one can claim Paul is enmeshed in, and possibly a critic of, his Roman imperial context.[10] Taking a cue from the work of Sanders, Stendahl, and others who associated with the New Perspective as a methodological lens, such empire-critical scholars have also contended that scholarly readings of Paul have traditionally been more heavily indebted to Protestant church dogma and theological concerns than historical analysis. These scholars have thus begun to work on understanding the Roman Empire as proper topographical locus of Pauline discourses. Highlighting the relationship between apostle and empire, then and now, this strand of scholarship assesses whether, and how, Paul's letters can be read as responding to Roman imperial ideology—as well as whether, and how, such a reading of Paul might serve as a resource for contemporary engagements with imperial designs and rhetorics.

Empire-critical scholarship offers an investigative site where texts, contexts, histories of interpretation, and identities and ideologies of readers coalesce. Over the past several decades of Pauline studies, the topic of Paul and empire has become a signifier for discussions about Paul and politics. In taking the Roman Empire as the political

[10] I have used the term "empire-critical" here and elsewhere in my own work, although the scholars I mention would not necessarily claim that term for themselves. In my view, "empire-critical," as heuristic, is related to postcolonial studies even as the former focuses more on ancient colonial and imperial discourses rather than the rhetorics at work in modern colonial encounters (particularly with those colonial powers that have deployed the Bible). For a brief elaboration on the difference between "empire-critical" and postcolonial approaches to New Testament studies, see Davina C. Lopez, *Apostle to the Conquered: Reimagining Paul's Mission*, Paul in Critical Contexts (Minneapolis: Fortress, 2008), 8–11. Nevertheless, scholars who take the Roman Empire seriously as a way to see Paul's program differently can also be seen as "critical" of empire in its contemporary configurations, including those that shape the work of New Testament scholarship. The literature on this front is fairly extensive; see, e.g., Richard A. Horsley, ed., *Paul and Empire: Religion and Power in Roman Imperial Society* (Harrisburg, Pa.: Trinity International, 1998); John Dominic Crossan and Jonathan Reed, *In Search of Paul: How Jesus's Apostle Opposed Rome's Empire with God's Kingdom. A New Vision of Paul's Words & World* (San Francisco: Harper, 2004); Neil Elliott, *The Arrogance of Nations: Reading Romans in the Shadow of Empire*, Paul in Critical Contexts (Minneapolis: Fortress, 2008); and Joseph A. Marchal, *The Politics of Heaven: Women, Gender, and Empire in the Study of Paul*, Paul in Critical Contexts (Minneapolis: Fortress, 2008).

background for the Pauline correspondence, usually represented as the "state" or "governing authorities" in the apostle's ancient world, the main question in this scholarly conversation hinges on whether and how Paul negotiated the Roman imperial power structures in which he was situated, marking him out as a potentially "political" figure rather than a "theologian" or "pastor." Within empire-critical scholarship, debates about Paul's possible political inclinations tend to focus on the characterization of the apostle as pro- or anti-empire, along with the implications of such portraits for contemporary ethics and theologies relying on Paul's letters as a scriptural resource. While there are a variety of possible responses to the question of Paul's relationship with the Roman Empire, scholars tend to agree that the history of interpretation has not taken this particular aspect of Paul's world seriously enough and that, similar to the New Perspective and its focus on Judaism, theological assumptions have kept scholars from engaging the potentially political dimensions of Paul's rhetoric.

The New Perspective and empire-critical approaches to Pauline studies have raised numerous critical methodological questions. As attractive as it might be to call the New Perspective and empire-critical work "new" as far as interpretive methods in Pauline studies are concerned, such claims to novelty are not quite accurate. This is especially the case with locating and interpreting Paul in light of the broader Roman world to which he belonged, which might be better termed "long overdue" than "new." More than a century ago, Adolf Deissmann challenged scholars to consider Paul and his letters to be fully associated with the history of religion, rather than solely a part of the history of dogmatics, as the epigraph to this chapter suggests. This reorientation required, in Deissmann's view, greater attention to the literature and monuments of the Roman world. Similarly, Sir William Ramsay argued that Paul constituted an important chapter in Roman history, and that the followers of the Tübingen School had ignored the Roman world to their great peril.[11] And notably, G. B. Caird emphasized the humanity of Paul's thought, which he considered to exemplify intellectualism at its "best," as well as a pattern of engagement that is at once theological and political.[12] Today in the field there are

[11] Sir William Mitchell Ramsay, *Pauline and Other Studies in Early Christian History* (New York: A.C. Armstrong, 1906), 49–50.

[12] G. B. Caird, *Principalities and Powers: A Study in Pauline Theology*, Chancellor's Lectures for 1954 at Queen's University, Kingston, Ontario (Oxford: Clarendon, 1956), esp. 1–30.

some who emphasize the historical dimensions, human touch, and Roman imperial situatedness of Paul's letters, but many also focus almost exclusively on what can be read as a rather forced question: was Paul pro- or anti-imperial?[13] Likewise, those who maintain that Paul's Jewishness ought to be fronted in interpretive efforts tend to ask exactly *how* Jewish Paul was, or *what kind* of Jew he was, or what sorts of activities he would have conducted that would mark him out as "Jewish." In the end, these are questions that say more about modern desires in which Paul serves various contemporary purposes (e.g., Should *we* be pro- or anti-imperial? Should *we* do more to be empathic to Jewish people?), than what we might know or infer about Paul's own motivations or his theological orientation and historical situation. And neglected in these questions are the rhetorical dimensions of Paul's letters—that is, that the letters themselves are highly occasional and written to persuade their audiences, and thus may not be transparent windows onto actual historical circumstances, feelings, beliefs, and practices. In other words, while Paul may seem to be pulling out all the stops in his letters, the question is to what persuasive ends might he be doing so, who would be (and would not be) persuaded, and on what terms.[14]

Nevertheless, briefly outlining the approaches of the New Perspective and empire criticism here helps to raise a point about methodology in the study of Pauline texts generally, and Romans in particular. If it is a goal of Pauline studies to figure out what Paul is up to in his letters, and if we think we can do that by comparing and contrasting his words with those of others in his milieu, then where we begin and what we use as the context for comparison make all

[13] The answer to this question, of course, tends to depend in large part upon whether an interpreter thinks Paul is at all interested in "politics," as well as what "politics" is taken to mean in the first place. For a discussion of this pattern among contemporary scholars, see Davina C. Lopez and Todd Penner, "Paul and Politics," in *The Oxford Handbook of Pauline Studies*, ed. R. Barry Matlock (New York: Oxford University Press, forthcoming).

[14] Mark Given explores the issues surrounding whether, and how, Paul might be telling the "truth" in his letters; see *Paul's True Rhetoric: Ambiguity, Cunning, and Deception in Greece and Rome*, Emory Studies in Early Christianity 7 (Harrisburg, Pa.: Trinity International, 2001). For a methodological overview of how readers might notice the multivalence of Paul's rhetoric in interpretational contexts, see Todd Penner and Davina C. Lopez, "Rhetorical Approaches: Introducing the Art of Persuasion in Paul and Pauline Studies," in *Studying Paul's Letters: Contemporary Perspectives and Approaches*, ed. Joseph A. Marchal (Minneapolis: Fortress, 2012), 33–52.

the difference in terms of the results that we achieve in our work. If we do want to understand Paul in his ancient context, as well as use the ancient context to more fully appreciate the contingent nature of his religious expressions and conceptions, we may in fact need to put Paul himself on the back burner for a bit or cast a wider ideological-contextual net, seeking to expand the basis for comparison in order to achieve a more robust configuration of religious and, indeed, theological expression in Paul's period more generally. Rather than something of a detour, putting Paul on the back burner and exploring the world that gave shape to his rhetoric can actually be quite illuminating for interpreters, as well as for examining some of the contemporary utility of Pauline literature, as the examples of the New Perspective and empire criticism show.

However illuminating it might be for New Testament scholars to entertain proposals about Paul's relationship with Judaism and/or the Roman Empire, such interpretive trajectories also have relied on neat distinctions between theology, history, religion, and politics that were nonexistent in Paul's ancient world (not that they are, arguably, all that distinct even in our own). Persistent oppositional discourses wherein theology is "opposed" to history and religion (read: Judaism) and politics (read: empire) downplay some important aspects of the Roman world, namely, the interdependence of mythological, historical, and theological narratives that the Romans themselves constructed and maintained, a narrativizing strategy that Paul and his ancient colleagues may have similarly deployed as a means to encounter and negotiate their world. In this setting it is quite plausible that there was no such thing as a Judaism devoid of politics, or a Roman Empire devoid of theology and religion. For example, narratives of the miraculous and/or predestined founding of the Roman state and the rehabilitation of the mythical "Golden Age" under Augustus defy easy categorization as merely "political" stories that are therefore irrelevant to situating the New Testament. Likewise, ancient Jewish materials are not simply focused on the elaboration and codification of religious practices and beliefs but have significant political dimensions that are worth exploring in relation to Paul's letters. The rhetorical power of such narratives, and specifically their capacity to dwell somewhere between history, politics, theology, and mythology, should be highlighted as a major potential component intersecting with Paul's own rhetoric. Indeed, perhaps such a shift in focus is no more important than in a reassessment of Romans 9–11, where fairly narrow notions of theology, religion, history, and politics have been operative for many scholars and defined the terms upon which these enigmatic Pauline passages have been understood. In the next section I unpack a little further what might be at stake in this shift in focus.

Paul at the Crossroads of Categories

In my view, both Paul's rhetoric and that of the world he negotiated belong at the intersection of history, mythology, theology, and politics, and here is where a history-of-religions approach to the material can be instructive. One relevant aspect of the legacy of the *Religionsgeschichte Schule* is the understanding of "myth." Calling something "myth" is not the same thing as calling it "untrue"; rather, myth denotes a highly textured use of religious rhetoric that has a deep level of persuasiveness, particularly when the distant past is used to tell stories about the present. In his recent comparative study of Norse stories of origins, Bruce Lincoln has argued that people tell stories about where they have come from and why it matters, and institutional entities like the state are especially good at telling such stories. Therein, according to Lincoln, part of the fascination with foundation stories lies in the ability to dwell somewhere between history and myth, which are not opposites but part of the broad narrative category called "nonfiction"—even as both myth and history can take on traits we might commonly associate with "fiction." That is, as far as narratives are concerned, myth

> reaches deeper into the past, concerning itself with the time of origins, foundations, creation. It also frequently (but not always) admits nonhuman actors and agency, including gods, spirits, animals, and other exotics, including ancestors of humanity who are not yet subject to all the limitations of our species. Again, this category usually claims for itself more than simple truth, constituting itself as a paradigmatic model for proper existence, always valid, always authoritative, always demanding of deep respect. Further, this category permits itself more imaginative flights of fancy than does its counterpart, acknowledging—at least in some variants—that the truths it conveys may be of a metaphoric, poetic, structural-logical, or theo-logical sort, not being willing to limit itself to truths of a literal nature.[15]

[15] Bruce Lincoln, *Between History and Myth: Stories of Harold Fairhair and the Founding of the State* (Chicago: University of Chicago Press, 2014), 115.

While positioning themselves as accounts of "what happened," mythological narratives reach far into the past, often to "the start of it all," the point of "holy beginnings," and allow for some measure of fantasy and imagination that some would ordinarily consider the provenance of "fiction." Historical narratives, of course, belong to a similar tradition: efforts to tell "what happened" through the "truth" of history, especially when significant time has elapsed between the events and their narration and the evidence is paltry, can lead to invention that is often welcome among audiences. Moreover, historical narratives can take on mythological qualities, in both "official" stories (e.g., those by/about "the winners") and in what Lincoln calls "revisionist" stories (e.g., those by/about "the losers").[16] In the case of both history and myth, the process of telling a story, especially when origins are concerned, serves to stabilize a past that is by its very nature profoundly unstable. And the success or demise of such narratives, historical and mythological alike, depends in part on the type of relationship the narrators and audience have with the story and with one another.

Origin stories may recall "what happened," to be sure, and also do more than that. By resisting the neat history/myth binary, such stories offer a certain ambiguity, perhaps some measure of comfort, and legitimation for what we might call "the way it is and ought to be." I find compelling the idea that stories that deploy the past, particularly those that are thought to be persuasive, do not belong to exclusive categories such as history or myth, but might best be characterized as something in between. Such in-betweenness can be a productive way to characterize Paul's rhetoric as well. On the one hand, Paul's letters are "other people's mail," wherein we are witnesses to what we have assumed is part of a conversation between the apostle and various communities and individuals across the ancient eastern Mediterranean world. These conversations are dominated by Paul's voice and perspective on things, making it difficult for us to reconstruct a reliable, stable historical situation within which to place these conversations. Within these letters, though, Paul narrates a variety of stories about the past, including those of his own life, wherein he deploys elements of accounts about distant, irretrievable (and perhaps, to his audiences, unintelligible) events that he argues are part of Israel's story of origins. These narratives serve to bolster Paul's authority, and they

16 Lincoln, *Between History and Myth*, 116–17.

also function to rhetorically link the audience to other people in other times and other places.

In the case of Romans, Paul narrates what appears to be an attempt to negotiate a contemporary conflict situation concerning Jews and Gentiles through the optic of history, including the mythical ancestral history of his "kinsfolk." This is especially noticeable in Romans 9–11, wherein Paul uses a genealogical argument about the history of Israel to make a case for the salvation of Jews and Gentiles alike, regardless of Israel's stumbling or the nations' arrogance. And among the rhetorical choices Paul makes when he is speaking to "you, nations" in this chapter of Romans is an allegory about a grafted olive tree, complete with roots, branches, suggestions about brokenness, and ideas about fruitfulness. Given that myth, history, theology, and politics enjoy more confluence and convergence than is usually thought, Paul's olive tree is suggestive of both the mythical ancestral history of Israel and the situation of his immediate addressees, thus being a particularly potent metaphor for his justification of a continuing covenant relationship between the God of Israel, Jews, and Gentiles alike.

Methodologically, the olive tree of Romans 11:11-24 has enjoyed a rich exegetical history in Pauline studies, and not just on account of Christian theological assumptions and interests. Clearly, Jewish-Gentile relations have been, and continue to be, a major area of scholarly and ecclesial attention, whether one concludes that the tree brings together Jews and Gentiles into a new Christian community or that Jews and Gentiles are to coexist across ethnic and religious differences. Rhetorically, Paul does appear to be making the case for a common mytho-historical ancestry for seemingly disparate groups through deploying arboreal genealogical imagery. Such a move could indicate that these groups were somehow configured as unrelated to one another—indeed, perhaps barely human to one another—in his and their own rhetorical situation. Caroline Johnson Hodge has suggested that such genealogical rhetoric could be considered a form of "ethnic reasoning," common in the ancient world,[17] the point of which is to argue for binding people together in kinship configurations

[17] Caroline Johnson Hodge, "Olive Trees and Ethnicities, Judeans and Gentiles in Rom 11.17-24," in *Christians as a Religious Minority in a Multicultural City: Modes of Interaction and Identity-Formation in Early Imperial Rome*, ed. Jürgen Zangenberg and Michael Labahn, JSNTSup 243 (New York: T&T Clark, 2004), 77–89. See also Hodge's *If Sons, Then Heirs: A Study of Kinship and Ethnicity in the Letters of Paul* (New York: Oxford University Press, 2007), esp. 19–66.

in persuasive ways, regardless of whether the people narrated are related by "blood." However, perhaps due to its apparent resonances with and allusions to the appearance of the olive tree in the Hebrew Bible prophets, scholars have also tended to imagine an almost exclusively Jewish background for this imagery (and thus for Rom 9–11 as a whole). When a broader rhetorical context for the olive tree language is considered, it is usually along the lines of reviewing ancient Greco-Roman horticultural techniques, some of which survive in agricultural handbooks from the likes of Columella and Theophrastus. Therein, scholars debate whether Paul understood grafting "correctly" in his own discourse; he apparently did not, given what the handbooks describe and what we know about ancient and modern farming practices. Given how much attention has been paid to such farming practices in modern studies of Romans 11, it is evident that scholars have found it important to assess Paul's intentions in using grafting procedures (whether correctly or not) to build his argument about Gentiles and Jews.[18] It is not evident, however, that such assessment has truly aided our understanding of Paul's argumentative strategy.

Curiously underexplored in discussions of Paul's olive tree allegory is the wider significance of such imagery in the Roman Empire, the capital of which is the location of Paul's implied audience. If one desires to front ancient Judaism in interpretive efforts, it is important to remember that this Judaism would have been shaped by encounters with Rome. Even those who undertake empire-critical studies have not done much to theorize the possible broader Roman dimensions of this passage, preferring instead to focus on more obvious "political" texts such as Romans 13:1-7. For example, Georgi places the

[18] The literature on Paul's olive tree allegory in Romans 11 is extensive and similarly oriented toward expositions of ancient olive cultivation. See Philip F. Esler, "Ancient Oleiculture and Ethnic Differentiation: The Meaning of the Olive-Tree Image in Romans 11," *JSNT* 26 (2003): 103–24, as well as Mark D. Nanos, "'Broken Branches': A Pauline Metaphor Gone Awry? (Romans 11:11-24)," in *Between Gospel and Election: Explorations in the Interpretation of Romans 9–11*, ed. Florian Wilk and J. Ross Wagner, WUNT 257 (Tübingen: Mohr Siebeck, 2010), 339–76, esp. 357 n. 44. The consensus seems to be that Paul got grafting "wrong," or at least he turns grafting backward in order to make a point about the Gentiles not "resting on their laurels" since Israel will also be "saved" in his final analysis. N. T. Wright, e.g., argues that Paul "knows" that he is talking about grafting "contrary to nature" regarding the Gentiles in order to make a parallel argument about their ontological status vis-à-vis Israel and God's plans for the world. See Wright, *Paul and the Faithfulness of God*, 2 vols. (Minneapolis: Fortress, 2013), 2:1043–268.

olive tree passage in the context of "theocracy" but does not otherwise observe imperial connotations or resonances that could connect Paul's olive tree to a broader Roman context.[19] Robert Jewett's recent commentary maintains that the Jewish background is most appropriate for interpreting this particular passage, even though he ventures into Roman imperial territory elsewhere.[20] Neil Elliott comes closest to shifting the conversation through the lens of what he calls "Roman imperial theology," treating the rhetoric of the passage as part of a larger discourse about the consonance of Pauline and Roman concepts and suggesting that Paul is advising the nations not to be too boastful, given their precarious grafted position on the larger tree of Israel.[21] Still, what it would truly mean to compare Paul's genealogical rhetoric with resonant examples from the Roman world remains understudied.

To highlight the complex issues that the olive tree allegory might raise, the images it might evoke in the hearers and readers of Paul's letter, and the images and discourses with which Paul might be interacting in his own rhetoric, in the next section I will move beyond well-trodden discussions of olive husbandry in the ancient Mediterranean and whether Paul got that right, as well as the questions about whether Paul is pro- or anti-Jewish and/or pro- or anti-imperial. To this end I will explore the imagery on the Ara Pacis Augustae, or Altar of Augustan Peace, and specifically the "acanthus scroll" that decorates the bottom register around the outside of the monument. I contend that such orderly agricultural visual rhetoric, far from being merely ornamental, is critical to the overall discourse of the altar, particularly the deeply rooted mythological genealogy of the Pax Augusta and emergent Roman Empire that it seeks to re-present to the audience. As rhetorical forms, public monuments such as the Ara Pacis are every bit as readable as words and letters, and, given the framework provided by Lincoln, they also represent a form of state historicizing wherein past myths are creatively reconfigured within new historical narratives. Indeed, as George Kennedy has noted, Augustus was likely one of the most skilled rhetoricians of the

[19] See Dieter Georgi, *Theocracy in Paul's Praxis and Theology*, trans. David E. Green (Minneapolis: Fortress, 1991).

[20] Robert Jewett, *Romans*, Hermeneia (Minneapolis: Fortress, 2007).

[21] Elliott, *Arrogance of Nations*, 19–20, 147–48.

ancient world, even as he was not noted for his oratorical prowess.[22] He needed to be, as his leadership capacity rested on his ability to convince a large and diverse populace. His rhetoric, as it were, was expressed in great part through the topography of the city of Rome and throughout the Roman Empire,[23] and herein the Ara Pacis could be considered one of the most important, and most readable, artifacts of the Augustan rhetorical program. Granted, the visual rhetoric on the Ara Pacis is not ostensibly about olives (or Israel) as such, nor does it correspond to Romans 11 in a straightforward way. However, such monuments do express dynastic and cosmic narratives about how the Roman Empire functions as "creation," and, in the case of the Ara Pacis, we find represented a "new creation" erected early in Augustus' reign wherein national origin and affiliation are negotiated and reimagined through representations of floral, faunal, and human hybridity as a foregone conclusion—as something the emperor controls as a "god." The Roman mytho-historical imagination placed in service of creating state stability, visible in monuments such as this, can illuminate the Pauline imagination, and that intersection can be quite useful as a lens through which to see these monuments and perhaps even monumental texts such as Romans 9–11.

Rhetorics of Grafting in the Augustan Golden Age and on the Ara Pacis Augustae

Roman imperial visual representation is a primary mode of communicating a theology of victory and imperial genealogical inclusion of the "other," one that Paul's addressees in Rome may have understood and perhaps even negotiated themselves as they moved to and fro in the cityscape, regardless of their own ethnic and/or "religious" affiliation. By engaging Roman imperial visual representation, particularly that of the Augustan age, we can see Paul's Roman world as that which is heavily laden with symbolic and theological, and not just "political," dimensions. I submit that we students of the New Testament, Christian origins, and early Christianity should be interested in visual materials like the Ara Pacis Augustae not simply as illustrations for words, but as powerful conveyers of ideas that reached vastly more ancient

[22] George Kennedy, *A New History of Classical Rhetoric* (Princeton, N.J.: Princeton University Press, 1994), 159–72.

[23] For an elaboration on how the rhetoric of empire was expressed topographically, see Claude Nicolet, *Space, Geography, and Politics in the Early Roman Empire*, Jerome Lectures 19 (Ann Arbor: University of Michigan Press, 1991).

people than literature did (especially given the scant "literacy" rates during that time). What we call "art" and/or "archaeological remains" has often been considered peripheral to New Testament studies, or relegated to a subordinate position to literary materials. And yet Roman imperial visual representation is fully a part of the ancient world that Paul and his addressees traversed on a daily basis, evidenced in everything from coins to houses to public complexes, the latter of which were erected and maintained in cities throughout Roman territory, and particularly in commemorative narration of events like war, international conquest, and the victories that make (it was argued) continued peace and fertility possible. While Paul may never have seen the Ara Pacis himself—in the end we cannot know for sure what he saw or did not see, read, or experience—this monument very likely stood in the city of Rome amid Paul's Romans in the first century C.E. It belongs in a long and remarkably consistent tradition of nonliterary, yet no less rhetorical, ancient evidence. Thus, attention to visual representation can highlight different elements and strategies in our own reading, in this case, the mytho-historical, theo-political, and socio-allegorical dimensions of Paul's rhetoric.

I imagine that Paul composed Romans in a world in which the Augustan Golden Age was the dominant mytho-historical metanarrative framework, which monuments like the Ara Pacis express visually. While the specifics of the political dimensions of each decade from Augustus to Nero might differ, in many ways the Augustan Golden Age is the ideological and theological configuration to which the rest of the "principalities and powers" responded, and which they appropriated, adopted, and adapted to their own ends. In the broadest possible terms, the Augustan Golden Age refers to the period during the end of the Roman Republic, during which time Rome and Italy were deeply scarred by civil unrest, violence, and oppression, and dominated by conflict between various civil and military leaders vying for power. After Octavian defeated Mark Antony and Cleopatra at the Battle of Actium (ca. 31 B.C.E.), power was effectively consolidated and the civil wars ended. Thereafter, and following important and decisive campaigns to squelch "barbarian" unrest in Spain and Gaul, Octavian became "Augustus" ("holy one," ca. 27 B.C.E.) and brought stability and peace to Rome, the new capital of a new territorial empire. The Pax Romana was configured as part of a renewal program that would rehabilitate the "old ways" (*mos maiorum*) and laws that marked the Romans out as a moral, righteous, faithful, and upstanding people. This Roman peace was to be characterized by economic and civic progress for all citizens, as well as fertility for future generations.

According to ancient writers such as Ovid, the Golden Age denotes a primevally just and merciful time when all peoples lived in harmony and peace with a minimum of hunger and violence. During this time, humans flourished on an abundant paradisiacal earth with a minimum of effort (e.g., they would not have to perform agrarian labor; see Ovid, *Met.* 1.89–112). This idyllic perpetual spring gave way to a "fall" during a battle between Saturn and Jupiter, after which seasons were introduced, people lived in disunity, and tilling a harsh earth became the symbol of survival. The Saturnian Golden Age was thereafter longed for as the "pristine" state for humanity. In linking the new reign (and state) of Augustus with the return of the Golden Age, the rhetorical effect is to identify this new reign with the reappearance of a "pre-fall," paradisiacal state. The Augustan Golden Age was narrated to the public via a comprehensive literary, architectural, and visual rhetorical program. Within these stories, which on the literary side include such epic contributions as Vergil's *Aeneid* and *Eclogues*, the poetry of the likes of Horace and Ovid, and the *Res Gestae* of Augustus himself, the city and its inhabitants were reborn as a "new creation" (in marble, from brick, as the emperor says), wherein Augustus, his family, the city, and the empire were reimagined as belonging to the mythical ancestral genealogy of Rome. That is to say, Augustus became more than himself: he was linked to Aeneas, the mythical epic hero who traveled to Italy to found Rome, and he was considered to be a new Romulus, the mythical founder of, and lawgiver to, the city itself. As a descendant of these mythical forefathers, and as the son of the divine Julius Caesar, Augustus was essentially a son of the gods, Mars and Venus in particular, as they were the divine progenitors of the Julian line. In the broad narrative arc of the Augustan Golden Age, it is the divine mission and destiny of Augustus to refound Rome and "save" the Roman people from oppression, violence, and poverty—his destiny was predicted from the beginning, at the point of Rome's origins, and decreed by the gods themselves.

Kathleen Lamp has called the story of the Augustan Golden Age the "political myth" of Augustan Rome, the importance of which cannot be overstated with respect to the success of Augustus' principate and the Julio-Claudian dynasty. This etiological narrative, Lamp notes, "informs virtually every rhetorical action taken by Augustus after 27 B.C.E., and if there is an Augustan ideology, it surely is evident in this political myth."[24] Indeed, the "Augustan ideology" embedded in the Pax Romana was revisionist and restorative: the Romans, devastated by civil war, poverty, and moral and material degradation, could, with the coming of Augustus, return to paradise and become "themselves" again and in new ways, becoming part of this new world order and cosmic family. As is well documented, peace at home through victory over others, and the resultant fertility, soteriological dimensions, and cosmopolitanism that can be enjoyed in the capital city as a result, are major themes of the Augustan Golden Age. And it is in this context that the Ara Pacis represents a significant communicative medium for the promotion and promise of eternal fecundity and stability through the figure and actions of Augustus and, by extension, his "children," the population at large—Roman and non-Roman, rich and poor, slave and free, male and female.

The Ara Pacis (fig. 3.1) is commonly thought to have been dedicated between 13 and 9 B.C.E. as part of a Senate decree to commemorate the return of Augustus to Rome following successful military "peacemaking" campaigns in Gaul and Spain. According to the *Res Gestae Divi Augusti*, the location of the altar was to be Campus Martius, where the magistrates, priests, and Vestal Virgins were to make an annual sacrifice to Pax Augusta, the divine female personification of Augustan peace (12:2). While it was popularly represented on coins and in literature of its time,[25] and its visual program and style were likely repeated in other subsequent ancient (and modern) monuments, the altar was actually lost for many centuries and has been part of a long and somewhat inconsistent recovery and reassembly process that stretches back to the Renaissance period. The Ara Pacis as we know it now is largely a product of the dictatorship of Benito Mussolini, who in 1937–1938 sponsored a campaign to rebuild significant portions of the monuments and topography of Ancient Rome in order to glorify

[24] Kathleen S. Lamp, *A City of Marble: The Rhetoric of Augustan Rome*, Studies in Rhetoric/Communication (Columbia: University of South Carolina Press, 2013), 18.

[25] For examples of the Ara Pacis on coins of the period, as well as for an introduction to the monument as such, see Erika Simon, *Ara Pacis Augustae* (Greenwich, Conn.: Graphic Society, 1968); and Diane Atnally Conlin, *The Artists of the Ara Pacis: The Process of Hellenization in Roman Relief Sculpture*, Studies in the History of Greece and Rome (Chapel Hill: University of North Carolina Press, 1991).

FIGURE 3.1
Ara Pacis Augustae, Rome. View of the "west" wall featuring the so-called Tellus relief (left) and the Roma relief (right) flanking an entryway to the interior and altar. The ceremonial festoons decorating the interior walls are partly visible here, as is one of the processional walls. The acanthus scroll reliefs line the bottom register. The approach platform is modern. Photo by Davina C. Lopez.

the mythical ancestral past of Fascist Italy.[26] Mussolini identified with Augustus as a leader of the Roman people and had a museum (the Museo dell'Ara Pacis) erected around the reconstructed altar, which was then moved to its current location near the restored Mausoleum of Augustus as part of a celebratory architectural location called the Piazzale Augusto Imperatore. The Ara Pacis was hailed as a masterpiece of Augustan (and Italian Fascism) visual communication and propaganda and became a symbol of Mussolini's reign and aspirations. With the collapse of that political regime, this altar faded from public

[26] For discussion of Mussolini's reconstructions of Ancient Rome, see Joshua Arthurs, *Excavating Modernity: The Roman Past in Fascist Italy* (Ithaca, N.Y.: Cornell University Press, 2012); Wayne Andersen, *The Ara Pacis of Augustus and Mussolini* (New York: Editions Fabriart, 2005); Borden W. Painter, *Mussolini's Rome: Rebuilding the Eternal City*, Italian and Italian-American Studies (New York: Palgrave Macmillan, 2007); and Claudia Lazzaro, "Forging a Visible Fascist Nation: Strategies for Fusing Past and Present," in *Donatello among the Blackshirts: History and Modernity in the Visual Culture of Fascist Italy*, ed. Claudia Lazzaro and Roger J. Crum (Ithaca, N.Y.: Cornell University Press, 2005), 13–31.

prominence and propagandistic deployment. Scholars now debate the accuracy of the 1938 reconstruction of the Ara Pacis—for example, whether the modern filling in of lost or misplaced fragments gives us a good picture of what the altar looked like in antiquity—and have made important revisions and adjustments to its sculptural program along the way, including analysis that has helped scholars to theorize what colors the altar was painted in its time. While such debates (which, as far as many ancient monuments are concerned, is fairly typical) continue and are important for the precise identification of the various human figures and other visual elements on the altar, it is also the case that the Ara Pacis in its present condition represents an informed consensus concerning its programmatic characteristics.

Sculptural programs on the inside and outside of the monument compose the Ara Pacis as a whole. Around the interior walls are reliefs of stylized palm branches and lotus flowers. The most extensive visual element is a relief pattern of hanging festoons made up of numerous types of leaves, shoots, and fruits from all over the world, such as corn, ivy, oak, poppy, apple, fig, and pomegranate. These garlands, which at once communicate ideas of victory (over the lands that produced some of these fruits) and of cosmopolitan abundance (the availability of these fruits to the Roman people under Augustus), are connected with sculpted ribbons and hang between ox skulls carved in high relief. The interior houses a now-fragmentary sacrificial altar that likely displayed multiple scenes related to the ritual that took place in the complex. This altar is visible from the outer walls, which are decorated in two distinct registers. The upper register features human figures in procession on the north and south walls; humans, personifications, mythological figures, and animals appear on the east and west walls. The bottom register is composed solely of a series of reliefs depicting a highly idealized plant motif with swans and smaller animals visible throughout its swirling branches; these plants wrap around all four exterior walls. Together these elements suggest a visual discourse that seeks to persuade the people of the city and empire that their leader was no mere mortal. Aside from saving the Roman population from civil wars, barbarian threats, and pirates in his own time, Augustus was positioned as someone through whom this "sacred power" of peacemaking via victory and conquest flowed freely.

When approaching the entryway to the Ara Pacis, one would ascend a bank of stairs and notice that the lower register of plant scrolls gives way to two allegorical mythological scenes on either side of the

FIGURE 3.2

Ara Pacis Augustae, Rome. Relief featuring a veiled woman sitting on a stone throne. Infants sit in her lap, as does a collection of various fruits. She is flanked by two personifications, perhaps of "Land" and "Sea." This figure has been identified as Tellus, Italia, and a variety of other goddesses/personified virtues. Photo by Davina C. Lopez.

entry opening, both containing female figures. The panel on the left side (fig. 3.2) is well preserved and has long been the subject of discussion. In this relief a fully clothed and veiled woman reclines on a stone pedestal, holding two babies and various fruits on her lap. The left infant faces her and appears to be tugging at her bosom, and the right infant is shown in profile holding a piece of fruit in her line of vision. Farm animals recline and graze at her feet, and plants shoot up around her. This woman is flanked by two other female figures, clothed from the waist down, riding on the backs of a swan or goose (left) and dragon-like creature (right), respectively. The presence of plants on the left, and water on the right, suggests an association of the swan-riding figure with an allegorical representation of "land" and the sea-creature-riding figure with "sea." Such a reading would be supported by visual representations of Augustus pictured striding between "land and sea" (for example, in a relief from the Aphrodisias Sebasteion) as well as reminiscent of Augustus' own statements: "I many times waged civil and foreign wars by land and sea over the whole world, and as victor I spared all citizens who asked for pardon" (*Res Gestae* 3.1).

Based on her positioning and attributes (agricultural products, infants), several suggestions have been made as to the identity of this woman. She could, for example, be Tellus or Ceres, the goddess/personification of the earth. Other possibilities include Fecunditas ("fecundity," often shown with infants), Abundantia ("abundance" and the guarantor of the Golden Age, often shown with infants and fruits), Venus (the mother of the Julio-Claudian line), and/or Pax herself, to whom the altar is dedicated and in whose name the sacrificial rituals would have been conducted. She could also be the personification of the nation of Italia, a nation that, in the logic of the Golden Age, now, with the help of Augustus, presides over land and sea, sure to enjoy a fecund future for its newly (re)born citizens. Persuasive cases have been made in favor of each of these figures. Rhetorically, depending on the viewer's frame of reference, social positioning, and relationship to the city, this woman could be any and all of these women. At a most basic level, this image is intelligible as an allegorical representation of the peace (through victory "over land and sea"), fertility (through the presence of infants and young animals), and abundance (through the depiction of various plants and fruits) that was prophesied about Augustus and that he himself claimed to bring to Rome.

The panel on the opposite side of the entryway from the veiled fertility figure (fig. 3.3) is the most fragmentary of all the exterior panels on the upper register of the Ara Pacis. Through comparison of surviving fragments with similar representations, art historians and archaeologists mostly concur that the relief depicts a female figure thought to be Roma, the goddess and personification of Rome. The reconstruction of this woman situates her in the common depiction of Roma: she is dressed in military garb and helmet, holds a spear, and is sitting on a pile of weapons and armor captured from the enemy. This is a common visual representation of Roma in the early Roman Empire. She is often shown on monuments that express victory in war, as well as dynastic commemoration, as is the case with the famous Gemma Augustea, where Roma sits next to Augustus as he is crowned with the *corona civica* by a personification of Oikoumene, the world.[27] On

[27] John Pollini has made this point most convincingly in his assessment of the Gemma Augustea; see Pollini, "The Gemma Augustea: Ideology, Rhetorical Imagery, and the Creation of a Dynastic Narrative," in *Narrative and Event in Ancient Art*, ed. Peter Holliday (New York: Cambridge University Press, 1993), 258–98. On the personification of Roma as a military-clad woman, represented as such across imperial territory, and especially in the east, see Ronald Mellor, *Thea **Rhōmē**: The Worship of the Goddess Roma in the Greek World* (Göttengen: Vanderhoeck & Ruprecht, 1975). In Aphrodisias, Roma is shown both in military costume and in traditional female dress;

FIGURE 3.3
Ara Pacis Augustae, Rome. Largely fragmentary relief of a helmeted female figure thought to be Roma, the personification of Rome. Lines denote modern reconstructive diagram. Photo by Davina C. Lopez.

this panel Roma is thought to be flanked by two figures that were also common in victory art: Honos, the personification of military honor and justice, and Virtus, the personification of virtue and bravery. Both of these figures appear on coins and relief sculptures commemorating war and conquest, such as the Boscoreale cups and the Arch of Titus.[28] Taken together, the left and right panels are multivalent. They portray allegorical representations of peace and victory along with imperial virtues. Although seemingly "calm," the imagery on the Ara Pacis suggests that a fecund, fertile present and future in the Augustan Golden

in one relief from the Sebasteion, she strides over a reclining personification of Gaia. See R. R. R. Smith, *The Marble Reliefs from the Julio-Claudian Sebasteion*, Aphrodisias 6 (Darmstadt: Verlag Philipp on Zabern, 2013).

[28] For discussion of the possible connections between the Boscoreale cups, the Arch of Titus, and the Ara Pacis, see Ann L. Kuttner, *Dynasty and Empire in the Age of Augustus: The Case of the Boscoreale Cups* (Berkeley: University of California Press, 1995).

FIGURE 3.4
Ara Pacis Augustae, Rome. Relief thought to depict an older, bearded Aeneas making sacrifice to the household gods. Two young attendants bring fruits and a sow. Photo by Davina C. Lopez.

FIGURE 3.5
Ara Pacis Augustae, Rome. Largely fragmentary relief interpreted as Romulus and Remus being suckled by the she-wolf near the sacred fig tree, flanked by Mars and Faustulus. Lines denote modern reconstructive diagram. Photo by Davina C. Lopez.

Age are in part activated by the conquest and inclusion of the "others," that is, the "enemies" at home and elsewhere.

The Ara Pacis panels on the outer entry wall opposite from the female fertility and Roma scenes feature two depictions from Rome's mythical history that involve predominantly male characters. On the left (fig. 3.4), fragments have been postulated to be Romulus and Remus, the twin founders of Rome, suckling at their she-wolf in the *lupercal* and flanked by the war god Mars (their "true" father) and Faustulus (the man who raised them), as well as the sacred fig tree from the banks of the Tiber River, which was associated with their infancy. This imagery appears to have been consistent across diverse media and was popular in Rome and throughout the empire; it would thus be quite plausible and intelligible to viewers of this particular monument. This visual reference to Rome's origins in this public, civic context would resonate with the Golden Age sentiment that Augustus was a "new" Romulus, a refounder of the city.

The second scene, on the right (fig. 3.5), is thought to depict sacrifice. An older, bearded man wearing a veil, signifying his piety, occupies the center of this relief, followed by a fragmentary other (male) figure to his right. The man appears to be pouring out a libation on a garland-decorated stone altar under an oak tree. Two young attendants bring him a platter of fruits and a sow. A garlanded temple with two reclining male figures sits in the background on a hill. This scene is often interpreted as an (older) Aeneas and his son, Julius-Ascanius (ancestor of the Julio-Claudian line), offering sacrifice to his household *penates* (who may be seated in the temple). The presence of the sow, oak, and temple in the background link this scene to the prophecy that Aeneas, upon his arrival in Latium, would find a Lavinian sow under an oak tree and make a sacrifice of her. Both reliefs on this side of the Ara Pacis involve mythological scenes that were decisive for the founding of Rome: Romulus and Remus for the city, and Aeneas and the sow for the *gens Julia*.[29] And yet these reliefs, particularly the depiction of sacrifice, are also connected to the "present" purpose of the altar. That is, the altar would have been used for sacrifice in its time, to be sure. However, the imagery of Aeneas sacrificing is also reappropriated in light of the dedication of the Ara Pacis after the return of Augustus to Rome. Herein the past is joined to the present, as participating in

[29] Mario Torelli, *Typology and Structure of Roman Historical Reliefs*, Jerome Lectures 14 (Ann Arbor: University of Michigan Press, 1982), 37.

FIGURE 3.6
Scale model of the Ara Pacis Augustae showing processional frieze and acanthus scroll relief filling the bottom register. Museo della Civiltà Romana, Rome. Photo by Davina C. Lopez.

sacrifice at the Ara Pacis connects one to a venerable tradition that reaches back to the founding of the Roman city and "first family."[30]

Further related to these themes, the mythological and allegorical scenes on the Ara Pacis are juxtaposed with sculptural reliefs of a procession—perhaps with a nod toward the ritual to take place at the Ara Pacis itself—that line the "north" and "south" outer walls of the monument (fig. 3.6). Again, in these scenes the present joins the past. There has been much discussion concerning the proper and precise identities of the various people in the processions. On one side, Augustus is featured wearing a veil, a symbol of his sacrificial piety. Joining him in this procession are members of four priestly colleges, his extended family, and other elites. Of particular interest is the depiction

[30] John Clarke has made this point well with regard to ordinary viewers' experience with the Ara Pacis; such viewers "would have connected Aeneas's act of sacrifice with the ritual that took place every year at the Ara Pacis: the slaughter of three animals (ram, steer, and heifer), the cooking of the choice parts (*exta*) as a sacrifice to the gods, and the joining in on the feast—eating roasted meat—afterwards" (Clarke, *Art in the Lives of Ordinary Romans: Visual Representation and Non-elite Viewers in Italy, 100 B.C.–A.D. 315*, Joan Palevsky Books in Classical Studies [Berkeley: University of California Press, 2006], 25).

of several children of various ages among those in procession. These children are not, for the most part, dressed "properly," that is, in Roman clothing. They are dressed as "barbarian" children, with the garb and jewelry of eastern and northern "outsider" nations, and in one case a young girl wears the toga, the common dress for adult male citizens and not children. These children, along with the adults immediately surrounding them, provide an interesting union of Roman and non-Roman families together in procession toward a common ritual—and common future as "Romans." The presence of these children could be read as a symbolic rendering of how including the non-Roman national (the "other") into the family of Rome is part of the power of the peace brought by the emperor. As with the infants on the lap of the fertility figure flanking the entryway, young children communicate hope for the future, familial affinity, and a dynastic connection, demonstrating, as Natalie Boymel Kampen has suggested, "the permanence and completeness of victory *and* dynastic continuity."[31] The delivery of foreign children to their new "father," the emperor, following conquest, is a common theme in the Roman art that commemorates victory, and the Ara Pacis appears to be an early example of this pattern. In these cases, rhetorically, the "nations" are "grafted" onto the Roman "root" and are given the promise of "becoming Roman" themselves. Furthermore, the Romans tended to represent their cosmopolitanism and international flair—their national diversity, if you will—in literature and visual representation deploying symbols of "all the nations" and their "fruits." This was accomplished in various media forms, and included explicit and implicit allusions to war alongside fertility motifs.

In all of this, of course, viewers become a part of this procession by walking alongside it as they approach, or just walk past, the Ara Pacis, even as the sacrifice would happen only once a year. As with the narrative reliefs on the interior of the Arch of Titus, wherein viewers walk alongside a procession of victorious Romans, personifications related to peace and war, and conquered Judeans carrying their own spoils from Jerusalem through a triumphal arch, the procession on the Ara Pacis is ongoing—in some sense, perpetually—with help from everyday, pedestrian viewers.

It seems natural to focus attention on identifying the human figures on the upper register of the Ara Pacis. It is also very likely; the

[31] Natalie Boymel Kampen, *Family Fictions in Roman Art* (New York: Cambridge University Press, 2009), 61.

case that these scenes were not fully intelligible in intricate detail to the average viewer, as the reliefs were positioned too high for full readability. What viewers could see clearly, and what was at eye level all the way around the outside of the altar, is the so-called acanthus scroll (fig. 3.1 and fig. 3.6, bottom register). Far from being merely decorative, these reliefs complement and enhance the visual program of the altar as a whole, exemplify an important idea about the relationship between people and the natural world, supplement the trees and fruits depicted elsewhere on the altar, and reinforce the overall themes of fertility, abundance, and peacemaking that characterized the Augustan Golden Age.[32] Each of these panels has a central "root" point in the representation of the base of an acanthus plant, a relatively common plant that still grows in temperate and warmer climates such as the Mediterranean basin and across south Asia. On the Ara Pacis, these root bases feature a single stalk shooting up out of the middle, as is common to the acanthus, and that is where the similarity with a recognizable real-life plant ends. Also growing out from each acanthus base are multiple scrolling, vine-like branches that appear to be swirling across the panels, taking up the entire space in symmetrical fashion. These branches, however, are not acanthus branches per se. The swirly tendrils, rather, have the distinctive attributes of different plants such as roses, poppies, grapevines, oak, and palms. Branches, leaves and flowers, and fruits of multiple plants are interspersed throughout the Ara Pacis, which, with these reliefs, contains what is probably the highest concentration of floral representation in Roman art of the period. Swans roost on the tops of several branches, six on the processional sides and two each on the walls under the four mythological and allegorical panels. Along with these large swans, small animals such as snakes and frogs, birds with nests and baby chicks, and insects such as grasshoppers and scorpions are shown living among the branches.

[32] For discussion of the mythological and theological significance of the acanthus scroll reliefs, see Hans Peter L'Orange, *The Roman Empire: Art Forms and Civic Life* (New York: Rizzoli, 1985), 211–28; David Castriota, *The Ara Pacis Augustae and the Imagery of Abundance in Later Greek and Early Roman Imperial Art* (Princeton: Princeton University Press, 1995); and John Pollini, "The Acanthus of the Ara Pacis as an Apolline and Dionysiac Symbol of *Anamorphosis*, *Anakyklosis*, and *Numen Mixtum*," in his *From Republic to Empire: Rhetoric, Religion, and Power in the Visual Culture of Ancient Rome*, Oklahoma Series in Classical Culture 48 (Norman: University of Oklahoma Press, 2012), 271–308.

The acanthus scrolls on the Ara Pacis, like their counterparts featuring human actors on the upper register, carry allegorical and mythological overtones. The acanthus was depicted in the age of Alexander as a symbol of immortality and in Hellenistic Egypt as a plant out of which Helios, the sun god, would rise. This plant also represented healing and rebirth, and in the Roman context could be linked to Apollo, whom Augustus adopted as his patron deity.[33] The fantastic hybrid plant on these reliefs features branches of plants and fruits common to places such as Pergamon, Greece, and Egypt, all important nations for the ascendancy of the Roman Empire. These "foreign" plants, moreover, can be associated with various ethnic/national gods, and their being grafted onto the acanthus collectively could symbolize concord between gods and nations, with Rome as the "support system," a theme that is highlighted by the internationalism and cosmopolitanism promised with the Augustan "new creation." As John Pollini has argued, "the miraculous acanthus scrollwork of the Ara Pacis serves as a metaphor for the new era of peace and prosperity that Augustus, as agent of divine will under the good auspices of his patron god Apollo, brought to Italy and the entire Roman world."[34] The visual adoption of the acanthus as a central element, as the root and base from which all other vines spring, onto which all manner of flora appear to be seamlessly grafted, and in which animals and insects from all over the world might dwell, can be read as a visual representation of the prophesied abundance and healing of the rifts between nations that will come to pass with the return of a Golden Age under Augustus.

The "graft" represented on the Ara Pacis is consistent with literary imagery of spontaneous, miraculous hybridity among plants and animals portending the Augustan Golden Age and the rebirth of the "new creation" of the Roman Empire. That is, grafting appears not to simply signify a means of doing farming in rural settings, but rather bears a weighty symbolic and theological import in the ancient Roman world, urban and rural. To be sure, in some respect the Romans tended to treat hybridity—as manifest in half-human, half-animal creatures or hermaphrodites, for example—as monstrous prodigies that were "contrary to nature" and expendable. However, as Dunstan Lowe has pointed out, miraculous grafting of, and hybridity in, plants is a common feature in Augustan literature and is a central part of early

[33] Pollini, "Acanthus of the Ara Pacis," 284–85.

[34] Pollini, "Acanthus of the Ara Pacis," 299.

imperial rhetorics of "utopian fantasy."[35] In the *Georgics* of Virgil, for example, we find the personification of a tree marveling at all manner of hybrid flora, for example: "the wild strawberry-tree is grafted with a walnut shoot, and barren plane-trees have carried vigorous apple; the beech has shown white with pale chestnut flowers, and the ash with the pear's" (*Georg.* 2.69–73). Herein grafting takes on an unlimited and fantastic character that signifies more than mere reporting of farm techniques. The mythical Golden Bough of *Aeneid* 6 is a miraculously grafted tree. Famous, also, is the link between such preternatural grafting and hybridity and the birth of an infant savior in *Eclogue* 4. This poem prophesies that a special child will be born into a new age wherein Apollo reigns and humans mingle with gods (*Ecl.* 4.10–15). Upon this child's birth, the earth (*tellus*) will, without agricultural labor, gift him from her miraculous "fruits," including ivy mixed with foxglove and Egyptian beans with "smiling acanthus" (4.19–23). Similarly, trading will need to stop, for "all lands will bear all things" (4.39). During this time, goats will miraculously have their udders filled with milk and the wool of rams will dye itself, rendering human labor unnecessary (4.42–45). Echoes of Virgil's grafting imagery can be found in subsequent literature of the likes of Pliny the Elder, who reports that elite Romans displayed family trees in their homes, and that often these trees, which included ancestral faces and masks, were revised with shifts in family structure and looked like fantastic, grafted, hybrid plants (*Hist. Nat.* 35.8).[36] Palladius devotes significant space to the agricultural "miracles" possible through grafting trees of different nations together (*De Ins.* 129–130; see also 53–54). Such themes resonate with the visual representation on the Ara Pacis, whose ancient viewers may have been familiar with such tales and prophecies as well.

[35] Dunstan Lowe, "The Symbolic Value of Grafting in Ancient Rome," *TAPA* 140 (2010): 461–88.

[36] Most of the evidence we have for the visual representation of ancient Roman family trees is from the imperial period. Other ancient authors who discuss the Roman display of family trees include Sallust, *Jugurtha* 85.10; Martial, *Epigrams* 4.40.1, 5.35; Juvenal, *Satire* 8.1, 6, 40; Suetonius, *Nero* 37.1, *Galba* 2, *Vespasian* 12; and Plutarch, *Numa* 21.4. On Roman family tree displays, see Harriet I. Flower, *Ancestral Masks and Aristocratic Power in Roman Culture* (Oxford: Clarendon, 1996). For extensive discussion of the visual representation of ancestral lineages in the Roman imperial world, see Olivier Hekster, *Emperors and Ancestors: Roman Rulers and the Constraints of Tradition*, Oxford Studies in Ancient Culture and Representation (New York: Oxford University Press, 2015), 1–30.

As an ancient visual element, grafting offers a powerful and multivalent metaphor. That is, the miraculously grafted hybrid acanthus scrolls are resonant with the idea of the prophetic return of the Golden Age characteristic of Augustan ideology, and to be sure there are other significations viewers might make as well. As part of the visual rhetoric of the Ara Pacis, the single root base spiraling out into multiple branches of plants from the world "contrary to nature" can serve as a means of portraying how the "new creation" of the Roman Empire is knit together, especially in cases where plants are associated with places, peoples, nations, and national deities. Given the mythological ancestral imagery and visual suggestions of fertility and abundance elsewhere on the Ara Pacis, it very well could be that the hybrid acanthus scrolls functioned as a "family tree" of sorts, wherein the nations of the empire, in all their various tendrils, spring up from a hearty Roman root base that has divine overtones.

Such an image as that which the acanthus and its myriad branches and vines provide seems serene and "peaceful." However, it is worth remembering that foreign nations were not "grafted" onto the Roman Empire miraculously or spontaneously, but through the "miracle" of war and territorial annexation. Becoming part of the Roman "family tree" if one were not natively of the national elite was accomplished through service in the army, manumission from slavery, or outright conquest. For the Romans, making "peace" meant, as Tacitus has the Caledonian chieftain Calgacus relay, "making a desolation and call[ing] it peace" (*Agr.* 30.4). Triumph over foreign people meant triumph over their land—and their flora and fauna—which was often rearranged and repurposed toward Roman ends (e.g., feeding an expanding population). Peace is signified by the ability of the Romans to control the land of others—to "graft" foreign branches onto their own tree. Visually, war is the most popular theme in Roman art, and representations of the "others"—the conquered and "grafted"—was especially popular in various media. Often portrayed as female figures with distinctive attributes, either standing, kneeling, or sitting, sometimes dead, often bound to trophies and/or trees, and in later periods seen shaking hands with emperors such as Hadrian, the "nations" became a common theme in public visual representation across Roman imperial territory. Rather than depict allegorical human personifications of conquered nations as a means to commemorate the "peace" Augustus made through the forced cessation of civil wars and campaigns in Gaul and Spain, the Ara Pacis represents such "peace" allegorically, mythologically, and genealogically. "Peace," here, is shown as being accomplished miraculously and spontaneously through domestic concord and international conquest, according to prophecy, with no effort or labor.

Through the symbolic visual rhetoric of the Ara Pacis, Augustus and, by extension, the Roman people are linked to a host of ideas, virtues, and genealogical configurations that reach back into the earliest moments of Roman existence.[37] Part of its genealogical discourse is achieved through the representation of utopian, miraculous grafting of foreign plants and animals onto a central, theologically significant acanthus base. Thus, it stands to reason that grafting, for the Romans, is not simply a banal agricultural technique that was relayed in agricultural handbooks for the sake of getting the procedure down correctly for good crops. The discourse of farming, of which grafting techniques is a part, is highly idealized among Roman elites—it is a mode of representation. Rhetorically, grafting is also a way of thinking through dynastic origins and legacies, as well as symbolizing the fertility and miraculous abundance of the Augustan Golden Age. To this end, hybrid plants serve miraculous and ambivalent functions, and the abundance of a vividly hybrid natural world is key to a Roman imperial theology of "peace through victory," bearing with it a cosmic significance. For his part, Augustus was an expander: he tried to put a positive, symbolic face on the mundane and challenging material realities of territorial empire. However, and this is important for Pauline studies, this representation only goes so far. The "others" were not necessarily happy to be included through war and conquest. Some Romans, including elites who produced literature, also held suspicions about who could belong and on what terms. In the end, then, this "golden age" of peace and fertility was a site for the negotiation of community, identity, and cosmic order in its own time. It seems reasonable to me that the Romans of Paul's most

[37] Carlos Noreña has argued that personifications served to express aspects of the emperor's personality, and specifically his personal and political virtues, e.g., Pax, Concordia, Tranquilitas, Fortuna, Abundantia, and so on. See Noreña, *Imperial Ideals in the Roman West: Representation, Circulation, Power* (New York: Cambridge University Press, 2011), 127–36. Given such a link between the emperor with the (usually female, but see the "maleness" of Honos and Virtus) personifications of virtues, we can see a rationale for the perhaps intentional ambiguity of the woman on the Ara Pacis commonly identified as "Tellus": her range of meaning could be intoned as any number of virtues, or all of them, by viewers.

famous letter would have participated in such negotiations, given the pervasiveness of the Roman metanarrative. The Ara Pacis Augustae, and Roman imperial theology more broadly, can thus be seen as an intriguing *comparandum* for the genealogical rhetoric about Jews/Israel and "others" that Paul offers in Romans 9–11.

The Rhetoric of the Graft in Romans 11: Peace and Fertility through Reversal and Restoration

Engaging Roman imperial ideology/theology provides us with a productive site of comparison wherein we might detect some points of intersection between Paul and his world. Seeing the Romans as theologically and mythologically inclined people, and not just as the people in the "political" background of Paul, can also help to broaden our view of Pauline literature as well as the New Testament as a whole, allowing us to ask different questions of early Christianity as a historical and religious phenomenon. Herein I maintain that narrow engagements with Romans 9–11 limit scholarly imagination in terms of what kinds of readings and reconstructions are possible with respect to Pauline personae, communities, and correspondence. It is my hope that understanding Roman imperial theology, even in the cursory way presented here, can also broaden our own views of what "theology" is, what it does, and what we make it do as a category and area of investigation.

One major anxiety in Pauline studies is that Romans 9–11 somehow needs to be read doctrinally and dogmatically, and only that way. Any attempt to do otherwise is problematic for any number of reasons, and scholars of Paul seem to spend more time defending dogmatic readings of this particular set of chapters than in asking what kinds of alternative historical or rhetorical questions could be posed. Again, at least one explanation for this myopic focus is that Romans 9–11 is seen as the "heart" or "pinnacle" of Paul's "theological treatise"—the summary of his theological reasoning for his mission to the Gentiles and his justification and logic for the church in its present form and its future hope. In addition, in terms of the loaded question of anti-Judaism in the New Testament, scholars have had to double down on defending Paul against accusations of being the "father" of anti-Judaism in the Christian tradition, and certainly Romans 9–11 is a *crux interpretum* in this respect.

Whatever the reason for the focus, however, the seeming intractability of this approach exposes, as I have stated above, two methodological problems. First, because Romans 9–11 is a venerable source for dogmatics, it is tempting to let those conclusions drive and circumscribe the questions posed. Herein the Romans become much less important as conversation partners for Paul. If Deissmann and the legacies of historical-critical (and literary-critical) New Testament scholarship are to be taken seriously, though, then we do need to acknowledge that doctrine was a later development through which interpreters deployed the Pauline letters, including Romans, as a means of support. "Doctrine" and "theology"—at least as we know those categories—cannot be found in these letters, at least not in the forms with which we are generally comfortable. Second, and related to the first, who we think Paul is and what he meant tend to dominate scholarly conversations about his letters, even if implicitly. It becomes difficult, as a result, to move from assumptions about authorial intent and the narrowing of resources for Paul's thought to the development and reception of Paul's rhetoric in his own milieu, although it is precisely the latter that opens up wider questions of interpretation for the passage. If we take seriously that texts are responses to the world in which they are situated and produced, then it stands to reason that we have often been neglecting to develop a fuller picture of Paul's world.

Understanding Paul's rhetoric in Romans, though, should move beyond questions about whether he had a traditional Greco-Roman education and/or access to the rhetorical handbooks that would have outlined proper modes of argumentation, as these foci are no less limiting in their scope. Whether or not Paul is a skilled rhetorician in the classical sense, his letters are rhetorical—that is, they are written to persuade his audience of something. Rhetoric is, ultimately, about the means and powers of persuasion and extends beyond words to the image-laden landscape in which Paul's addressees would have lived their daily existence. Visual rhetoric such as that displayed on the Ara Pacis and throughout the Roman world offers a way into understanding the theological and religious landscape of the world to which Paul responds and negotiates.

Given this broader dimension of rhetoric, Paul's genealogical grafting discourse in Romans 9–11, and in chapter 11 specifically, can be understood a little differently. A primary question is how and on what terms these "new" people can be included into an "old" community, or at least a community that has a long historical genealogy. Along these lines, I note that a rhetorical theme of Romans as a whole can be summed up with the term "contrary." That is, in

Romans Paul appears to be mounting a case for his addressees that would run "contrary" to ideas and practices with which they would be familiar, including what "others" need to do or be in order to be a part of "Israel." The olive tree allegory may seem to be backward or "contrary to nature," and yet perhaps that would fit with the mytho-historical, genealogical discursive thrust of Romans as a whole. A "reversed" grafting procedure calls attention to the genealogical reversal and restoration paradigm to which Paul is alluding in Romans 9–11 overall. That is, in the Pauline imagination the integration of Jews and Gentiles into "Israel" is positioned as that which is contrary to social and ethical "laws." In this schema, which reaches back to the "origins" of Paul's current addressees, the firstborn does not acquire the promise of guaranteed inheritance, as would be "natural." Contrary to what is "natural," the Gentiles are grafted in without any effort on their part or the grafter's. Importantly, though, the Gentiles are grafted into this venerable (and certainly prophetic and miraculous) olive tree without being conquered or otherwise forced, which is also quite contrary to the Roman imagination of what would be "natural." In light of these observations, in my reading Paul's argument unfolds in three parts over chapters 9 through 11: genealogical argumentation concerning the origins and heritage of Israel, prophetic justification for the inclusion of those thought to be excluded according to the genealogical discussion, and the integration of myth and history, past and present, and Jews and nations. Ultimately, this rhetoric appears to be aimed at configuring and managing a current understanding of some social situation in the immediate context of his audience, a situation that Paul connects to the "seeds" sown in the distant, mythological past of Israel.

In light of a contrarian genealogical theme, Paul's basic argument to his addressees seems quite simple: contrary to what they have read or heard or thought, or what they have read or heard in regard to the history of Israel and the Hebrew Scriptures, those Scriptures are clear throughout that the history of Israel itself runs "contrary to nature," that is, contrary to what one would expect of a small minority nation that has long been under threat and dominance from foreign, much larger, empires. Israel, in this case, offers a strong foundational story and community upon which the "nations" can be grafted and flourish. To further his argument, in Romans 9 Paul makes a distinction between "my brothers" and "my kinsmen," the Israelites to whom adoption, covenants, laws, promises, and fathers were originally given and from whom they come, and the idea that not all Israelites belong to Israel. That is, not all of the children of the ur-ancestor Abraham, the "father of many nations" both before and after his circumcision (Rom 4:9-12), are his "seed"—for Paul, children are not the same as "seed," and only the children of Isaac, the second-born of Abraham with Sarah "according to promise," are "seed" (Rom 9:8; cf. Paul's assertion that Christ is somehow the activated long-dormant "seed" of Abraham in Gal 3:15-20). Paul continues his genealogical argument about the composition of the "new creation" in Christ using Genesis, the mythological story of origins, as well as Hosea. In Genesis, he argues, the "seed" comes not from the firstborn, which is linked to the "flesh," but from the "promise" given to those who come afterward, which, in the case of the genealogy and his own addressees, is the "nations." These are those who, according to Hosea, "were not my people" and now are "called my people" (Rom 9:25-26). For Paul, this dynamic plays out through the difference in the pursuit of righteousness by Israel and the nations: Israel pursued righteousness by "law" and did not achieve it, while the nations did not pursue righteousness and achieved it by "faith" (Rom 9:30-31). Those who pursued righteousness and fell short are "broken off" later in Paul's olive tree allegory, while those who did not pursue righteousness become the ones who are "grafted in." As it is now, so it has been throughout Israel's history: the family tree includes multiple parties.

Paul continues his argument in chapter 10, when he turns his attention to "you, brothers." Herein he uses the prophets to support his claims for the kind of union between Jews and nations under the banner of "Israel," as well as an elaboration of those claims based on what seeking and not seeking righteousness has entailed according to the history of Israel. It is in Christ, Paul states, that there is no distinction between "Jew and Greek" (Rom 10:12), and all those who call on the Lord will be saved, regardless of ethnic origin (Rom 10:13). And in chapter 11, Paul brings genealogical and prophetic discourses together. After speaking about the ways in which some Israelites have fallen short of their birthright and calling in relation to God, Paul rejects the idea that the Israelites have been rejected and identifies himself as an Israelite, "out of the seed of Abraham, the tribe of Benjamin" (Rom 11:1-2). He then speaks explicitly to "you, nations" as (an Israelite who is) the apostle to the nations, glorifying that mission in order to provoke jealousy in "those of my flesh" (Rom 11:12-14). In noting that both the roots and branches of a tree are holy, Paul then calls "you" ("nations") a "wild olive shoot" that is grafted in place of "broken branches" ("Israelites") (Rom 11:17). However, perhaps contrary to what his wild-olive-shoot addressees might assume, Paul admonishes them not to be arrogant, as the (holy) root supports "you" and not the other way around (Rom 11:18). Paul then speaks as if he can anticipate the response of his grafted audience, letting them know that even as they might contend that they have been grafted onto the holy root in place of the branches that were broken off—indeed, those very branches that were broken off for the express purpose of such a graft—they should still not boast (Rom 11:19-20); their situation is perhaps just as precarious. After all, Paul says, the "natural" branches that were broken off can easily be grafted back in—much more so than the wild shoots who were grafted in "contrary to nature" (Rom 11:23-24).

As far as Paul is concerned, his argument seems to indicate that the Gentiles/nations will be restored to Israel, just as the paradigm suggests in the genealogical and prophetic discourses he has been deploying throughout Romans 9–11. The branches in Paul's olive tree allegory have been a focus of interpretive efforts, but perhaps the more significant point of interest in the Pauline imagination is the root or base itself. This holy root, of course, represents Israel—the nation, the ideal—and the "natural" branches represent the Israelites. While some of those "natural" branches are broken off, the root is no less vigorous, and it can "support" the wildest of grafted shoots such as those represented in the "nations." The rest of this discourse serves to make the point that the genealogical myth of Israel's ancestral heritage forms the basis for his mission to the "nations" and his idea that faith in Christ is the way to become a part of this tradition that goes all the way back to the beginning with Abraham and his holy seed. With this in view, it could very well be that, rhetorically, the hierarchical arrangement of the branches—wild or "natural"—actually does not matter that much to his argument. In the Pauline imagination, the branches all relate to the common root regardless of their origin.

Given the ubiquity of Roman imperial theology, and particularly expressions of the return of the Golden Age through Augustan peacemaking, I imagine that Paul's addressees—some of whom, perhaps, belong to the "nations" brought to Rome and grafted onto the acanthus base through the "miracle" of war—would be challenged by Paul's genealogical discourse through the olive tree allegory. Paul's effort to respond to perceived objections would suggest that he at least anticipated a struggle over his ideas here. If one looks at it in light of the Roman imperial visual representation that I have outlined above, Paul's argument in Romans 9–11 looks much more like an imaginative and generous expansion of God's promise, one that in some sense is more "peaceful," inclusive, and even more radically transformative than what we find in the Roman imagination. The Pauline imagination is willing to see the basis of the root transformed in light of a new revelation and new faith that is connected to the very origins of Israel itself. When the "nations"—Gentiles and Israel—come together, things do not stay the same. It is not just that Gentiles join the "in-group" and move up or down on the existing hierarchy. Rather, the very basis of what is "in" changes—including who is "out."

Compared to the Roman vision of genealogical rhetoric, Paul's vision comes as a radical reorientation and dislocation, a topsy-turvy view. It is not what the many who viewed Roman imperial representations such as those on the Ara Pacis would have anticipated: it is a reimagination of community and the potential of people to work out new relationships in communion. Whatever Paul's orientation to Roman imperial theology may have been, one thing is clear: the rhetoric has mythological dimensions and is multivalent. In my view, reading the olive tree allegory in light of Roman imperial theology and mytho-historical representation offers a glimpse at a vision of peace among the nations through restoration and reversal, rather than conquest and assimilation. This practice of peacemaking would be "contrary to nature," a note Paul accents when he implores his addressees in Romans 12:2: "do not be conformed to this age, but be transformed by the renewal of your minds." Only then—through dwelling in those ideas and narratives that seem "contrary" to what is all around them, in "this age" of mythmaking and rebirth (which is painful! See Rom 8:22) in a "new creation" that has been freed from slavery (Rom 8:21)—can Paul's Romans discern the "will of God." And in such discernment, one can detect traces of a peacemaking process that can lead to mutual abundance and fertility among nations, "weak" and "strong" alike, in a world in Christ that is itself contrary to what is "natural" as far as the metanarrative of the Roman Empire is concerned.

The olive tree allegory in Romans 11:11-24 is particularly arresting in this light. Much has been said about the complexity of Paul's argument here. At its base, however, Paul appears to be invested in understanding something of how the nations/Gentiles join an old and venerable tradition and how it is, in the process, that that tradition morphs and changes to the extent that those who once thought they were a part of this "family (olive) tree" are, in Paul's eyes, potentially no longer so. In Paul's world, the imagery of grafting and abundance was critical to the Romans in their imperial imaginings, as was the rhetoric of the (re)dawning of the Golden Age, the peace of which is accomplished through the intermixing of diverse people groups who are joined together at the Roman root. Indeed, this theme is quite prevalent throughout the imagery and the literature of the Roman period. Obviously, the Romans are not broken off from their own rooted tradition—rather, others are grafted in. And here we do see a difference in comparison with Paul, much like Sanders saw the difference in Paul's conception of entrance into the convental-nomistic framework over against other Jewish perspectives. Yet, the differences are probably less important and interesting than the similarities. And those differences may also be less revealing for Pauline theology generally.

Conclusion: The Graft as a Comparative Question in Pauline Studies

The Romans, as a people and nation, have been read as the "politics" to the "religion" of Christianity, especially in Anglophone contexts. Because the Romans are not quite on the "religion" radar of Christian origins, we have not trained ourselves to examine this world in as much depth as we could. Furthermore, the Romans have been used as a way to underscore contemporary political theologies (e.g., American imperial theology, as articulated by some empire-critical scholars), which in my view exemplify important shifts in how we wish to relate to the early Christians and the Bible as a whole. However, these distinctions, while valuable in our world, do not quite capture the multivalence of the ancients.

The rhetoric of Romans 9–11 looks different in this context, and this is where, for me at least, engaging Pauline discourses can get interesting. That is, the imagery in Romans is not just biblical, but Roman as well. At the very least, we need to entertain the possibility that the hearers and readers of Paul's letter—quite a diverse bunch if Romans 16 is to be believed—would have been familiar with this world of Roman imperial images I have cursorily presented here. It need not be the case that they saw the Ara Pacis, even if it was in the city where

Paul's addressees lived. The point I have made is that the imagery presents a consistent and coherent and pervasive rhetoric through visual means for an audience that is visually literate in the service of encouraging them toward a particular set of relationships with their immediate surroundings, their situatedness in the Roman Empire, and their status as inhabitants of a Roman *kosmos* or "new creation." Whatever else Paul is doing or not doing in his letters, I would want to maintain that this world of images is a part of it, even if just part of the reservoir from which arguments are formed and informed. We need not focus on whether Paul is resisting the Roman theo-political mythology or simply drawing on its themes, given that they were particular potent modes of communication. Such moves very quickly begin to narrow down the avenues that can be explored through such comparison.

Thus, while some have supposed that Paul performs as a "good Roman," familiar with, and aspirational for, the *auctoritas* that marked educated male elites with exceptional rhetorical prowess,[38] perhaps the most we can say for sure is that Paul is a good negotiator of the Roman world. His rhetorical language, themes, and structure channeled multiple resonances of the broader Roman world for his audience. From a comparative standpoint on the history of religions and/or cultures, we learn that Paul's genealogical argumentation and presentation in Romans 9–11, regardless of how we make sense of it, does cohere rather readily with images and texts that we find in both the Roman and Jewish worlds in which Paul lived, moved, and had his being. Paul's argument in Romans 9–11 may ultimately be beyond our full understanding. It may have in fact been beyond Paul's own understanding! That is, he may not have been fully consistent or coherent in the argument he sought to make in this cluster of texts. Wherever scholars end up on that score, we can say that there is something rather cosmic for Paul in the merging of Gentiles and Jews in a new familial faith, which is also a very old faith, one that reaches back to Israel's "origins of things." Paul is seeking to negotiate the old and the new, and particularly the way in which the new might now be seen in light of the old, and the consequent implications thereof for rethinking the old itself within, and in relation to, the completely new situation of his addressees.

[38] The case for Paul having much *auctoritas* in the Roman sense has most recently been argued by J. Albert Harrill in *Paul the Apostle: His Life and Legacy in their Roman Context* (New York: Cambridge University Press, 2012).

Returning to Lincoln's observations about the relationship between history and myth, and the different ways and means that such narratives are composed and the ways that readers and interpreters put them to meaningful uses, it is productive for us to see two ancient mytho-historical traditions side by side. It would be easy to suggest that the Ara Pacis and Augustan Golden Age rhetorics represent "myth" in that they reach into the distant past, offering an account of the origins of the Augustan family tree that presents itself as natural, inevitable, universal, divinely ordained, and historically stable. In this respect, Paul's rhetoric appears to be no less mythological, at least in Romans 9–11. At the same time, it would be very tempting to call the Roman imperial metanarrative an "official history" of the state, in that it offers something powerful on behalf of the elite, establishing that elite as holding an orthodox position while subordinating and suppressing other positions. It would be even more tempting to say, then, that Paul's narrativizing in Romans represents the "revisionist" account of history, or history written "from the margins" of an "official" version, be that Roman, Jewish, or even inter-Christian. As Lincoln puts it, "official" history "tends to legitimate, stabilize, and naturalize things as they are, thereby helping the advantaged consolidate and preserve their benefit," while "revisionist" history "tends to destabilize, afflicting the comfortable and comforting the afflicted."[39] And yet "official" and "revisionist" histories are similar in that both types of narrative use the past in strategic ways to shape the present and future, and both can display significant mythologizing tendencies. In this respect, it is worth remembering that the Augustan version of events as represented on the Ara Pacis was, at some point, a "revisionist" narrative in that it redrew the story of Rome so as to minimize the previous "official" narratives that fronted kings and republicans—it became convincing as an "official" story only after some time had passed. And Mussolini's deployment of that narrative nearly two millennia after its first articulation was also both "revisionist" and "official." So too with Paul: perhaps Romans is a "revisionist" account that is also configured as an "official" story. Either way, both the Ara Pacis and the Letter to the Romans sit somewhere, somewhat uncomfortably, between myth and history, between the state and the not-state, between authority and resistance. In the case of Israel and the nations in Romans 9–11, Paul is offering a revisionist use of mytho-history, reconfiguring the

[39] Lincoln, *Between History and Myth*, 116.

epic story of his people to different ends. Maybe what separates Pauline rhetoric from the Roman imperial theology is that these mythohistorical narratives have a different status vis-à-vis their audiences. However, Paul's version of the graft and its implications for peace and fertility does not wholly preclude the Roman one, and vice versa. Both of these can converse and even coexist—in fact, in either system, one or the other could be absorbed.

The modern theological implications of Romans 9–11—and the historical consequences of some of these modern theological implications in particular!—are well known in terms of their respective assessment and treatment of Judaism and Jews. The theological interests that have driven the interpretation of Romans 9–11 have also in some ways redirected us away from looking at the broader pattern of ancient ways of imagining communities and the integration of outsiders. Cultures constantly have to deal with the "root" and the "branches" and the "fruits" in the process of developments and shifts and changes. It is interesting here to examine the ways in which such mergences and migrations are conceptualized and visualized. And in a historical moment like our own, which is focused on issues of immigration and inclusion, origins and legacies—as well as all the accompanying promises and problems—this topic sure hits us at "home." Indeed, perhaps there is no better analogy to both the Roman and the Pauline situation than what we find here, where for some American identity is seen to be compromised by the influx of immigrants and others who might just be granted pathways to inclusion and citizenship, a grafting on to the venerable root.

This is not a new problem, of course. The Rev. Dr. Martin Luther King Jr., in fact, addressed precisely this issue and did so in the very logic of Paul in Romans. Formulating his own narrative of origins, drawing heavily on the imagery of the book of Romans, he outlines in his Lincoln Memorial address—the famous "I Have a Dream" speech—the very grafting of new (black) Americans onto the old (white) American tradition. In King's rhetorical imagination, blacks and whites are given a promissory note from their "fathers" to which they have fallen heir. This promissory note, which King's addressees had come to Washington to "cash" in, is represented by the Constitution and Declaration of Independence, documents that compose a critical part of the mythohistorical origins of America as a nation. Whether the founding fathers, the ur-ancestors of this nation, had King's particular vision in mind is not the point. King is speaking genealogically, tying his addressees to a common past and deploying that past to imagine a different future. In his view, which was persuasive to a great many people, both black and white Americans come together in a "new creation" to inherit on equal footing and in equal measure the "land where my fathers died, land of the Pilgrim's pride." Herein we can see the potentially powerful force of mytho-historical reasoning, where we find echoes and resonances of the Pauline argumentative structures . . . as well as their very powerful potential outcomes. And in such cases, we can also see broken branches, broken promises, and miracles and dreams deferred, then and now.[40]

[40] I am grateful to Beverly Roberts Gaventa, Bruce Longenecker, and Todd Still, the organizers of the 2014 Drumwright New Testament Colloquium at Baylor University, for the extremely warm, abundant welcome to that place and conversation. Professor Still deserves special mention for his admirable shepherding and listening skills. Memorable discussion with colleagues and graduate students at the Colloquium yielded comments and questions that were quite instructive and for that I give thanks. Conversations with Todd Penner about the historical and rhetorical trajectories of Pauline studies have been invaluable for this chapter in the form presented here. I offer this piece in memory of two women who taught me much about the rhetoric of the ancient and modern worlds, in word, image, and deed: Beverly Wildung Harrison (1932–2012) and Natalie Boymel Kampen (1944–2012).

4
"Enemies" Yet "Beloved" Still
Election and the Love of God in Romans 9–11

J. Ross Wagner

> κατὰ μὲν τὸ εὐαγγέλιον ἐχθροὶ δι᾽ ὑμᾶς, κατὰ δὲ τὴν ἐκλογὴν ἀγαπητοὶ διὰ τοὺς πατέρας; ἀμεταμέλητα γὰρ τὰ χαρίσματα καὶ ἡ κλῆσις τοῦ θεοῦ.
>
> —Romans 11:28-29

In Romans 11:28-29 Paul sums up the tortuous argument of Romans 9–11 with three crisp lines. The artful couplet of v. 28 neatly captures the dynamic dialectic of gospel and election that drives his discourse: "With respect to the gospel, they are enemies for your sake; but with respect to election, they are beloved for the sake of the ancestors."[1] And a concise explanatory coda anchors Paul's hope for Israel—and for the nations—in the gracious and unchangeable character of the divine love: "For the gifts and calling of God are bestowed without regret" (Rom 11:29).[2]

The rhetorical prominence of these verses recommends them as a vantage point from which to survey the entirety of Romans 9–11. Paul's striking formulation in 11:28—brisk, balanced clauses enhanced by a twofold end rhyme (ἐχθροί/ἀγαπητοί; ὑμᾶς/πατέρας)—appears at the high point of the discourse, the apostle's disclosure of the "mystery" of the ingathering of the nations' "fullness" and the final

[1] Contributors explore this dialectic from numerous angles in Florian Wilk and J. Ross Wagner, eds., *Between Gospel and Election: Explorations in the Interpretation of Romans 9–11*, WUNT 257 (Tübingen: Mohr Siebeck, 2010).

[2] While no one writing in English can entirely escape the influence of the Authorized Version, translations of Scripture are my own unless otherwise noted.

salvation of "all Israel" (11:25-27).[3] Following hard on the heels of the divine speech in 11:26-27, vv. 28-29 provide an epigrammatic commentary on this "mystery," one that Paul further unpacks in vv. 30-32 and finally celebrates in a glorious hymn of praise (11:33-36). Moreover, Romans 11:28-29 forms an *inclusio* with Romans 9:1-13, reprising themes sounded prominently in the opening stages of the argument, including election (11:28; 9:11), calling (11:29; 9:7, 12), gifts of divine favor (11:29; 9:4-5), and God's gratuitous love for Israel's ancestors (11:28; 9:5, 7-13).[4] Examining Romans 9–11 through the lens of 11:28-29 reveals that Paul's hope for Israel and for the nations rests solely on the divine self-determination to be the God of steadfast love: a sovereign self-commitment articulated in God's promises to the ancestors, attested by Israel's Scriptures and embodied in Jesus Christ.

"With Respect to the Gospel, They Are Enemies for Your Sake" (Rom 11:28a)

We begin with the apostle's blunt declaration: "They are enemies." To discover who "they" are, it is necessary to go back to the beginning of Romans 11, where Paul reveals that since the coming of the Messiah, Israel has been divided internally. In the present time, there exists "a remnant chosen by grace" (λεῖμμα κατ᾽ ἐκλογὴν χάριτος, 11:5); "the rest" of Israel, however, have been "hardened" (οἱ λοιποί ἐπωρώθησαν, 11:7). While he regards the "remnant" as incontrovertible evidence of God's unremitting faithfulness to God's chosen people (11:1-2), it is "the rest," the hardened "part" of Israel (cf. 11:25), that Paul has particularly in view from Romans 11:8 onward.

"With Respect to the Gospel, They Are Enemies. . . ." In what sense, then, are the rest of Israel "enemies"? Paul qualifies his claim in two ways. First, they are enemies "with respect to the gospel." By this point the Roman house churches have already learned a great deal from the apostle about the good news he has been called to proclaim. From the

[3] On Paul's formulation, which Folker Siegert identifies as an instance of *parhomoeōsis*, see idem, *Argumentation bei Paulus, gezeigt an Röm 9–11*, WUNT 34 (Tübingen: J. C. B. Mohr, 1985), 173–74. On Rom 11:25-32 as the climax of Paul's argument, see Florian Wilk, "Rahmen und Aufbau von Römer 9–11," in Wilk and Wagner, *Between Gospel and Election*, 227–53; Filippo Belli, *Argumentation and the Use of Scripture in Romans 9–11*, AnBib 183 (Rome: Gregorian and Biblical Press, 2010), 361–64.

[4] See the thorough analysis of the structure of Rom 9–11 by Wilk ("Rahmen und Aufbau"); for verbal and thematic links between 11:25-36 and 9:1-5, see esp. 239–41.

first lines of the letter, Paul has reminded them that God promised the gospel long beforehand through his prophets in Israel's sacred writings (1:1-2). Now, through the faithful obedience of Jesus, the divine promises have at last come to fruition. In raising Jesus from the dead, God has publicly identified this scion of David as the powerful Son of God: the Messiah of Israel and the one Lord of all nations (1:3-4; cf. 10:9-13).

Paul depicts his apostleship as priestly service (1:9; 15:16, 19), for as the good news is proclaimed God himself is powerfully at work to bring salvation to all who trust.[5] In the gospel, God displays his own righteousness (δικαιοσύνη) as the one who delivers Jew and Greek alike from the power of sin and death through the faith of Jesus Christ (1:16-17; cf. 3:21-31).[6] Thus, although Paul understands his particular commission to center on bringing about "the obedience of faith among all the Gentiles" (1:5), the gospel addresses Jews as well as Gentiles. Indeed, the good news is "for the Jew first."[7]

It is the absence of the obedience of faith among so many of his fellow Jews that prompts Paul's anguished wrestling with the fate of Israel in Romans 9–11. Despite the immense privileges God has granted them as "Israelites" (9:4-5), a significant number of his kinspeople are presently cut off from their Messiah (9:1-3).[8] From Paul's perspective, they stand in desperate need of "salvation" (10:1; cf. 1:16-17). In attempting to account for this anomaly, Paul does not shy away from assigning blame to his fellow Israelites. "The rest" of Israel are not merely indifferent to the apostolic message; "with respect to the gospel, they are enemies" (11:28). Their zeal for God, Paul charges, is unenlightened, for they remain "ignorant of God's righteousness" (10:2-3). This ignorance, moreover, is willful: "They have not submitted to God's righteousness" (10:3b).[9] Instead, they seek "to establish their own righteousness"

[5] Rom 1:16. The phrase "all who trust" recurs in Rom 3:22, 4:11, 10:4, and 10:11.

[6] A massive literature has grown up around the meaning of "the righteousness of God" in Paul. Richard B. Hays ("Justification," in *The Anchor Bible Dictionary*, ed. David Noel Freeman [New York: Doubleday, 1992], 3:1129–33) provides an incisive introduction to the issues.

[7] The priority of Israel in God's plan runs like a refrain throughout Rom 1–11. See 1:16; 2:9, 10; 3:9, 29; 9:24; 10:12.

[8] To share their plight Paul would have to be "cursed [and so cut off] from Christ" (9:3). Compare the metaphor of branches "broken off" the olive tree in Rom 11:17, 19-21.

[9] For ἀγνοεῖν in the sense, "disregard," see BDAG (s.v. ἀγνοέω, 2). The closest parallel in Romans is Paul's description of "the mind of the flesh," which is "enmity

(10:3a) by pursuing the Law "as if it were a matter of [human] works" rather than a matter of "trust" (9:31-32).[10] But the end and goal (τέλος) of the Law, Paul avers, is none other than Jesus the Messiah, in whom alone is found "righteousness for all who trust" (10:4).[11]

Paul's account of "the righteousness of God" finds confirmation in the speech of the personified "Righteousness from Faith." Taking on her lips the admonition of Deuteronomy 30:12-14, she affirms the nearness of "the word of faith" that Paul preaches: "It is in your heart and in your mouth" (10:8). Radical trust in the God who raised Jesus from the dead, eliciting a public acknowledgment of Jesus as Lord, leads to "righteousness" and "salvation" because, as Paul has already explained, Jesus was "handed over for our trespasses and raised for our justification" (4:25).[12] Now exalted as Lord over all, he responds with lavish generosity to all—Jew and Gentile alike—who call on him in faith (10:11-13).

Nevertheless, "not all have obeyed the gospel" (10:16). Prominent among them are many of Paul's fellow Israelites. As the apostle considers whether all have indeed "heard" and "known" the good news, his focus quickly narrows to his own people. They are among those who have "heard" the gospel, he insists, for heralds have been sent out to the ends of the earth (10:14-15, 17-18). What is more, Israel has "known" that Gentiles would obtain the righteousness from faith as God's free gift (cf. 9:30), for Moses and Isaiah together testify to God's scandalous embrace of the nations (10:19-20). Yet despite hearing and knowing the good news, they stubbornly resist the gospel call to trust in God by confessing Jesus as Lord. In the face of God's tireless entreaties, they remain a "disobedient and rebellious people" (10:21).

References to Israel's culpability become still more pointed in Romans 11. That God has not forsaken his people can be seen in the preservation, even now, of a remnant of "Israelites" like Paul, chosen by grace (11:1-7). When it comes to the rest of Israel, however, Paul talks

---

with God" in that it does not—indeed "cannot"—"submit" to God's Law (8:7).

10 Cf. Rom 3:21-22 and compare Phil 3:7-11, where Paul contrasts his quest for "my own righteousness that comes from the Law" with "the righteousness that comes through the faith of Christ, the righteousness from God on the basis of faith" (3:9).

11 I defend this interpretation of Rom 9:30–10:4 at length in *Heralds of the Good News: Isaiah and Paul in Concert in the Letter to the Romans*, NovTSup 101 (Leiden: Brill, 2002), 120–70.

12 In his reworking of Deut 30:10-14, Paul replaces each reference to human doing with a reminder of what God has done in sending Christ and in raising him from the dead (Wagner, *Heralds of the Good News*, 162–65).

of their "trespass" (παράπτωμα, 11:11, 12)[13] and discourses frankly about their "unbelief" (ἀπιστία, 11:20, 23; cf. 3:3),[14] "ungodliness" (ἀσέβεια, 11:26), unforgiven "sins" (ἁμαρτίαι, 11:27), and "disobedience" (ἀπείθεια/ἀπειθεῖν, 11:30-32; cf. 10:21).[15] Despite the considerable variety in expression, Paul's complaint comes down to this: heralds have gone forth with the good news that "now, apart from the law, the righteousness of God has been revealed," namely, "the righteousness of God, through the faith of Jesus Christ, for everyone who trusts" (3:21). To respond to this proclamation, not by trusting in what God has done through the death and resurrection of the Messiah, not by acknowledging Jesus as Lord, but by continuing to seek "[one's] own righteousness" (10:3a), is to make oneself an enemy of the gospel.

". . . They Are Enemies for Your Sake." Though he names the rest of Israel "enemies with respect to the gospel," this is by no means all Paul has to say. Addressing the Gentile members of the Roman house churches, he adds a further qualifier: the enmity of his fellow Israelites toward the gospel is, in fact, "for your sake."[16] Without minimizing

[13] Paul's choice of words creates a certain ambiguity here, perhaps deliberately: παράπτωμα could be taken to mean "misstep" or, more negatively, "trespass." Talk of their "stumbling" (πταίειν) in Rom 11:11a suggests "misstep" would be an appropriate translation. Yet the apostle has also spoken forthrightly of Israel's disobedience and rebellion (10:21), and he will continue to do so with increasing frequency as the argument proceeds. Thus, one should probably hear a distinct overtone of culpability in παράπτωμα in Rom 11:11, 12. Compare Paul's earlier use of παράπτωμα in 5:15-21; the fact that the term occurs parallel to ἁμαρτία, παρακοή, and παράβασις removes any ambiguity as to the sense intended there.

[14] See further Rom 3:2-3, where Paul observes that although the Jews have been entrusted with "the oracles of God," some have proved "unfaithful" (ἀπιστεῖν/ἀπιστία); contrast Abraham's refusal to give way to ἀπιστία in the face of the divine promise (Rom 4:20).

[15] Paul quotes the complaint of Elijah against his fellow Israelites (11:2-3), implying that some of the apostle's kinspeople, too, display their enmity toward the divine plan through active opposition to him and to other heralds of the good news (cf. 1 Thess 2:15-16; 2 Cor 11:24, 26). In Rom 15:31 Paul explicitly asks the Roman churches to pray that during his upcoming visit to Jerusalem he may be delivered from "the disobedient (οἱ ἀπειθοῦντες) in Judea."

[16] The distinction between "you" and "they" goes back to Rom 11:13, where Paul directs his comments specifically to "you Gentiles." His subsequent references to "you," whether singular (11:17-24) or plural (11:28-32), similarly target the Gentile Christ-followers in his audience. While ἀδελφοί in 11:25 does not exclude Jewish listeners, the admonition against holding an inflated self-opinion (repeated from 11:18, 20) suggests that even here Paul remains focused on the Gentiles.

their culpability, Paul finds the divine hand at work in the recalcitrant response of "the rest" to God's saving deeds. Indeed, Paul keeps a tight focus on divine agency as he describes the present division within Israel. The same God who has graciously preserved a remnant (11:5-6) has also "hardened" the rest of Israel in their disobedience (11:7). Paul substantiates the latter claim with scriptural testimony carefully shaped to highlight the active role God has assumed: "God has poured out on them a spirit of stupor, eyes so as not to see and ears so as not to hear, to the present day" (11:8).[17] Far from being stymied by the resistance of the rest, God has commandeered their rebellion, intensifying it and channeling it to achieve God's own ends.

Paul's conviction that the disobedience of his fellow Israelites actually serves the divine purpose for the nations ("for your sake") emerges with increasing clarity from Romans 11:11 onward. By the trespass of the rest, "salvation" has come to the Gentiles (11:11b). Indeed, their trespass has brought "wealth to the world" (11:12a) and their loss "riches to the nations" (11:12b), for their estrangement has led to "the world's reconciliation" to God (11:15a).[18] These "natural" Israelite branches have been broken off so that, "contrary to nature," wild Gentile branches might be grafted into the rich rootstock of the cultivated olive (11:17-24). As he discloses the "mystery" of God's surprising plan for Israel and the nations, Paul drives the point home: God's partial hardening of Israel has in view the accomplishment of the divine purpose for the Gentiles. It is only through the ingathering of the nations' "fullness" (11:25) that the way will be finally opened for the realization of Israel's own "fullness" (11:12), the salvation of "all Israel" (11:26-27).

Paul asserts that the rest of Israel are now enemies of the gospel "for your sake" one last time in Romans 11:30-32. In the summary

[17] Contrast the more indirect locution in LXX Deut 29:4, "The Lord your God has not given you a heart to understand and eyes to see and ears to hear, to this day." For the details of Paul's conflation of Deut 29:4 with Isa 29:10 in Rom 11:8, see Wagner, *Heralds of the Good News*, 240–65.

[18] The word ἀποβολή might be understood as "loss," in parallel with ἥττημα in v. 12b; however, the contrast with πρόσλημψις, "acceptance, welcome" (cf. προσλαμβάνειν; 14:1, 3; 15:7), in v. 15b favors the sense "casting off." Although NRSV renders ἀποβολή as "rejection," I have preferred "estrangement" in order to avoid confusing English readers, who will have just heard Paul expressly deny that God has "rejected" (ἀπωθεῖν) his people (11:1-2). On God's reconciling the world to himself in Christ, see 2 Cor 5:18-21.

statement that leads directly to his concluding doxology Paul explains, "You [Gentiles] were once disobedient to God, but now you have been shown mercy by means of their disobedience" (11:30). So crucial is this point for understanding the divine purpose in Israel's hardening that Paul immediately repeats it: "They have disobeyed for the sake of the mercy shown to you" (11:31a).[19] In God's unfathomable wisdom, these Israelites serve—in their very resistance to God—as instruments of divine mercy to the Gentiles. For just this reason, however, there remains a future for the rest of Israel as well. "They have disobeyed for the sake of the mercy shown to you in order that they, too, may now be shown mercy. For God has imprisoned all people in disobedience that he may show mercy to all" (11:31-32).

"With Respect to Election, They Are Beloved for the Sake of the Ancestors" (Rom 11:28b)

Paul's confidence that the rest of Israel will not finally be excluded from God's mercy is grounded in the conviction he expresses in the second half of the couplet: "With respect to election, they are beloved for the sake of the ancestors" (11:28b). "They," of course, are the "enemies" of 11:28a: "the rest" of Israel, whom God has presently hardened for the sake of the Gentiles (11:7, 25); those from "Jacob," whose ungodliness and sins the redeemer has yet to remove (11:26-27). It is precisely these "enemies" that the apostle names "beloved." As in the first half of the couplet, so here also Paul supplements his statement with two crucial qualifications: they are beloved "with respect to election" and "for the sake of the ancestors." It will soon become clear that these are not two reasons, but one. The rest of Israel remains beloved by God solely because of God's free and gracious self-determination to bind himself forever in love to Israel's ancestors: "Jacob have I loved" (9:13).[20]

[19] The phrase τῷ ὑμετέρῳ ἐλέει should be understood as a dative of interest modifying ἠπείθησαν (Siegert, *Argumentation*, 274); NRSV and many English translations wrongly take it as part of the following purpose clause ("in order that, by the mercy shown to you, they too may now receive mercy"). For Paul, there remains a fundamental asymmetry between the role of Israel and that of the nations in God's plan. See J. Ross Wagner, "'Not from the Jews Only, but Also from the Gentiles': Mercy to the Nations in Romans 9–11," in Wilk and Wagner, *Between Gospel and Election*, 417–31, esp. 425–28.

[20] Alongside Abraham, Isaac, and Jacob, Paul mentions Sarah (9:9; cf. 4:19) and Rebekah (9:10-12) by name as recipients of God's promises. For this reason I have chosen to render πατέρες by "ancestors" as well as "patriarchs."

Election and the Love of God in Romans 1–8. To grasp the logic of Romans 11:28b, we must go back beyond Romans 9:13 ("Jacob have I loved") and even beyond Romans 9:5 ("theirs are the ancestors") to the very beginning of the letter. The close connection in Paul's thought between election and divine love becomes apparent from the opening salutation. As those "beloved by God" (ἀγαπητοὶ τοῦ θεοῦ), Paul's addressees—Gentiles as well as Jews—are "called" to be God's holy people (κλητοὶ ἅγιοι), children of a gracious Father and servants of the Lord Jesus Christ (1:7).[21]

Paul finds the election of Jew and Gentile in Christ revealed in God's promise to Abraham, "our forefather" (4:1). The divine promise is not elicited by anything Abraham has done. It represents neither "wages" for work performed (4:4-5; cf. 4:2, 6) nor repayment of a debt owed by God (4:4; cf. 11:35). Rather, God makes the first move. For Paul, the promise is sheer gift (κατὰ χάριν, 4:4, 16), a blessing (μακαρισμός, 4:6-9) prompted by nothing beyond God's own character. Most astounding of all, God bestows this blessing on those who are absolutely undeserving.[22] In his interactions with the ancestors, God reveals himself to be the God "who justifies the ungodly" (ὁ δικαιῶν τὸν ἀσεβῆ, 4:5): those, like David, who justly stand convicted of sins and lawless deeds (4:6; cf. 3:19); those, like uncircumcised Abraham, who can claim no righteousness of their own (4:10-16) but must depend utterly on the righteousness that comes from the faith engendered by God's free and gracious word of promise (4:11).[23]

[21] Cf. 1 Thess 1:4 (NRSV): "For we know, brothers and sisters beloved (ἠγαπημένοι) by God, that he has chosen you (τὴν ἐκλογὴν ὑμῶν). . . ." That Paul's letter is directed to Gentile Christ-followers is apparent not only from Rom 1:5-6, 13 but also from the explicit address to Gentile believers in 11:13. Yet Paul has a wider audience in view as well, addressing his letter to "all those in Rome who are beloved by God" (1:7) and greeting a number of his kinspeople in the Roman house churches by name (Rom 16:1-16).

[22] On the "incongruity" of grace in Paul's thought, see especially John Barclay, *Paul and the Gift* (Grand Rapids: Eerdmans, 2015).

[23] While the narrative of Genesis 17 stresses Abraham's immediate and complete obedience to the command to practice circumcision (vv. 23-27), Paul emphasizes that Abraham was justified by no "works" of his own. Rather, "Abraham trusted God, and it was reckoned to him as righteousness" (Rom 4:3, quoting Gen 15:6). Only subsequently did Abraham receive circumcision; and this, Paul asserts, was but a "sign" (cf. Gen 17:11) and a "seal" of the righteousness of faith that God had already credited to the as-yet-uncircumcised patriarch (4:11).

The notion of "promise" proves crucial to the apostle's account of election in Romans, for it allows Paul to maintain God's sovereign freedom in election while simultaneously affirming God's unwavering fidelity to the particular people of Israel "for the sake of the ancestors."[24] Nicholas Wolterstorff observes that promise has the character of a "speech-action," a communicative act that generates a new social reality.[25] In taking the initiative to establish a relationship with Abraham through promise, God assumes the rights and responsibilities of a speaker, including the right to be trusted as truthful and the responsibility to act truthfully by fulfilling one's promises. Henceforth, God's own righteousness (δικαιοσύνη, Rom 3:5) is inextricably bound up with God's fidelity (πίστις, 3:3) and truthfulness (ἀλήθεια, 3:7; 15:8; ἀληθής, 3:4) to the promise spoken in freedom and grace to the ancestors.

Abraham, in turn, exemplifies the only proper human response to the divine promise, which is to take God at his word. As Paul retells the ancestral story, Abraham recognizes that he has no capacity in himself to bring the promise to fruition. He sees clearly that his hundred-year-old body is "as good as dead," as is the womb of his elderly wife (4:19). Nevertheless, he entrusts himself to the God "who gives life to the dead and calls into being that which does not exist" (4:17). Empowered by God with a trust that hopes beyond hope (4:18),[26] Abraham refuses to doubt the divine promise.[27] Instead, he "gives glory to God" by remaining fully convinced that God "is able (δυνατός ἐστιν) to do what he promised" (4:20-21). Such trust, the Scripture says, "was reckoned to him as righteousness" (Rom 4:22, quoting Gen 15:6). These words were written not for Abraham's sake alone, Paul concludes, but for "our sake" as well (4:23), for in the death of Jesus Christ "for our transgressions" and in his resurrection "for our justification," God has fulfilled his oath (4:25). Through Jesus' faithful obedience,

[24] In fact, Paul uses the term "promise" in Romans only when he is talking about God's relationship to the ancestors and their descendants: 4:13, 14, 16, 20, 21; 9:4, 8, 9; 15:8. Cf. 1:2, where the gospel was "promised beforehand (προεπαγγέλλεσθαι) through [God's] prophets in sacred writings."

[25] Nicholas Wolterstorff, *Divine Discourse: Philosophical Reflections on the Claim That God Speaks* (Cambridge: Cambridge University Press, 1995), 75–113.

[26] The verb ἐνεδυναμώθη in Rom 4:20 should be taken as passive: "he was strengthened in trust (by God)" (contra NRSV, "he grew strong in his faith"); cf. Phil 4:13.

[27] Abraham's refusal to give way to unbelief (ἀπιστία, 4:20) thus contrasts sharply with the ἀπιστία of the "broken branches" (11:20, 23).

God's promise to the "father of many nations" has now been confirmed to "all the seed" (4:16)—to all, circumcised and uncircumcised alike, who share Abraham's trust in the God "who raised Jesus our Lord from the dead" (4:24).[28]

Just as God's fidelity finds its conclusive confirmation in Jesus' death and resurrection "for us," so also God's love attains its consummate expression in Jesus' self-giving to the point of death "for our sake." The early Christian confession, "Christ died for us," recurs repeatedly in Paul's letters.[29] In Romans 5, however, the apostle lingers to reflect on the character of those for whom Christ gave himself up: the "weak" (ἀσθενεῖς, 5:6) and "ungodly" (ἀσεβεῖς, 5:6; cf. 4:5), "sinners" (ἁμαρτωλοί, 5:8), and "enemies" of God (ἐχθροί, 5:10). Paul could not more clearly underscore that the divine love is not aroused by any inherent loveliness in its object. Rather, God's love springs solely from the unceasing and inexhaustible overflow of God's own gracious and compassionate nature.[30] God's love in Christ Jesus, who died and who rose again, justifies sinners (5:1, 9) and reconciles enemies (5:1, 10-11), providing the powerless with a sure hope of salvation and future glory (5:2, 9-11).

So potent is the divine love, so far-reaching in its effects, that it transforms God's enemies into lovers of God. "The love of God has been poured out into our hearts through the Holy Spirit given to us" (5:5), evoking the cry of filial trust and love: "Abba, Father" (8:15). This Spirit-inspired response to God's prior, unmerited love is thus itself a sign of divine election. "Those who love God," Paul explains, are "those who are called according to God's purpose" (οἱ κατὰ πρόθεσιν κλητοί, 8:28).[31] And God's purpose in election is nothing less than to transform enemies into children and heirs by conforming them to the image of his beloved Son (8:29). As Romans 12–15

[28] Compare the argument of Rom 9:6-29: in Jesus Christ, God is calling Abraham's "seed" (9:7-8)—"children of promise" (9:8-10)—"not only from among the Jews but also from among the Gentiles" (9:24).

[29] E.g., 1 Cor 8:11; 15:3; 2 Cor 5:14-15; Gal 2:20; 3:13; Eph 5:2; 1 Thess 5:9-10; Titus 2:4. In Romans, see 4:25; 8:32, 34; 14:15.

[30] Accordingly, in Rom 5:15-21 Paul repeatedly emphasizes the gift-character of God's action in Jesus Christ: χάρισμα (5:15, 16), χάρις (5:15, 17, 20, 21), δωρεά (5:15, 17), δώρημα (5:16).

[31] Note the cluster of expressions for election here: κατὰ πρόθεσιν (8:28), κλητός (8:28), προγινώσκειν (8:29), προορίζειν (8:29), καλεῖν (8:30), ἐκλεκτοὶ θεοῦ (8:33).

will make clear, this process is already at work in the community of faith. Through the life-giving Spirit, God is even now transforming the minds of Jesus' Jewish and Gentile followers (12:2) so that together they may come to share the mind of Christ (15:5). The same Spirit that infuses the human heart with the love of God enkindles among God's beloved ones the love of neighbor that epitomizes and fulfills the divine Law (13:8-10).[32] In this way, those who walk by the Spirit come to embody in their individual and communal lives the sacrificial self-giving of Jesus (15:1-6) as they pour themselves out in love for brothers and sisters (12:9-13),[33] for strangers (12:13), and even for enemies (12:14, 19-21).

Romans 1–8 concludes with a triumphant celebration of divine love for those who were once enemies. God's immeasurable, inexhaustible love has been conclusively demonstrated in the fact that God did not spare even his own Son but willingly handed him over "for us all" (8:32). God's almighty, death-defeating love has been definitively displayed in God's raising Jesus from the grave and exalting him as Lord of the living and the dead (8:34; cf. 14:9). And because the divine love depends finally on nothing other than God's fidelity to his own character—God's unconstrained self-determination to be God *for us* (8:31)—"neither death, nor life, nor angels, nor rulers, nor things present, nor things to come, nor powers, nor height, nor depth, nor anything else in all creation, will be able to separate us from the love of God in Christ Jesus our Lord" (Rom 8:38-39 NRSV).

Election and the Love of God in Romans 9. This joyous celebration of the invincible love of God "for us" leads Paul at last to face squarely the problem that has dogged his heels since Romans 3:1-8.[34] What, then, of God's love for Israel, the people God has adopted as his own and upon whom he has showered such incomparable gifts?

> They are Israelites, to whom belong the adoption and the glory and the covenants and the giving of the law and the divine service and

[32] For the Spirit as the source of love within the community, see further Paul's appeal in Rom 15:30 to ἡ ἀγάπη τοῦ πνεύματος as he asks the Roman churches to struggle alongside him in prayer.

[33] This includes the "weak" in their midst (14:1–15:6), whom the "strong" are to serve in love (κατὰ ἀγάπην, 14:15) in imitation of the example of Christ (κατὰ Χριστὸν Ἰησοῦν, 15:5).

[34] "[The Jews] were entrusted with the oracles of God. What then? If some proved unfaithful, their unfaithfulness will not nullify the faithfulness of God, will it?" (3:2-3). Paul's response in 3:4-8 largely sidesteps the specific question of Israel's fate.

> the promises; theirs are the ancestors, and from their midst comes the Messiah according to the flesh. (9:4-5)

In light of what we have already seen in Romans 1–8, it should not surprise us to find that in Romans 9, too, Paul draws heavily on the language of love and grace, election and promise, as he struggles to comprehend the divine purpose for his fellow Israelites.[35]

Denying that God's word has "fallen" (9:6), the apostle begins by retelling the story of Israel's origins. In doing so, he takes up a central theme of the ancestral narratives: "It is not the case that all from Israel are Israel, nor that all [Abraham's] children are Abraham's seed" (9:6-7). From the first, God's free and gracious election of Abraham and his descendants has entailed a selection from among the patriarch's bodily offspring, and the divine preference for the younger son has repeatedly upset human notions of merit and desert.[36]

Paul insists on God's freedom in election throughout Romans 9:6-29. Yet this is not a shapeless freedom, an arbitrary will to power, but a freedom determined by the character of the God who makes himself known in the very particular history of God's dealings with humanity. There, the divine freedom is revealed to be the freedom to make promises (9:6-9).[37] "It is the children of promise who are reckoned as 'seed'" (9:8). As the story of Abraham demonstrates, divine freedom is God's unimpaired capacity and unswerving commitment to remain true to himself and so to keep faith by performing what he has freely promised to do (Rom 4:21). Likewise, God's freedom is the freedom to call whomever he chooses (9:10-13). Paul contends that election has nothing whatsoever to do with human deeds, whether good or bad. It rests solely on God's reality-creating calling (9:12; cf. 4:17),[38] which is constrained only by God's sovereign self-determination (ἡ κατ' ἐκλογὴν πρόθεσις τοῦ θεοῦ, 9:11) to be the God of mercy and truth.

[35] As Leander Keck rightly observes, "One cannot insist too strongly that while Rom 9–11 is elicited by the need to account for the Jews' No to the gospel, the real problem is the faithfulness of God, for only a faithful God is righteous" (*Romans*, ANTC [Nashville: Abingdon, 2005], 224).

[36] See the now classic study of Jon Levenson, *The Death and Resurrection of the Beloved Son* (New Haven, Conn.: Yale University Press, 1993).

[37] In Rom 9:7 and 9:9, Paul carefully selects quotations that allow the divine voice to speak the word of promise in the first person.

[38] See Beverly Roberts Gaventa, "On the Calling-Into-Being of Israel: Romans 9:6-29," in Wilk and Wagner, *Between Gospel and Election*, 255–69.

Thus, the divine freedom is, at its heart, the freedom to love—gratuitously, extravagantly, constantly. In the end, Paul can offer no explanation for election beyond God's love itself. God simply confesses, "Jacob have I loved" (9:13, quoting Mal 1:2). With this citation, Paul situates his account of divine freedom in election within a broad and deep scriptural tradition that testifies to "Israel's fixed resolve to take God, in his self-determination in terms of the Grace-formula [Exod 34:6-7], at his word": that is, as the God of steadfast love.[39] This tradition comes to find the divine freedom manifested, above all, as God's freedom to show mercy to his unfaithful people. Not by chance does Paul cite God's response to the intercession of Moses after Israel's shameless betrayal of the divine love: "I will show mercy to whom I show mercy, and I will take pity on whom I take pity" (Rom 9:15, quoting Exod 33:19). Only God's faithfulness to his own character can explain God's stubborn mercy to faithless Jacob. Just as the election of Israel depends not on human deeds but "on the one who calls" (9:12), so the preservation of God's elect people hinges not on human will or effort but "on the God who shows mercy" (9:16) to those God has freely chosen in love.

What is more, because the divine freedom is governed by nothing external to God's own self, God remains free to show compassion not only to "beloved" Jacob but even to "hated" Esau. Now, in Christ, God has bestowed "his glorious riches on vessels of mercy that he prepared beforehand for glory" (9:23): namely, on "us whom God has called not just from among the Jews but also from among the Gentiles" (9:24). "Not-loved" Gentiles, those once "not-my-people," suddenly find themselves the "beloved" objects of God's gracious calling. They, too, are mercifully embraced by God's self-giving love in Jesus Christ. Through the divine Spirit they, too, are adopted as "children of the living God" (9:25-26; cf. 8:14-17).

39 Hermann Spieckermann, "Die Liebeserklärung Gottes. Entwurf einer Theologie des Alten Testaments," in idem, *Gottes Liebe zu Israel*, FAT 33 (Tübingen: Mohr Siebeck, 2004), 218 (my translation). Appeal to God's love for the ancestors as the grounds for Israel's election has strong roots in the Deuteronomic tradition; see especially Deut 4:37-38; 7:7-8; 10:14-15. See further Hos 1:1; Mic 7:18-20; Isa 41:8; 44:2 (where "Jeshurun" is interpreted by the Greek translator as ὁ ἠγαπημένος Ἰσραήλ; cf. Deut 32:15); Isa 51:2 (where LXX adds that God "loved" [ἀγαπᾶν] Abraham); Jer 31:1-4, 31-37. The idea lives on in the literature of early Judaism, notably in traditions of communal confession and penitential prayer. See, e.g., Pr Azar 3:34-37; Bar 2:27-35; Pss Sol 9:8-11; 4Q393 frg. 3 6-7; 4Q504 frgs. 1+2 recto ii:7-11.

At the same time, despite the undeniable tragedy of his fellow Israelites' present enmity toward the gospel, Paul finds that God's "calling" of "seed" for Abraham from among the children of Israel (9:6-7) continues uninterrupted in the "remnant" (9:27-28), the "vessels of mercy whom [God] has called . . . from among the Jews" (9:23-24). As "seed" (9:29), they are "children of promise" (9:8) whose survival can be explained only by reference to God's unwavering faithfulness to his pledge: "God's word has not fallen to the ground" (9:6).

These selective soundings in Romans 1–9 should make it clear that "for the sake of the ancestors" (διὰ τοὺς πατέρας) in Romans 11:28b must be understood to mean "for the sake of *God's gracious promises to* the ancestors." Not only does Paul conspicuously fail to mention the virtues of Israel's forebears, he unequivocally denies that the calling of Abraham, Isaac, and Jacob had anything at all to do with human "works" or merit (4:2, 5-6; 9:12).[40] Israel's election depends solely on the love of God, who has freely chosen to bind himself to this people through the promises made to their ancestors. It is just this conviction that grounds the apostle's hope for his kinspeople who presently stand alienated from their Messiah. For God is not one to regret his gracious calling of Israel or to revoke the gifts he has freely given them (Rom 11:29).

"The Gifts and Calling of God Are Bestowed without Regret" (Rom 11:29)

With the language of "gifts" and "calling" Paul circles back to where he began in Romans 9. The rest of Israel, though estranged, are "Israelites" nonetheless. To them God has granted "the adoption and the glory and the covenants and the giving of the Law and the divine service and the promises" (9:4). At present they are enemies, yet they remain beloved by God. For God remains true to himself. God neither

[40] To the extent that Paul's thought can fruitfully be compared and contrasted with later rabbinic traditions, it is noteworthy that, of the multiple ways *bizekut ʾabot*, "for the sake of the ancestors," functions in Tannaitic reflections on divine election (on which see the carefully nuanced treatment of E. P. Sanders, *Paul and Palestinian Judaism* [Philadelphia: Fortress, 1977], cf. 84–107, 183–98), only the view that God acts because of his promise and that "no meritorious [human] deed is involved" (Sanders, *Paul and Palestinian Judaism*, 195) finds expression in Paul's letters. Paul's account of the patriarchs represents a notable exception to the widespread tendency in Second Temple literature to amplify the ancestors' virtues. See further Francis Watson, *Paul and the Hermeneutics of Faith* (London: T&T Clark, 2004), 167–269.

reneges on the promises made in love to the ancestors nor rescinds the gifts graciously bestowed on their descendants. Rather, in his unfathomable wisdom God has resolved to harden "part" of Israel in their disobedience, for a time, in order that he might now extend mercy to disobedient Gentiles (11:30-31a; cf. 11:25). Moreover, having hardened them for this purpose, the God who shows mercy to whom he chooses (9:14-18) will now show mercy to his disobedient people as well (11:31b; cf. 11:26-27). "For God has imprisoned all people in disobedience that he may show mercy to all" (11:32).

Paul has worked steadily toward this conclusion since first speaking of the division of Israel into "the remnant" and "the rest" (11:5-10). The apostle insists that while the rest of Israel have stumbled, they have not tripped so as utterly to "fall" (11:11a); rather, the coming of salvation to the Gentiles will be God's means of provoking his own people to jealousy so that they, in turn, may find salvation (11:11b). Their present loss is to be followed by a "fullness" (τὸ πλήρωμα αὐτῶν, 11:12) corresponding to the "fullness" of the Gentiles toward which Paul labors (τὸ πλήρωμα τῶν ἐθνῶν, 11:25). Their estrangement will give way to renewed "acceptance" by God (11:15). Paul concludes his metaphor of the olive tree by observing that the broken branches of Israel will be grafted back in "if they do not remain in unbelief" (ἐὰν μὴ ἐπιμένωσιν τῇ ἀπιστίᾳ) for, without question, "God is able" (δυνατός ἐστιν ὁ θεός) to regraft them (11:23-24). Paul's reference here to the reversal of human "unbelief" and his insistence on God's "ability" to restore what is lost recall his programmatic characterization of the gospel as "the ability of God" (δύναμις θεοῦ) to save everyone who "believes" (παντὶ τῷ πιστεύοντι, 1:16). At the same time, his affirmation echoes the firm conviction of Abraham that what God has promised, "he is indeed able to do" (δυνατός ἐστιν καὶ ποιῆσαι, Rom 4:21).

As Paul shares with his brothers and sisters in Rome the "mystery" that has been revealed to him, it becomes absolutely clear that God's ability—and reliability—to make good on his promises is the sole foundation of the apostle's hope for the rest of Israel.[41] When the appointed

[41] As Markus Bockmuehl observes, Paul is careful to connect this "mystery" closely with Israel's Scriptures, read in light of God's apocalypse in Christ Jesus (*Revelation and Mystery in Ancient Judaism and Pauline Christianity*, WUNT 236 [Tübingen: J.C.B. Mohr, 1990], 174). Nevertheless, "[o]nly this revealed piece of divine wisdom could provide the answer to a question of theodicy which otherwise eluded human reason" (173).

time comes, when the fullness of the Gentiles has been gathered in through the preaching of the good news, then at last God will act to bring in the fullness of his chosen people Israel. Through the coming of "the redeemer," who will "turn away ungodliness from Jacob," God promises to do for the hardened rest what they have proven unable to do for themselves.[42] The one who "loved Jacob" before the patriarch had done anything, good or bad, will once again seize the initiative in a work of sheer grace: "I will take away their sins."[43] In just this way (καὶ οὕτως) will "all Israel" be saved (11:25-27).

The reference to "all Israel" (πᾶς Ἰσραήλ) in Romans 11:26 presents interpreters with something of a puzzle. Yet Paul provides important clues as to his meaning. In Romans 11:7, he acknowledges that "Israel" is currently divided against itself. That he subsequently refrains from calling either the remnant or the rest "Israel" strongly suggests that neither group by itself constitutes Israel in his eyes. When Paul next speaks the name, it is once again to stress Israel's present lack of wholeness: "A hardening has come upon Israel in part" (πώρωσις ἀπὸ μέρους τῷ Ἰσραὴλ γέγονεν, 11:25). In the context of Paul's argument, this calloused portion of Israel must be "the rest," whom God has hardened (11:7) until the appointed time when "[he] will take away their sins" (11:27). Only when the yet-to-be redeemed "rest" join

[42] The apostle's expectation that God himself will act to transform faithless Israel into a faithful people corresponds to the hope voiced repeatedly by the prophets (e.g., Hos 2:14-23; 14:4-7; Isa 63:7–64:12; Jer 31:31-34; Ezek 36:26). Deuteronomy 30:6 provides the classic statement: "Moreover, the LORD your God will circumcise your heart and the heart of your descendants, so that you will love the LORD your God with all your heart and with all your soul, in order that you may live" (NRSV). Hermann Spieckermann comments, "God will do for Israel of the present and the future that which Israel itself has not been capable of doing at any stage of its history. In [Deut] 30:6, circumcision of the heart has lost the gloomy undertone of 10:16. It is now no longer in the first place Israel's renunciation of its own stiff-necked stubbornness but rather God's work, by which he awakens Israel's love of God—because God wills life for Israel" ("Mit der Liebe im Wort: Zur Theologie des Deuteronomiums," in idem, *Gottes Liebe zu Israel*, FAT 33 [Tübingen: Mohr Siebeck, 2004], 157–72, 170; my translation).

[43] Paul's choice to retain the name "Jacob" in the quotation evokes his earlier reference to God's love for the patriarch ("Jacob have I loved," 9:13, also a scriptural citation). These are, in fact, the only occurrences of the name in the entire Pauline corpus.

the present "remnant," then, will πᾶς Ἰσραήλ—Israel as a whole—have come to know the salvation of their God.[44]

When does Paul envision this taking place? On the one hand, it is clear that God is already working out the salvation of Israel through the apostolic mission. Paul and his fellow Christ-followers from among the Jews constitute a "remnant chosen by grace" whose existence even now confirms God's unremitting faithfulness to the people he has called his own. On the other hand, the apostle remains deeply distraught over the rest of Israel, the part that God has hardened "until the fullness of the Gentiles" has been gathered in. Working tirelessly for the salvation of the nations, Paul seeks to provoke his fellow Israelites to jealousy and so to save "some of them" also along the way (11:13-14). At the same time, it seems clear that he cherishes a far more expansive hope for his people. Paul expects their estrangement to give way to an acceptance by God that will signify nothing less than "life from the dead" (11:15). To understand the apostle's language here simply as a vivid metaphor for individual conversion hardly does justice to the place resurrection holds in his soteriology.[45] In speaking

[44] "How many Israelites constitute πᾶς Ἰσραήλ?" has seemed a pressing question to many interpreters, but it does not appear to have been Paul's concern. In view of Rom 9:6, the apostle cannot be thinking of "all Israel" as comprising every single biological descendant of Jacob ("all from Israel"). As Karl Barth observes, "The Bible nowhere reckons with unqualified totalities of this kind" (*Church Dogmatics*, vol. II: *The Doctrine of God, Part 2*, ed. G. W. Bromiley and T. F. Torrance [Edinburgh: T&T Clark, 1957), 300). The concept of *kol Yisrael* in m. Sanh. 10 is frequently adduced as a parallel to Paul's πᾶς Ἰσραήλ. Here, the affirmation that "all Israel" has a share in the world to come is immediately followed by a catalogue of those from Israel "who have no portion in the world to come." Certainly Paul's avowal of "intense grief and unceasing sorrow of heart" is no mere rhetorical affectation (9:1-3; cf. 10:1). As he considers his kinspeople according to the flesh, Paul finds more than enough to evoke tears of lamentation: ignorance and rebellion against God, stumbling and hardness, transgression and loss. All the same, Otfried Hofius is correct to emphasize the clear note of "hope and expectation" in Paul's πᾶς ("Das Evangelium und Israel: Erwägungen zu Römer 9–11," in idem, *Paulusstudien*, WUNT 51 [Tübingen: J.C.B. Mohr, 1989], 175–202, 195–96; my translation). "To speculate whether this person or that could be excluded from this πᾶς is prohibited by the express intention [*Aussageintention*] of the text" (196). It remains unclear to me whether Paul envisions "all Israel" in Rom 11:26 as comprising, in addition to "the remnant" and "the rest," the "fullness of the Gentiles" as well (cf. the vigorous debate over the referent of "the Israel of God" in Gal 6:16).

[45] Contra N. T. Wright, *The Climax of the Covenant: Christ and the Law in Pauline Theology* (Edinburgh: T&T Clark, 1991), 248; Wright, *Paul and the Faithfulness of God*, 2 vols. (Minneapolis: Fortress, 2013), 2:1199–1201.

of life from the dead, Paul envisions the final realization of the hope for which the entire cosmos presently groans: the release of all creation from bondage into the glorious freedom of the children of God (Rom 8:18-30). The most satisfactory reading of Romans 11:25-27, then, finds Paul looking for a dramatic and widespread turning of his presently hardened kinspeople to their Messiah at the parousia,[46] as their "unbelief" (11:20) and refusal "to submit to God's righteousness" (10:3) give way at Christ's appearing to a wholehearted embrace of "the righteousness of God, through the faith of Jesus Christ, for everyone who trusts" (3:21).[47]

The "mystery" of Israel's salvation revealed to the apostle is consonant with the living scriptural traditions of Israel, whose many voices testify in concert to God's steadfast love and unshakable faithfulness toward his unfaithful people.[48] Even more fundamentally for Paul, it is congruent with the revelation of Jesus Christ. For Paul finds the definitive demonstration of God's invincible love for Israel—indeed for all nations—in the gracious self-donation of Jesus, whom God has raised to life and exalted as Lord of all.[49] At present, the rest of Israel remain

[46] Paul's statement that "the redeemer (ὁ ῥυόμενος) will come from Zion" (Rom 11:26) finds its closest parallel in 1 Thess 1:10. The Thessalonian believers now "wait for [God's] Son from heaven, whom he raised from the dead—Jesus, the one who redeems us (ὁ ῥυόμενος ἡμᾶς) from the wrath that is coming." The tight connection in Paul's thought between the parousia of Christ and the resurrection of the dead is widely attested in his letters (e.g., 1 Thess 4:13-18; 1 Cor 15:23; Phil 3:20-21).

[47] So Hofius: "Israel will . . . hear the gospel from the mouth of the returning Christ himself—the saving word of his self-disclosure, which effects the faith that lays hold of God's salvation" ("Evangelium," 197; my translation). For Paul, trust in what God has done through the death and resurrection of Jesus is at once a work of divine grace and a genuinely human act, the willing response of a human agent who has been freed to trust by God's life-giving, reality-creating calling. Might the apostle have in mind here his own experience as an Israelite ignorantly zealous for God (Gal 1:12-14; cf. Rom 10:3) whose life was radically transformed by the revelation of Jesus Christ to him, an event that Paul ascribes to God's sovereign pleasure to call his apostle "from the womb" (Gal 1:15-16; cf. Rom 9:10-12)? Johannes Munck (*Christ and Israel* [Philadelphia: Fortress, 1967], 131) credits this suggestion to Adolf Jülicher's Romans commentary of 1917, while Hofius ("Evangelium," 198 n. 89) traces it to a 1903 essay of the theologian and Methodist preacher Ernst F. Ströter.

[48] See n. 39 above.

[49] Cf. Barth (*CD* II/2, 302): "[Romans 11:29] is a confession of the Christian hope which clearly has in mind, as its object, the unshakeableness of the divine mercy in the resurrection of Jesus from the dead; which has encountered God in this deed of His as the eternally faithful God, and takes account of Him as such."

ungodly (11:26); but God has revealed himself in Jesus Christ as "the one who justifies the ungodly" (4:5). The rest of Israel now live as enemies of the gospel (11:28a); but God has reconciled us to himself, "while we were enemies, through the death of his Son" (5:10). The rest of Israel still labor under the burden of "transgressions" (11:11-12) and "sins" (11:27); but God has handed Jesus over for our "transgressions" and raised him for our justification (4:24-25). Once for all, God has demonstrated his own boundless love toward "us," Jew and Gentile alike, in that "while we were sinners, Christ died for us" (5:8). In Jesus Christ, every one of God's promises—not least those made in love to Israel's ancestors—receives a resounding Yes and Amen.[50]

[50] As the apostle himself concludes in Rom 15:8-9, "Christ has become a servant of the circumcised on behalf of the truth of God in order to confirm the promises made to the ancestors. . . ."

5
Locating Christ and Israel in Romans 9–11

Simon Gathercole

It has at various times been thought that chapters 9–11 of Romans—and especially chapters 10–11—are "unchristological," and some have found this cause for celebration. A few scholars have talked of a "special way" or *Sonderweg*, a term usually associated with Franz Mussner,[1] and picked up by Lloyd Gaston: "If Christ is meant [as Israel's deliverer in Romans 11], then it is Christ in a different role, Christ as the agent of the 'Sonderweg' of Israel's salvation."[2] For Gaston, Israel's salvation is emphatically "*not* by individual Jews converting to faith in Christ," but nor is it an "end-time conversion."[3] When Paul speaks of God's saving covenant for Jacob in Romans 11:27, this "is, of course, the Sinai covenant."[4] John Gager similarly remarks that in Romans 11 "when Paul thinks and speaks of Israel's imminent restoration *he does not construe this to imply conversion to Christianity*."[5]

Although Krister Stendahl (perhaps surprisingly) rejects the language of a "Sonderweg," he maintains that Paul is being "overtly

1 F. Mussner, *Traktat über die Juden* (Göttingen: Vandenhoeck & Ruprecht, 2009 [1979]), 57. Mussner notes the earlier usage of the word in D. Zeller, *Juden und Heiden in der Mission des Paulus: Studien zum Römerbrief* (Stuttgart: Verlag Katholisches Bibelwerk, 1976 [1973]), 245.

2 Lloyd Gaston, *Paul and the Torah* (Vancouver: University of British Columbia Press, 1987), 148.

3 Gaston, *Paul and the Torah*, 148.

4 Gaston, *Paul and the Torah*, 143.

5 J. G. Gager, *The Origins of Anti-Semitism: Attitudes towards Judaism in Pagan and Christian Antiquity* (New York: Oxford University Press, 1983), 261. Emphasis original.

non-christological" in Romans 11.[6] Even on 11:26 and the reference to the deliverer coming from Zion, he writes,

> Instead of speaking about Jesus in Romans 11.26, Paul says something mysterious—"For it is out of Zion that the rescuer will come." We Christians read that immediately as a reference to Jesus. But it could just as well be read as a Pauline form of the famous statement in the Gospel of John (4:22), when Jesus says to the Samaritan woman, "For salvation is from the Jews."[7]

He goes on to emphasize that because the Jews are in God's hands, "God has the power to realise their salvation, which is definitely not cast in christological terms."[8]

Rather than criticize this viewpoint, which has been done often enough already,[9] this chapter will explore the grain of truth in the theory that Romans 9–11 is "unchristological." This grain of truth is that there is a relative lack of focus on Jesus Christ's *agency* in those chapters.

If we examine the foregoing chapters of Romans, we see in Romans 1 that Christ is raised from dead as the son of God in power and gives grace to Paul (1:4-5); even in the *Verdammnisgeschichte* in Romans 2 Jesus is the agent of divine judgment (2:16); in Romans 3 he accomplishes atonement (3:21-26), and in Romans 4 is delivered to death for our sins and raised for our justification (4:25); in Romans 5 he brings righteousness and life through his one act of righteousness (5:12-21), and in Romans 6 he dies to sin once for all and rises from the dead, including believers with him (6:1-11); even in Romans 7, believers die to the Law in order to belong to him and Christ is clearly involved in deliverance from the body of death (7:1-6, 25). In chapter 8 he comes as sacrifice for sin, dies for us, is raised, and intercedes at the right hand (8:3, 32-34).

By comparison, in Romans 9–11 Christ *does* much less. The only action of Christ thematized in these chapters is the—admittedly

[6] Krister Stendahl, *Final Account: Paul's Letter to the Romans* (Minneapolis: Fortress, 1995), 39.

[7] Stendahl, *Final Account*, 39–40.

[8] Stendahl, *Final Account*, 40.

[9] See, e.g., Bruce W. Longenecker, "Different Answers to Different Issues: Israel, the Gentiles and Salvation History in Romans 9–11," *JSNT* 36 (1989): 95–123; Terence L. Donaldson, "'Riches for the Gentiles' (Romans 11:12): Israel's Rejection and Paul's Gentile Mission," *JBL* 112 (1993): 81–98.

momentous—one in which "the deliverer comes from Zion," and thereby brings salvation to all Israel. There is also a more fleeting reference, in the πλουτῶν in 10:12, to Christ's bestowal of riches (cf. 2 Cor 8:9).

The contention of this chapter, however, is that despite this lack of emphasis on Christ's agency until the very end, he occupies in Romans 9–11 a crucial place. Or rather, he occupies a number of crucial places—quite literally, because it is the *locations* of Christ in relation to Israel and the world that come to the fore in Romans 9–11, even though this has scarcely been noted by interpreters. The following pages, then, will explore the *positions* or locations of Christ in Romans 9–11, especially Christ's locations vis-à-vis Israel.

Romans 9:1-5

In the first place, the whole impulse for Romans 9–11 arises from Paul's relation to Christ. (There are three references to Christ in the first five verses.) The meaning of "in Christ" here is not straightforward: the point may be that Paul's oath[10] here is taken in some sense "in the presence of Christ,"[11] though perhaps the language is vague and there is an element of the "locative" sense.[12] Without a locative sense of "in," the point would still be that Christ stands before Paul perhaps as a judge, with Paul stating that he is conscious of standing in the presence of Christ as he declares Romans 9:1-5, and therefore aware that if he is not speaking the truth he would be lying while Christ looked on. Even if the point is not that Paul occupies a position *in* Christ here, then, Christ is invoked as situated before, in the presence of, Paul here, and so the close proximity between the two is emphasized.

A second impulse that gets Romans 9–11 off the ground (there are others) is that Israel—in contrast to Paul—is alienated from Christ. The strong implication here is that Israel is in the situation ἀπὸ τοῦ

[10] I am grateful for an informative conversation with Michael Wolter about the oath character of Rom 9:1-5. On the oath element, see further G. Stählin, "Zum Gebrauch von Beteuerungsformeln im Neuen Testament," *NovT* 5 (1962): 115–43, 133; Otto Michel, *Der Brief an die Römer*, 5th ed., KEK 4 (Göttingen: Vandenhoeck & Ruprecht, 1978), 291–92.

[11] Thus Ernst Käsemann, *Commentary on Romans*, trans. G. W. Bromiley (Grand Rapids: Eerdmans, 1980), 257.

[12] In the LXX the phrase ἐν κυρίῳ ὄμνυμι is very common (e.g., 1 Kgs 1:17), but the oath character is not quite so explicit in Paul here because of the use of the more general verb λέγω (admittedly in conjunction with ἀλήθειαν).

Χριστοῦ that Paul imagines theoretically for himself (cf. Exod 32:32). As Heikki Räisänen comments, the reason for Paul's anguish must be Israel's lack of belief in the Gospel—"no other reason makes sense."[13] Or as he puts it elsewhere, Paul's language "implies that they must be in the very plight he is willing to enter for their sake: they are anathema."[14] The nation is at present (as 10:1 makes explicit) not heading for salvation and consequently separated from Christ. As Michael Wolter comments, the problem of Romans 9:1-5 is the discrepancy between Israel's privileges and her *Heilsferne*.[15] In other words, Christ's position vis-à-vis Israel is in contrast to his position in relation to Paul—Paul speaks ἐν (whether "in" or "before"), Israel is ἀπό.

The awful irony here is that the Israel ἀπὸ τοῦ Χριστοῦ is the same entity that gave birth to Christ according to the flesh. Christ is ἐξ the Israelites in 9:5a. Israel and Christ have, therefore, at one level a most intimate relationship, that of mother and child. On the other hand, however, Israel has been a neglectful mother.

This is not so much in defiance of maternal στοργή, but rather in defiance of Christ's lordship, because Jesus in Romans 9:5 here is not merely ἐξ the Israelites τὸ κατὰ σάρκα but also ὁ ὢν ἐπὶ πάντων θεὸς εὐλογητὸς εἰς τοὺς αἰῶνας. This is of course, however, a proposition in need of defending.[16]

Arguments pro and con seeing an identification of Christ as θεός in Romans 9:5 center on four main areas: (1) syntax/punctuation, (2) Pauline theology, (3) Paul's style, especially his lexicon, and (4) early interpretation.

Syntax/Punctuation. In brief, there is general agreement that the syntax points in favor of Christ as θεός. Arguments have been mounted in the past on both sides. In defense of the identification of Jesus as θεός,

[13] H. Räisänen, "Paul, God and Israel: Romans 9–11 in Recent Research," in *The Social World of Formative Christianity and Judaism: Festschrift for H. C. Kee*, ed. J. Neusner et al. (Philadelphia: Fortress, 1988), 178–206, 180.

[14] H. Räisänen, "Torn between Two Loyalties: Romans 9–11 and Paul's Conflicting Convictions," in *The Nordic Paul: Finnish Approaches to Pauline Theology*, ed. L. Aejmelaeus and A. Mustakalio, LNTS 374 (London: T&T Clark, 2008), 19–39, 25.

[15] Michael Wolter, *Paulus: Ein Grundriss seiner Theologie* (Neukirchen: Neukirchener Verlag, 2011), 426.

[16] For a helpful survey of many of the arguments on both sides and a large bibliography, see now George Carraway, *Christ Is God over All: Romans 9:5 in the Context of Romans 9–11*, LNTS 489 (New York: Bloomsbury, 2013). It must be noted, however, that the book has an inauspicious first line: "When Paul wrote his letter to the Romans more than twenty centuries ago . . ." (1).

some have maintained that τὸ κατὰ σάρκα "suggests" an antithesis that is found in the counterbalancing assertion of Jesus' exalted status.[17] (At the very least, one can say that, as it turns out, there is an elegant one.)[18] On the other hand, F. C. Burkitt contended that the clause is a formal benediction added parenthetically in which Paul calls upon God as his witness: of course the advantage of a parenthesis is that it solves at a stroke any syntactic difficulties.[19] Most of the emphasis, however, has lain upon word-order in 5b. As the words stand, one would expect Christ to be the antecedent of both ὁ ὢν and εὐλογητός.[20] There is no independent doxology here: the rule for such doxologies is that εὐλογητός is *followed* by the object of praise ("Blessed be X . . ."). As a result εὐλογητός is simply part of the larger sentence.

Both J. D. G. Dunn and Gordon Fee recognize the prima facie force of the argument from syntax, even if they go on to argue on other grounds for a non-christological reading.[21] Cranfield is therefore

[17] C. E. B. Cranfield, *A Critical and Exegetical Commentary on the Epistle to the Romans*, 2 vols., ICC (Edinburgh: T&T Clark, 1979), 2:467.

[18] N. T. Wright, *Paul and the Faithfulness of God*, 2 vols. (Minneapolis: Fortress, 2013), 707–8; B. M. Metzger, "The Punctuation of Romans 9:5," in *Christ and Spirit in the New Testament: Studies in Honour of Charles Francis Digby Moule*, ed. B. Lindars and S. S. Smalley (Cambridge: Cambridge University Press, 1973), 95–112, 103–5.

[19] F. C. Burkitt, "On Romans ix 5 and Mark xiv 61," *JTS* 5 (1904): 451–55, 452.

[20] The usage of εὐλογητός can be summed up as following two patterns:

(a) Most frequent is at the beginning, i.e., *introducing a beatitude*, where εἶ or ἐστιν is understood: e.g., Εὐλογητὸς ὁ θεός . . . followed commonly by a relative clause or a ὅτι clause or a participle, "Blessed be God, who has/for he has. . . ." E.g., εὐλογητὸς ὁ θεὸς σήμερον ὃς ἔδωκεν τῷ Δαυιδ υἱὸν φρόνιμον . . . (1 Kgs 5:21). In a few instances it can introduce a blessing of a human being: εὐλογητὸς ὁ ἄνθρωπος ἐκεῖνος τῷ θεῷ (Gen 43:28).

(b) It can occur anywhere in the way *a normal adjective* might, e.g., καὶ ἔσῃ εὐλογητός (Gen 12:2); καὶ νῦν σὺ εὐλογητὸς ὑπὸ κυρίου (Gen 26:29). εὐλογητὸς ἔσῃ παρὰ πάντα τὰ ἔθνη (Deut. 7:14); εὐλογητὸς, ὁ υἱός μου, τῷ κυρίῳ (Judg 17:2).

There are eight instances of εὐλογητός in the NT. Half of them (Luke 1:68; 2 Cor 1:3; Eph 1:3; and 1 Pet 1:3) fit exactly within the pattern of (a). The others, including Rom 1:25; 2 Cor 11:31 fit roughly into (b). Mark 14:61 is unusual in that it functions as a substantive (σὺ εἶ ὁ χριστὸς ὁ υἱὸς τοῦ εὐλογητοῦ). Rom 9:5 works in exactly the same way as Rom 1:25 and 2 Cor 11:31. As far as its syntax is concerned, it should not be treated as unusual.

[21] J. D. G. Dunn, *Christology in the Making: An Inquiry into the Origins of the Doctrine of Incarnation* (London: SCM Press, 1980), 45; G. D. Fee, *Pauline Christology: An Exegetical-Theological Study* (Peabody, Mass.: Hendrickson, 2007), 273.

justified in saying that the burden of proof rests rather more on the shoulders of those wanting to argue for a non-christological reading.[22]

Pauline Theology. As far as theology is concerned, there has been a considerable shift in the past generation or so toward seeing Paul as having a "divine" Christology of sorts across the epistles as a whole.[23] Passages such as 1 Corinthians 8:6, Philippians 2:6, Philippians 2:9-11, and other OT christological κύριος texts (including Rom 10:13) have all contributed to a growing majority of scholars seeing Paul's Christ as sharing in the identity of the one God, or as the object of a "binitarian" worship.[24] In the current climate, then, those who argue for a theological difficulty are increasingly in the minority. In the near vicinity, for example, we have the characterization of Christ as κύριος πάντων in Romans 10:12, strongly redolent of the ἐπὶ πάντων in 9:5. Thereafter in 10:13 Paul writes of the need to call upon the name of Jesus in the terms of calling upon the name of YHWH from Joel 2. Furthermore, as we will see, Paul ascribes Jesus the divine title of "deliverer" in Romans 11:26. These might add weight to the argument that the language of 9:5b is christological.

Paul's Style. In terms of style, it is interesting that a scholar such as Gordon Fee who shares this view of a divine Christology more widely in Paul nevertheless considers the reference in Romans 9:5 to be to God, not Christ, on the grounds that Paul carefully distinguishes elsewhere between the Father who is the θεός, and Christ who is the κύριος.[25] Fee's point is correct as far as it goes. However, Paul not only has a high theological conception of Christ, but also sometimes veers in the direction of using "god-language" in connection with Christ.

[22] C. E. B. Cranfield, "Some Comments on Professor J. D. G. Dunn's *Christology in the Making* with Special Reference to the Evidence of the Epistle to the Romans," in *The Glory of Christ in the New Testament: Studies in Christology in Memory of George Bradford Caird*, ed. L. D. Hurst and N. T. Wright (Oxford: Clarendon, 1987), 267–80, 273.

[23] In fact, on the basis of Philippians 2, Burkitt ("On Romans ix 5 and Mark xiv 61," 452) had already pronounced that the difficulty was not a theological one.

[24] I have summarized my own approach to this matter in brief compass in "Pauline Christology," in *The Blackwell Companion to Paul*, ed. S. Westerholm (Oxford: Blackwell, 2011), 172–87. See further, e.g., D. B. Capes, *Old Testament Yahweh Texts in Paul's Christology* (Tübingen: Mohr, 1992); Fee, *Pauline Christology*; R. J. Bauckham, *Jesus and the God of Israel: God Crucified and Other Studies on the New Testament's Christology of Divine Identity* (Grand Rapids: Eerdmans, 2008); Wright, *Paul and the Faithfulness of God*, 644–709.

[25] Fee, *Pauline Christology*, 274.

In Colossians, for example, Jesus embodies πᾶν τὸ πλήρωμα τῆς θεότητος (Col 2:9).[26] On this whole question, one must also bear in mind Bruce Metzger's point, which is worth citing in full:

> To deny that an author may on occasion, if he wishes, vary his style would mean that there could be no *hapax legomena* in his writings. But if one allows that such a principle holds good in purely lexical matters, there seems to be no reason why it should not also be allowed to operate with reference to *hapax legomena* among doctrinal statements. Let it be supposed, for the sake of argument, that Paul on one occasion wanted to state that "Christ is over all, God blessed for ever." If now the exegete rigidly adheres to the principle that Paul's Christological statements elsewhere in his epistles must be regarded as the controlling factor in estimating the meaning of any one particular statement, it is obvious that such a principle of interpretation will prevent the exegete from learning the mind of the apostle in the sole passage that stands outside the general run of such statements.[27]

Supposed objections to the christological interpretation on grounds of style, then, can carry little weight.

Early Interpretation. A further dimension not usually given much consideration is the early history of interpretation. In fairness, of course, one reason for the neglect may be that early interpretation is not always a reliable guide. Burkitt highlighted the fact that 1 Clement 31–32 alludes to Romans 9:5,[28] noting that the doxology there is

[26] Judgments here depend to some extent on one's view of how many letters are authentically Pauline, as the parallel most often cited is Titus 2:13: προσδεχόμενοι τὴν μακαρίαν ἐλπίδα καὶ ἐπιφάνειαν τῆς δόξης τοῦ μεγάλου θεοῦ καὶ σωτῆρος ἡμῶν Ἰησοῦ Χριστοῦ. The Colossians parallel is potentially more useful than that in Titus, because Titus 2:13 is itself ambiguous as far as Christology is concerned: see the discussions in I. H. Marshall, *The Pastoral Epistles*, ICC (London: T&T Clark, 1999), 276–82, and Fee, *Pauline Christology*, 442–46. Marshall takes this passage as a reference to Jesus as God; Fee takes the contrary view.

[27] Metzger, "Punctuation of Romans 9:5," 110–11. He goes on to say there are limits, of course, imposed by Paul's theology, but because of the clear high statements of Christology elsewhere in Paul there is no difficulty in the case of Rom 9:5.

[28] 1 Clem 32.4: ὁ παντοκράτωρ θεὸς . . . ᾧ ἔστω ἡ δόξα εἰς τοὺς αἰῶνας τῶν αἰώνων ἀμήν. This passage has also been used to suggest an emendation of Rom 9:5: for the literature on this, see Douglas J. Moo, *The Epistle to the Romans*, NICNT (Grand Rapids: Eerdmans, 1996), 565 n. 58.

clearly not ascribed to Christ.[29] Cranfield looks further afield in the early use of the verse, and finds the evidence divided.[30] The manuscript evidence is also inconclusive, despite the conclusions of Sanday and Headlam about the importance of the early punctuation;[31] Metzger rightly avers that the punctuation is a very unclear guide.[32] Another dimension of the early interpretation that has not been given much attention is the way in which Romans 9:5 is treated in the versions. Here again, however, as in the case of the use of Romans 9:5 by those not merely copying or translating, the evidence does not consistently point in one particular direction.[33] As is often the case, then, the history of interpretation can only issue a verdict of *non liquet*.

In sum, the first observation, on the syntax, is most important, and is supported by the second on Paul's Christology, with the stylistic objection powerless to undermine the case. As a result, one should regard the reference in Romans 9:5b as probably to Christ. The key point here, therefore, is that the high point (literally) of the depiction of Jesus in Romans 9:1-5 is that he is "above all" or "over all," a designation that complements his depiction as "from the Israelites."

Interim: Romans 9:6-29

After Romans 9:1-5, in the course of discussing the mode of God's election in Scripture, Paul makes no mention of Christ in 9:6-29, or to put it another way, Paul does not "cheat" and insert Christ into the story inappropriately. He *is* focused there, however, on saying that the way in which God is acting in Christ in the present follows the same pattern according to which God has acted in the past. The emphasis is that the quality of mercy is not strained. As John Barclay and Beverly Gaventa have rightly emphasized, God acts purely on the basis of

[29] Burkitt, "On Romans ix 5 and Mark xiv 61," 455.

[30] Cranfield, *Epistle to the Romans*, 2:469–70.

[31] See W. Sanday and A. C. Headlam, *A Critical and Exegetical Commentary on the Epistle to the Romans*, 5th ed., ICC (Edinburgh: T&T Clark, 1902), 234.

[32] Metzger, "Punctuation of Romans 9:5," 97–100. See already C. Lattey, "The Codex Vaticanus on Romans ix 5," *ExpTim* 34, no. 7 (1923): 331; and idem, "The Codex Ephraemi Rescriptus on Romans ix 5," *ExpTim* 35, no. 1 (1923): 42–43.

[33] Of the early versions, the Old Latin and the Vulgate woodenly translate the Greek; the Syriac Peshitta provides a clear interpretation in which Christ is God, and the main Coptic versions are divided: the Bohairic probably treats Christ as God (though it is a very wooden translation), while the Sahidic takes the blessing of God as a doxology independent of the reference to Christ. Cf. also Metzger, "Punctuation of Romans 9:5," 100–101.

unprompted mercy, which has hardening as its counterpoint.[34] This hardening/mercy contrast emerges from the fact that (as seen in 9:24-29) there is a clear imbalance in numbers at present between believing Jews and believing Gentiles,[35] as Isaiah's prophesied salvation of a mere remnant and seed implies. (This also implies a hope for the future of Israel, however, because the ideas of "seed" and "remnant" imply a new beginning as well.) This imbalance is a further impulse for the way in which Romans 9–11 proceeds: these chapters would clearly have looked very different if Gentiles had responded with the same antipathy to the gospel as Jews had.

Romans 9:30-33

Paul also communicates this "imbalance" through the use of racing imagery, imagery that we need to explore as the context for the "stumbling stone." The race is extremely difficult to picture, however, and has generated some unlikely sporting scenarios.

For example, Ross Wagner proposes a scenario that seems unlikely, namely, that Israel is pursuing a figure called Nomos who is himself a runner in the race, running after righteousness.[36] This seems to me to overcomplicate the lineup of contestants involved.

[34] See especially three essays by J. M. G. Barclay: "Grace within and beyond Reason: Philo and Paul in Dialogue," in *Paul, Grace and Freedom: Essays in Honour of John K. Riches*, ed. P. Middleton, A. Paddison, and K. Wenell (London: T&T Clark, 2009), 9–21; "Unnerving Grace: Approaching Romans 9–11 from the Wisdom of Solomon," in *Between Gospel and Election: Explorations in the Interpretation of Romans 9–11*, ed. F. Wilk and J. R. Wagner, WUNT 257 (Tübingen: Mohr Siebeck, 2010), 91–109; and "'I Will Have Mercy on whom I Have Mercy': The Golden Calf and Divine Mercy in Romans 9–11 and Second Temple Judaism," *EC* 1 (2010): 82–106. See also B. R. Gaventa, "On the Calling-Into-Being of Israel: Romans 9:6-29," in Wilk and Wagner, *Between Gospel and Election*, 255–69, 257: "Paul writes nothing about an Israel that can be isolated as an ethnic entity of a 'nation,' but only as God's creation in each patriarchal generation."

[35] Johnson is thus right to say that the problem is not just Israel's unbelief but Israel's unbelief and Gentile belief: E. E. Johnson, "Romans 9–11: The Faithfulness and Impartiality of God," in *Romans*, vol. 3 of *Pauline Theology*, ed. D. M. Hay and E. E. Johnson (Minneapolis: Fortress, 1995), 219; S. Stowers, *A Rereading of Romans: Justice, Jews, and Gentiles* (New Haven, Conn.: Yale University Press, 1994), 298.

[36] J. R. Wagner, *Heralds of the Good News: Isaiah and Paul in Concert in the Letter to the Romans*, NovTSup 101 (Leiden: Brill, 2002), 158: "In Paul's metaphor, the Law is running after righteousness, and Israel is pursuing the Law," adding that the Law leads to righteousness because its *telos* is Christ.

Stanley Stowers seems to have it right in his remarks that what we have in Romans 9:30-33 is "somewhat inchoate agonistic imagery" in which "the development of the metaphor lacks just enough clarity that reading the text variously exercises the imagination," but which in the end is marked by a fair degree of "obscurity."[37] What can be said minimally, if one makes use of the parallel racing language in 1 Corinthians 9 and Philippians 3, is that the imagery of the Roman race runs as follows.[38]

Verse 9:30. The Gentiles were not going for righteousness; the point here is not so much that they were not chasing it—like the greyhounds chasing the hare, or one runner in hot pursuit trying to catch up with another; rather, Paul is saying that they did not have righteousness in their sights as a goal to be reached. In the racing imagery in Philippians 3:11-16, διώκω has that sense of what you are heading for, namely, in Philippians 3:11-12 the resurrection of the dead, and in 3:14 the prize. This fits with the use of καταλαμβάνω in the main clause in Romans 9:30, which in the race contexts in both 1 Corinthians 9 and Philippians 3 refers to scooping up the prize.[39] They did not head for righteousness at all, but won it nevertheless.

Verse 9:31. Israel for his part set his sights on the righteousness-Law as his goal (Ἰσραὴλ δὲ διώκων νόμον δικαιοσύνης); it is, again, *probably* (though no more than that) not that he was chasing after the Law trying to catch up with it.[40] Rather, he was aiming at the Law, in order to reach it or fulfill it at the finish line (cf. ἐπιζητεῖ Ἰσραήλ in Rom 11:7). The main clause (εἰς νόμον οὐκ ἔφθασεν) could then mean either that he did not get to the Law *first* (φθάνω in the sense of "reach ahead of"), that is, that the Gentiles *did* get to the Law in some sense first and did light upon what the Law was always

37 Stowers, *Rereading of Romans*, 303.

38 In the stadium race imagery in 1 Cor 9:24-27, (κατα)λαμβάνω τὸ βραβεῖον is to scoop up the prize at the end (9:24), as is στέφανον λαμβάνω (9:25). Again in Phil 3:11-16: καταλαμβάνω and λαμβάνω are used to refer to scooping up what one hopes to get in the race, pursuing it in the sense of seeking it (διώκω). In the course of the race, the runner "chases after" (διώκω εἰς) the prize, and "chases" (διώκω) to get the end. In this passage, εἰς X φθάνω means to arrive at X (already?).

39 Compare also Sir 27:8: ἐὰν διώκῃς τὸ δίκαιον καταλήμψῃ καὶ ἐνδύσῃ αὐτὸ ὡς ποδήρη δόξης, where we have (a) the aim at the goal in the race, (b) the obtaining of it, and (c) the prize of the glorious robe.

40 I have chosen "he" as the personal pronoun for Israel here because Israel in a sense is embodied in the male figure of Jacob, but also because athletes in the ancient world were usually men.

about. Or it could simply mean that Israel did not arrive at the Law, as per the weaker sense of φθάνω in Philippians 3:16. Either way—*9:32*—he went off course, having taken a wrong turn, running not by faith but treating the race as if it should be run by works and treating the Law as though it could be reached that way (οὐκ ἐκ πίστεως ἀλλ᾽ ὡς ἐξ ἔργων). So he tripped over the stumbling stone (προσέκοψαν τῷ λίθῳ τοῦ προσκόμματος).

In summary, the Gentiles in the contest have somehow received the prize of righteousness (9:30; cf. 10:20), and—contrary to what one would expect, as in the fable of the tortoise and the hare—Israel has not got there because he went the wrong way (9:31). One might have thought that Israel would run ahead of the Gentiles and beat them in the race, but, after all, Paul has already said a few verses earlier that it is not a matter of running, but of the merciful God (9:16).

Israel did run the wrong way (οὐκ ἐκ πίστεως ἀλλ᾽ ὡς ἐξ ἔργων), but this is not the only reason for their losing the race to the Gentiles: Israel stumbled over the stumbling stone. This is not an accident, and not merely because of Israel's bad running, but because God had put the stone there: "Behold, *I place* a stone *in Zion*" (9:33b, citing Isa 28:16). Zion is of course the headquarters of Israel, whether understood as Jerusalem tout simple (e.g., in 2 Chr 5:2) or as a specific mountain in or near Jerusalem (e.g., Isa 10:12; Joel 2:32). The point, then, is that the stumbling stone is placed in the very midst of Israel.

Jesus implicitly appears here: I do not think that there can be much doubt about the christological referent of the stone.[41] The stone cannot be faith, because the stone is the object of faith (9:33c). Nor is it likely to be the plan of God embodied in the Law (as well as in Christ):[42] in the imagery here, the Law is depicted in the race as something that Israel heads for but does not reach, and so tripping over the Law would be impossible. If there is any ambiguity at all in the identity of the stone, this lasts only until Romans 10:11-13 as Wagner has shown, because when Paul cites Isaiah 28:16 again there, the reference is clearly christological. This can be seen from the parallel between Romans 10:11 and 10:13: "everyone who believes in him will not be put to shame," and "everyone who calls upon the name of the Lord will be saved."

[41] Rightly Cranfield, *Epistle to the Romans*, 2:511–12.

[42] Cf. N. T. Wright, *The Climax of the Covenant: Christ and the Law in Pauline Theology* (Edinburgh: T&T Clark, 1991), 244. See also Wagner, *Heralds of the Good News*, 156 n. 112, noting scholars who argue in favor of the Law.

The cause of Israel's stumbling is the divine placement of the stone in Zion, then, and therefore here at the end of Romans 9 Zion is the particular *location* of Christ. God installs Christ in Zion, in the midst of Israel, to be the object of faith leading to glory (οὐ καταισχυνθήσεται), but also to be a stumbling stone to trip up Israel. Mercy and hardening come to clear expression at one and the same time in this "stone," which can be both relied upon and tripped over. The one event of the coming of Christ is simultaneously the occasion of both trust and unbelief, mercy and hardening.

The implication of this is that Israel is therefore not distant from Christ because they have not been introduced to one another, but precisely because of an encounter—tripping over the stone set in Zion. Again, then, the location in which God places Christ is a key element in Paul's argument. It has multiple functions: (1) highlighting that Israel's sin is the result of an encounter with Christ, rather than of mere ignorance, and (2) identifying Israel's rejection of the Gospel as divinely caused—a point that naturally serves to reinforce the point in 9:6 that the purposes of God cannot possibly have failed. On the contrary, Israel's rejection of the gospel now begins to be seen as the positive fulfillment of "the word of God"—specifically the word of God in Isaiah 28:16 as combined with Isaiah 8:14.[43] The principle of divine action in mercy accompanied by hardening, enunciated in the first half of Romans 9, is seen specifically here fleshed out in christological terms.

By contrast, in 9:33, Gentiles have believed "upon" him, have rested upon him as a "precious cornerstone and a sure foundation" (Isa 28:16); for them according to Isaiah 8:14 Christ is the divine sanctuary rather than a stumbling stone.[44]

Romans 10:1-4

At the beginning of chapter 10, we see spelled out more clearly the situation that was only mutedly implicit at the beginning of Romans 9. The fact that Paul is praying for Israel's *salvation* very obviously implies

[43] The point is mutatis mutandis the same as that in 1 Peter 2: Jesus is the living stone who is believed in by those who will not be put to shame, but also "a stone that causes people to stumble and a rock that makes them fall," as a consequence, "they stumble because they disobey the message—which is also what they were destined for."

[44] Isa 8:14 says of the Lord, ἔσται σοι εἰς ἁγίασμα, although Paul does not cite this part of the verse.

that Israel appears to be standing subject to God's judgment, in a state of *Unheil*. Romans 10:2-3 diagnoses their condition: (1) zeal without knowledge, and (2) ignorance of the righteousness of God as they seek to establish their own.

There is probably an implied christological reference in the "righteousness of God" in Romans 10:3: the point there is probably not so much that Paul's kinsmen according to the flesh were unaware of the divine attribute of righteousness, but rather that they had not recognized the specific instance of God's righteousness enacted in Christ. But this is not clearly stated.

So, after a moment with no clear statement of Christ (10:1-3), the racing imagery—and with it, Christ—probably returns in 10:4. Here in Romans 10:4, Christ has another role in the athletic image: as Stowers and Wagner comment,[45] the τέλος recalls the racing imagery.[46] Jesus therefore marks the finish line of the race, where the prize of righteousness, or what 2 Timothy calls the "garland of righteousness" (2 Tim 4:8), is given to those who believe (10:4).

Romans 10:5-15

To counterbalance my discussion of reference to Christ as God in Romans 9:5, I want to argue the opposite line for 10:5—namely, that the verse is non-christological. For some, "doing these things" in Leviticus 18:5 (ὁ ποιήσας αὐτὰ ἄνθρωπος ζήσεται ἐν αὐτοῖς) as cited by Paul is about seeing faith in Christ as in some sense fulfilling the Law. Avemarie, for example, sees "doing these things" as "to *understand* the law as *a testimony* to Christ."[47] More to the point, however, is the observation made by Dunn and Westerholm, that a reference to righteousness through faith, and then righteousness through something else, linked with a δέ, is fairly obviously a contrast—as in similar

45 Stowers, *Rereading of Romans*, 304; J. R. Wagner, " 'Not from the Jews Only, but Also from the Gentiles': Mercy to the Nations in Romans 9–11," in Wilk and Wagner, *Between Gospel and Election*, 417–31, 423.

46 For some examples of τέλος in an athletic context, see R. Badenas, *Christ the End of the Law: Romans 10.4 in Pauline Perspective* (Sheffield: JSOT, 1985), 200 nn. 44–45.

47 F. Avemarie, "Paul and the Claim of the Law according to the Scriptures: Leviticus 18:5 in Galatians 3:12 and Romans 10:5," in idem, *Neues Testament und frührabbinisches Judentum*, WUNT 316 (Tübingen: Mohr Siebeck, 2013), 511–29, 525. Similarly Wright, *Climax of the Covenant*, 149.

statements elsewhere.[48] The parallel citation of Leviticus 18:5 in Galatians 3 has apparently no christological reference, and indeed is part of a contrast between righteousness by faith and righteousness through the Law—as appears to be the case in Romans 10.[49] The relationship between Romans 10:5 and 6 is, as most scholars and translators instinctively recognize, an antithetical one, rather than one in which these verses complement or explain one another. Interesting though the suggestion is, there is little positive reason to see a reference to the Law-Christ relationship here.

When Deuteronomy comes into play in the subsequent verses, however, Christ comes back into prominence, though initially in two counterfactuals. Christ is imagined solely up in heaven (10:6), or still down in the abyss (10:7). Neither location is quite true. Rather, in v. 8 Christ is *near*, and indeed *in* the mouth that proclaims the gospel and confesses it, and in the heart that believes it (10:8), as 10:9 expands upon. Here, the location of Christ is the proximity of Christ to the believing community. This emphasis on the immediate nearness of Christ in the gospel reinforces further the point that one does not need to run or chase for it—Romans 9:16 made it clear that running made no difference—but simply believe it.

In 10:9-13 thereafter, a number of the locations of Christ that we have already seen come back. Recapping, then, 10:9-10 expand upon the preceding verse, and so are a kind of exegesis of Deuteronomy 30:14: "No, the word is very near you; it is in your mouth and in your heart."[50] Verse 11 cites Isaiah 28:16 again, which we have already seen in chapter 9: here Christ, the stone, is not the obstacle for tripping over but the firm foundation for the believer. Verse 12, calling Jesus κύριος πάντων, recaps the position of Christ "over all" in Romans

[48] J. D. G. Dunn, *Romans*, 2 vols., WBC 38 (Dallas: Word, 1988), 2:602, cited in S. Westerholm, "Paul and the Law in Romans 9–11," in J. D. G. Dunn, ed., *Paul and the Mosaic Law* (Grand Rapids: Eerdmans, 2001 [1996]), 215–37, 232 n. 55.

[49] S. J. Gathercole, "Torah, Life and Salvation: Leviticus 18:5 in Early Judaism and the New Testament," in *From Prophecy to Testament: The Function of the Old Testament in the New*, ed. C. A. Evans and J. A. Sanders (Peabody, Mass.: Hendrickson, 2004), 131–50, and see further P. M. Sprinkle, *Law and Life: The Interpretation of Leviticus 18:5 in Early Judaism and Paul*, WUNT 241 (Tübingen: Mohr Siebeck, 2008), 131–90. Avemarie notes that, on his view, of the various OT verses that Paul cites twice, Lev 18:5 is one of the "rare exceptions" in which his interpretations differ, indeed, the interpretations are "entirely different" ("Paul and the Claim of the Law," 529).

[50] As Westerholm notes, Paul omits the "that you may obey it," or "so that you may *do* it," as per the LXX ("Paul and the Law in Romans 9–11," 231 n. 51).

9:5. (There is, moreover, in 10:12 a brief suggestion of the *agency* of Christ in his exercise of his riches, πλουτῶν.) The rest of the passage, from the end of v. 12 on into v. 15, continues to emphasize that Christ passes in the proclaimed gospel from the mouth of the preacher, to the ear of the hearer, to the heart of that hearer who believes, issuing forth in vocal confession.

Romans 10:16-21

In contrast to the believing community, of course, is the disbelieving community portrayed in 10:16-21; indeed, the latter is the majority, as Paul's citation "Lord, who has believed our message?" implies. It is perhaps no coincidence that this question comes from the beginning of Isaiah 53 and so introduces the poem about the suffering servant, but it is hard to know quite what significance might be attached to this. There may well be something bubbling under the surface in Paul's linkage between Isaiah's ἀκοή in the introduction to Isaiah 53 (Rom 10:16) and the ἀκοή of the gospel in 10:17, but at this point it remains under the surface.[51] Another key theme, introduced for the first time here, is that of *provocation*, which at this stage is apparently entirely negative. In addition, the final citation of Isaiah in Romans 10 is a reminder that Israel is not merely ignorant, but in disobedient rebellion against God. What comes out here in Paul's Old Testament quotations, however—and this will be crucial to Romans 11—is that (1) God is still communicating with Israel even if that is through provocation (v. 19), and (2) God has not rejected this disobedient and rebellious people, but has been spreading out his hands toward them all day long (v. 21).

Romans 11:1-10

The key question of God's ongoing commitment to Israel is broached here, and Paul asserts that God has not rejected his people. This does not come out of nowhere: as we have just seen in chapter 10, God has remained in constant communication with Israel; and back in chapter 9 we saw, even in the midst of Paul's indictment of Israel, reference to a remnant returning (9:27) and God leaving a seed (9:29). Paul picks up the seed language again here—he is from the (surviving) seed of

[51] On Paul's application of the servant language of Isaiah 53 to Jesus, see further S. J. Gathercole, *Defending Substitution: An Essay on Atonement in Paul* (Grand Rapids: Baker, 2015), 55–79.

Abraham. There is now a remnant in the present just as there was in Elijah's day, just as there was even in the bleak situation of Isaiah 1 (as cited in Rom 9:29): in both cases God has left a remnant behind (καταλείπω/ἐγκαταλείπω). But apart from citing himself as an instance of the surviving remnant, Paul conducts the argument in 11:1-6 on the basis of Scripture. The same is true of the references to divine hardening in 11:7-10. Here again, as for the bulk of chapter 9, Paul does not cheat and introduce Christ as *deus ex machina* to solve problems, which is not to say, however, that Paul's use of Scripture is uninformed by the coming of Christ and Israel's response.

Romans 11:11-24

Despite this hardness in Israel, then, because of the biblical promises one cannot draw the conclusion that Israel's tripping over means that he is out of the race (11:11a). No—his tripping over, which is both a "tripping" and a "trespass,"[52] had a purpose: salvation for the Gentiles, which in turn has the aim of provoking Israel to jealousy (11:11b).

The racing imagery from Romans 9:30–10:4 continues into 11:12, where Israel's stumbling means that he has lost the race: ἥττημα is translated by the NRSV as "defeat," but there is some merit in the translation "loss" (NIV), which captures the sense of both "defeat" but also "reduction in numbers" (cf. KJV's "diminishing"). None of the major translations, however, carries this over to what is contrasted with the ἥττημα, namely, the πλήρωμα, which can have connotations of both "fullness" and "completing."[53] "Completion" is perhaps

[52] Stowers, *Rereading of Romans*, 313, though this may be at odds with the attempt to diminish Israel's culpability earlier in the book (see, e.g., *Rereading of Romans*, 305).

[53] To confine the discussion to examples in the NT, πλήρωμα appears seventeen times in the NT:

(1) in eleven occurrences it means something like "full measure," "fullness," "full complement" (Mark 6:43; 8:20; John 1:16; Rom 11:25; 15:29; Gal 4:4; Eph 1:23; 3:19; 4:13; Col 1:19; 2:9), which is usually taken to be its meaning here in Romans 11:12 (cf. v. 25);

(2) in two places it means "the action of completing/fulfilling," in Rom 13:10 and probably Eph 1:10;

(3) in two places (Mark 2:21/Matt 9:16) it means "the component which brings completion" or which makes something complete;

(4) in one place, "that which completely fills" (1 Cor 10:26, citing Ps 24:1); this overlaps so much with sense (1) that some of those places could have this sense.

For πληρ- language in the context of finishing a race or course, see Acts 13:25 (ὡς δὲ ἐπλήρου Ἰωάννης τὸν δρόμον); cf. also Epiphanius, *Pan.* 70.13.1: τοῦ γὰρ

the best word, retaining the ambiguity of both "Israel completing the race" and "Israel being complete."

Shortly after, the imagery shifts in an agricultural direction. The firstfruits, that is, those of Israel already saved, are holy, therefore so will the rest of the batch be; the existing root is holy, so then will be the branches (11:16). Granted, branches have been broken off because of unbelief (11:20a), but they will be grafted back in if they believe (11:23a). In fact, this "if" appears to acquire the certainty of a "when" according to the logic of v. 24: "After all, if you (Gentiles) were cut out of an olive tree that is wild by nature, and contrary to nature were grafted into a cultivated olive tree, how much more readily will these, the natural branches, be grafted into their own olive tree!" (NIV).

Romans 11:25-27

Here at the end of Romans 9–11, Christ reappears as the Savior of Israel. He is the deliverer who comes forth from Zion and appears to establish a new covenant with Israel, forgiving their sins. As Daniel Kirk has noted, any interpretation of Romans 11:25-27 should be competent to address the following four problems: (1) the καὶ οὕτως, (2) the sense of "all Israel," (3) how Paul envisages the Isaiah quotation as supporting his argument, and (4) the meaning of ἐκ Σιών—irrespective of whether Paul made the change or not.[54]

I will give a brief account of the first three points to set the context for the fourth, which is naturally the main subject to be addressed here.

καὶ οὕτως. Israel's hardening leads to an influx of Gentiles: καὶ οὕτως all Israel will be saved. This may appear to be new information—Paul after all says that he is declaring a mystery. On the other hand, however, the γάρ, the warning to the Gentiles, and the theological content of Romans 11:25-27 all strongly suggest that what is said in these verses is not something especially new, but rather a summary of what has already been said in the earlier part of the chapter. In this chapter we have close parallels to the three points in 11:25-26: (a) hardening, (b) fullness of the Gentiles, (c) Israel's salvation—repeatedly.

ἐνιαυτοῦ κατὰ τὸν ἡλιακὸν δρόμον πληρουμένου ἐν τριακοσίαις ἑξήκοντα πέντε ἡμέραις καὶ ὥραις τρισί. . . .

[54] J. R. D. Kirk, "Why Does the Deliverer Come ἐκ Σιών (Rom 11.26)?" *JSNT* 33 (2010): 81–99, 81. On this last point, the "change" refers to the difference between the ἐκ Σιών in Rom 11:26 and the ἕνεκεν Σιών in Isa 59:20 LXX.

- To begin with, in 11:11, we have (a) Israel's stumbling, (b) salvation for the nations, and (c) the consequent provocation of Israel, even though Paul has not yet made this provocation clear as something positive.
- In 11:12, again there is (a) Israel's stumbling and defeat,[55] which brings (b) riches for the nations of the world, but also (c) Israel's own fullness, or completion of the race.
- In 11:13-14, Paul then applies this to his ministry, where the positive provocation comes in: on the surface his ministry is work for (b) the salvation of the Gentiles, but this has an ultimate goal of (c) provocation and salvation of Israelites. Paul's language of "saving some" might sound rather anemic as a depiction of the salvation of *all* Israel, but this objection is mitigated by two factors. First, Paul is not the only apostle engaged in the salvation of Jews; others will also play a part (cf. Gal 2:8-9). Second, Paul's language of "saving some" is not particularly modest: he can alternate between talking of saving "some" in 1 Corinthians 9:22 and the salvation of "the many" in 1 Corinthians 10:33 in reference to the very same category of people.[56] Paul's participation in this process of saving Jews strongly suggests that this provocation and salvation of Israel takes place during the course of the Gentile mission in the last days.
- In 11:15, (a) Israel's hardening leads to (b) the fullness of the Gentiles, but (c) then comes Israel's salvation (which in turn then leads to the eschaton). The parallelism makes it clear that Israel's salvation is not the same as the resurrection from the dead, but its immediate precursor. As is evident from table 5.1, the ζωὴ ἐκ νεκρῶν in 11:15 belongs with the πόσῳ μᾶλλον in 11:12, both of which are marvelous *consequences* of the completion of Israel.[57]

[55] Thus Stowers, *Rereading of Romans*, 366 n. 55, citing Philo, *Omn.* 111, where ἧττα means defeat in a wrestling context, and other places where ἡττ- forms contrast with νικ- language.

[56] Compare:

9:22: . . . τοῖς πᾶσιν γέγονα πάντα, ἵνα πάντως τινὰς σώσω.

10:33: . . . μὴ ζητῶν τὸ ἐμαυτοῦ σύμφορον ἀλλὰ τὸ τῶν πολλῶν, ἵνα σωθῶσιν.

[57] Cranfield, *Epistle to the Romans*, 2:563 is right to suggest the final resurrection as the most likely meaning of "life from the dead" here, though he downplays the last-days mission to Jews.

TABLE 5.1

11:12a	his stumble ➛	riches for the world		
11:12b	his loss ➛	riches for the nations		
11:12c			his "completion" ➛	?!
11:15a	his casting off ➛	reconciliation of the world		
11:15b			his acceptance ➛	life from death!

- In 11:16-17, (a) branches of Israel are broken off, (b) so that Gentile branches can be grafted in, (c) after which Israel's branches are ingrafted again. This is followed by the application to the Gentiles in the audience in 11:18. The warning in 11:18 means that the address to the Gentiles in 11:25 is not a new point.
- In 11:19, (a) Israel's unbelief meant branches being broken off, but this led to (b) the fullness of Gentiles. As in 11:18, this is followed by the application to Gentiles in the audience in 11:20-21. Again, this application here means that the instruction to the Gentiles in 11:25 recapitulates what has already been said. Compare Paul's overall aim expressed in 11:25 (ἵνα μὴ ἦτε [παῤ] ἑαυτοῖς φρόνιμοι) with, for example, μὴ κατακαυχῶ τῶν κλάδων· εἰ δὲ κατακαυχᾶσαι . . . (11:18) and μὴ ὑψηλὰ φρόνει ἀλλὰ φοβοῦ (11:20).
- In 11:22-23 again: (a) Israel's hardening leads to (b) the fullness of Gentiles, so that (c) they are ultimately grafted back in if they do not remain in unbelief. Like Paul's participation in the mission, this also suggests a "last-days" process of Jews coming to faith.
- Then 11:24 focuses just on elements (b) and (c): (b) the ingrafting of Gentiles logically implies (c) the reingrafting of Israel.

In sum, in vv. 11-24 we see that the stumbling of Israel—which Paul implies is temporary and not final—leads to the repositioning of God's saving purpose in the midst of the Gentiles, which in turn redounds to the redemptive provocation of Israel.

TABLE 5.2

11:25-26	(a) Israel hardened	(b) Gentiles' fullness	(c) all Israel saved
11:11	(a) Israel's stumbling	(b) salvation for the nations	(c) the consequent provocation of Israel
11:12	(a) Israel's stumbling and defeat	(b) riches for the nations of the world	(c) Israel's completion
11:13-14		(b) Paul's ministry of salvation of the Gentiles	(c) provocation and salvation of Israelites
11:15	(a) Israel cut off	(b) reconciliation of the Gentiles	(c) Israel accepted (leading to the eschaton)
11:17	(a) branches of Israel are broken off	(b) so that Gentile branches can be grafted in	
11:19-20a	(a) Israel's unbelief meant branches being broken off	(b) inclusion of the Gentiles through faith	
11:22-23	(a) Israel falls through God's severity ("cutting off")	(b) Gentiles the objects of God's kindness	(c) they are ultimately grafted back in if they do not remain in unbelief
11:24		(b) the ingrafting of Gentiles	(c) the reingrafting of Israel
11:28	(a) Israel enemies	(b) for the sake of you Gentiles	(c) their future is guaranteed through election
11:30	(a) Israel disobedient	(b) Gentiles thereby receiving mercy	
11:31	(a) Israel now disobedient	(b) for mercy to come to Gentiles	(c) so Israel might also (now) receive mercy

The mystery described in 11:25-27, then, is what has been talked about all along in Romans 11: as Nils Dahl put it, Paul here "draws the conclusion of the preceding arguments."[58] He speaks in 11:25-26 of the hardening of Israel and mercy to the Gentiles as the *means*

[58] N. A. Dahl, *Studies in Paul: Theology for the Early Christian Mission* (Minneapolis: Augsburg, 1977), 152. See also Wright, *Paul and the Faithfulness of God*, 1232: "every element in verse 25 is thus simply a summary of what has gone before"; cf. his statement that the mystery is "the entire sequence of through from 11.11 onwards" (1233).

(καὶ οὕτως) by which Israel is saved, that is, the space created for the Gentiles means Israel's being provoked into salvation. The rhetorical punchline to the Gentiles in 11:25 also simply recaps what has already been said earlier in 11:13, 17-24 (see table 5.2). That this is a missionary process taking place through the course of the last days (rather than in the blink of an eye at the parousia) comports with both of Paul's statements, that his ministry is part of this process (11:14) and that Israel's salvation depends on her not remaining in unbelief—which he is certain they will not (11:23-24).

The Sense of "All Israel." This then implies a specific meaning to "all Israel," to move on to the next point. By this rationale, all Israel has the sense of "the full complement of Israel which comes to faith in Christ"—that is, the great number of Israelites who will in the end be grafted back into the olive tree when they abandon their unbelief. It is not "every Israelite who has ever lived," or even every single Israelite among Paul's contemporaries. It is those who have been provoked by the mission to the Gentiles to embrace the gospel. Just as there will be a *pleroma* of Gentiles, there will also be, Paul predicts, a great number of Israelites saved when the *pleroma* of Jews comes to faith. Israel's salvation is not so much after the Gentile mission but, as E. P. Sanders has put it, "as a result of the Gentile mission, through faith in Christ."[59]

A potential objection to this line of reasoning is that Paul writes πώρωσις ἀπὸ μέρους τῷ Ἰσραὴλ γέγονεν ἄχρι οὗ τὸ πλήρωμα τῶν ἐθνῶν εἰσέλθῃ, with the ἄχρι οὗ suggestive of two successive stages, the hardening followed sequentially by the influx of the nations. This need not be the sense of ἄχρι οὗ, however. In Hebrews 3:13, the writer issues the exhortation to "encourage one another daily, as long as (ἄχρις οὗ) it is called 'Today.'" In 2 Maccabees 14:10 it is said that "as long as Judas lives (ἄχρι γὰρ Ιουδας περίεστιν), it is impossible that the government should be calm." Liddell-Scott gives two glosses for ἄχρι under "as Conj." and "of Time" (3:1): the first (more common) is "until," the second—rarer, but especially relevant here—"so long as."[60] One of the examples for the latter comes from Lucian, who notes that it may be an added bonus if an athlete is handsome, but it makes no difference to his running: "So it is with history—if she were to make the mistake of dealing in pleasure as well she would attract a

[59] E. P. Sanders, *Paul, the Law and the Jewish People* (Philadelphia: Fortress, 1983), 195.

[60] As opposed to its syntax as an adverb or preposition, and its semantics "of space" or "of degree."

host of lovers, but as long as (ἄχρι δ' ἂν) she keeps only what is hers alone in all its fullness—I mean the publication of truth—she will give little thought to beauty."[61] In view of this second gloss provided by Liddell-Scott, it is perfectly reasonable to translate Romans 11:25b (or 25c) as "there is[62] a hardening of some sort[63] on Israel *as long as* the fullness of the Gentiles comes in."

The Isaiah Quotation. The Isaiah quotation, ἥξει ἐκ Σιὼν ὁ ῥυόμενος, ἀποστρέψει ἀσεβείας ἀπὸ Ἰακώβ, is vital to the argument because it precisely reaffirms the point that God, according to Paul, remains committed to Israel. Deliverance will come precisely from the midst of Zion, and the result will be that God will purify Jacob (ἀποστρέψει ἀσεβείας ἀπὸ Ἰακώβ), and that he will forgive their sins (ὅταν ἀφέλωμαι τὰς ἁμαρτίας αὐτῶν). God is still committed, if I might paraphrase Paul's quotation this way, to the apocalyptic liberation of Jacob from sin and the forensic pardoning of his covenant people. The hardening of his people, which makes space for Gentiles, which in turn leads to the salvation of Israel, means that Paul can certainly say that the word of God has not failed.

The Deliverer from Zion. Finally, then, this is the key part of the "mystery" for our purposes because it is about locating Christ in relation to Israel.

The identity of the redeemer as Christ seems to me fairly obvious. Stendahl's argument mentioned at the beginning that the statement might simply mean something like "salvation comes from the Jews" goes off track because there is clearly a personal redeemer envisaged here. This personal redeemer here could hardly be Paul, as suggested as a possibility by Mark Nanos—that would be a step *too* mysterious, I think.[64] God, not Christ, is a possibility, but the evidence that

[61] Lucian, *Quomodo Historia conscribenda sit* 9. The English above is Kilburn's Loeb translation of τοίνυν ἡ ἱστορία, εἰ μὲν ἄλλως τὸ τερπνὸν παρεμπορεύσαιτο, πολλοὺς ἂν τοὺς ἐραστὰς ἐπισπάσαιτο, ἄχρι δ' ἂν καὶ μόνον ἔχῃ τὸ ἴδιον ἐντελές—λέγω δὲ τὴν τῆς ἀληθείας δήλωσιν—, ὀλίγον τοῦ κάλλους φροντιεῖ.

[62] γέγονεν is also an interesting case; the perfect tense of γίνομαι is not simply always "have come." For the sense above, compare, e.g., Rom 11:5; 2 Cor 1:19.

[63] Cf. Stendahl, *Final Account*, 38, on ἀπὸ μέρους as "sort of." According to the *TLG*, the phrase ἀπὸ μέρους appears approximately forty times up to and including the first century C.E. Of these, seven are in the LXX, two in Philo, five in Paul, and one in Josephus. Paul's own use perhaps suggests that a vague meaning "to some extent" might apply.

[64] Mark D. Nanos, *The Mystery of Romans: The Jewish Context of Paul's Letter* (Minneapolis: Fortress, 1996), 281 n. 118.

ὁ ῥυόμενος is an epithet frequently used to describe God is—for someone with Paul's Christology—no argument against a designation of Christ.[65] A reference to Christ is especially supported by Paul's instruction in 1 Thessalonians that we should wait for Ἰησοῦν τὸν ῥυόμενον ἡμᾶς ἐκ τῆς ὀργῆς τῆς ἐρχομένης (1 Thess 1:10). The data marshalled by Stanley in which God is ῥυόμενος simply provide further evidence for the high Christology of Paul in these chapters, rather than speaking against a reference to Jesus. The point made by Kavin Rowe and Ross Wagner about the Christology of chapter 10 applies here in chapter 11 as well: what we have here is, in Wagner's words, "Paul's careful interweaving of the identity of Jesus Christ with the identity of Israel's God."[66]

What then of his coming ἐκ Σιών? In line with the view outlined above, according to which the salvation of Israel takes place not en bloc at a moment at the very end of history, but through the course of the last days, I would take this to be a reference to the incarnation. A reference to the parousia does not seem likely to me, given what Paul has previously said about the salvation of Israel in the earlier part of chapter 11, still less, as Bruce Longenecker has shown, that Israel could be saved at the end without faith in Christ.[67] It also need not reflect a diaspora perspective, as some have argued.[68] Lloyd Gaston is also probably right to say that it is too contrived to see Jesus qua stumbling stone departing from Zion, because Jesus in Romans 11 here is coming qua deliverer.[69] Rather, it could very well be taken as a standard Messianic reference. The coming would then be a reference to the incarnation, with ἥξει in the future because it was in the future from the prophet's perspective.[70] One can compare Numbers 24:17, "a star will arise ἐξ Ιακωβ and a man [MT: scepter] rise up ἐξ Ισραηλ,"

65 As argued by C. D. Stanley, "'The Redeemer Will Come ἐκ Σιών': Romans 11:26-27 Revisited," in *Paul and the Scriptures of Israel*, ed. C. A. Evans and J. A. Sanders, JSNTSup (Sheffield: Sheffield Academic, 1993), 118–42, 137–38.

66 Wagner, "'Not from the Jews Only,'" 429 n. 50. See also C. K. Rowe, "Romans 10:13: What Is the Name of the Lord?" *HBT* 22 (2000): 135–73.

67 Longenecker, "Different Answers to Different Issues," 99–101.

68 Stanley, "'Redeemer Will Come ἐκ Σιών,'" 138; Wagner, *Heralds of the Good News*, 284: "Paul's quotation depicts the Lord's coming in person *from* a restored Zion to bring deliverance to his people who are scattered among the nations."

69 Gaston, *Paul and the Torah*, 144.

70 This perspective, from which the speaker of the oracle speaks during a time in which the oracle is not yet fulfilled, is also found in, e.g., Rom 9:7, 9, 12, 25-26, 27-28.

or Isaiah 11:1, "and a staff will come forth ἐκ τῆς ῥίζης Ιεσσαι and a flower will go up ἐκ τῆς ῥίζης." In this light, it is perfectly natural that Paul should take Jesus to come as redeemer ἐκ Σιών, not least because he has stated at the beginning of the argument that Christ came ἐξ the Israelites (9:4-5); indeed, at the very start of Romans, he is defined as ἐκ σπέρματος Δαυὶδ κατὰ σάρκα (Rom 1:3). Christ's point of origin in Romans 11, again κατὰ σάρκα at any rate, is Zion, the headquarters of Israel.

Conclusion

With Paul's conclusion here, then, we come full circle. In Romans 9:1-5, we saw that the implication of Paul's imaginary spiritual suicide is that Israel is cut off, ἀνάθεμα . . . ἀπὸ τοῦ Χριστοῦ, despite the fact that Israel had given birth to this very Christ, at least physically speaking. He came ἐξ the Israelites, yet his own received him not, because they did not recognize that he is actually "God over all." It was this lack of recognition that provoked the possible response that the word of God had failed. The first indication that confutes this objection is that Israel's condition, far from contradicting Scripture, in fact fulfills Scripture: this is not least because according to Romans 9 Isaiah foresaw God both installing Christ in Zion in order to trip Israel over, and bringing Gentiles to believe "upon" Christ and to rest upon him as a sure foundation. For those Gentiles, Christ in Romans 10 stands at the end of the race, granting the prize of righteousness miraculously to those who had not left the starting blocks. The salvation of these Gentiles has been the result of apostolic proclamation, as Christ has passed—enveloped in the word—from apostolic mouths to the ears and hearts of others, and ultimately to those others' mouths as well. Hence, he need not be searched for up in heaven or down in the abyss but rather is very "near" in chapter 10.

Coming to the end of the argument in Romans 11, then, we see two things. First, Israel's condition will in the end be reversed, no longer ἀνάθεμα . . . ἀπὸ τοῦ Χριστοῦ, but saved. Second, the coming of Christ may have temporarily exercised a hardening function and Christ may have served in the first instance more as stumbling stone, but the coming of Christ ἐκ Σιών at the incarnation has as its *ultimate* goal this salvation of his people, Jacob. And all this takes place not in opposition to, but in fulfillment of, the word of God—which has not failed.

In these chapters, then, Paul's interest in Christ is in his "nearness" to those who call upon his name, but his distance from Israel as a nation. This is only a distance from one point of view, however, because in another sense Christ is emphatically located in Israel, in Zion, though as a stumbling block. This is because God has in part relocated Christ as a saving presence outside of Israel, though this has the subsequent aim of fulfilling the purpose of Christ's incarnation and his coming forth in Israel—namely, Israel's salvation.

Romans 9–11 then, rather than being "Christology-light," in fact provides a unique perspective on Paul's Christology not really found in the same concentration anywhere else. It provides a perspective on Christ's locations that can supplement the standard topics of discussion such as "how divine" Paul's Christology is and what functions Paul sees Christ as carrying out. As we have seen, in Romans 9–11 Christ occupies a number of different locations. These locations might not be as numerous as those in Gerard Manley Hopkins' poem "As Kingfishers Catch Fire," in which "Christ plays in ten thousand places," but he is found in Romans 9–11 nevertheless to play in quite a lot of places.

6

Not the End

The History and Hope of the Unfailing Word in Romans 9–11

Jonathan A. Linebaugh

> The whole of history [is] a concealed witness, a riddle that cannot be solved, without plowing with another heifer than our reason.
>
> —Johann Georg Hamann[1]

Paul knows the future. That, at least, is what the contrast between the present Paul describes in Romans 9 and 10 and the mystery he unveils in Romans 11:25-32 suggests. With grief, pain, and prayer (9:2; 10:1), Paul confronts the apparent collateral damage of the "word" by which God has "called a not-my people, my people" (9:25): the advent and proclamation of Israel's Christ (9:5; 10:14-18) has occasioned Israel's stumble (9:32; cf. 11:11). In the words of Romans 3:3, "some did not believe" (ἀπιστέω); and in Romans 9–11 that "some" sounds more like "most" (9:27; 11:2-5, 7). The Israelites, Paul's "kindred according to the flesh" (9:3; cf. 11:1), to whom "belong the adoption, the glory, the covenants, the giving of the law, the promises, and the patriarchs" (9:4-5), are, in Paul's present, "hardened" (11:25) and "disobedient" (10:21; 11:30-32); they are, through unbelief (ἀπιστία, 11:20, 23), like branches broken off from the root that the sustains their life (11:17). "Great sorrow" and "unceasing anguish" indeed.

But what did Bob Dylan say? "When you're standing at the crossroads / that you cannot comprehend / just remember that death is not the end." Paul, in Romans 9–11, is standing at a crossroads, and Paul remembers: "now" is "not the end." While the present requires two

[1] J. G. Hamann, *Sämtliche Werke*, 6 vols., ed. J. Nadler (Vienna: Herder, 1949–1957), 2:65.

terms to describe Israel, the "remnant" (11:5) and "the rest" (11:7), this is, for Paul, the middle rather than the end of history: it is a "now" that persists only "until." And it is that "until," described in Romans 11:25 as "until the fullness of the Gentiles comes in," that names the horizon of hope: "all Israel will be saved" (11:26).

It is here, however, that the sphinx of Romans 11 poses its riddle: How does Paul know the future? By what theological and emotional path does Paul travel from the anguished prayer that opens chapters 9 and 10 to the euphoric poem that closes chapter 11? How, to put it plainly, does Paul know "all Israel will be saved"? As Ernst Käsemann asked the question, how can "the long detour" of Romans 9–10 be understood as a "meaningful and necessary" road to Romans 11:25-32?[2] At its root, this question about the relationship between Romans 9–10 and Romans 11 is a specific way of asking the perennial question about the relationship between, in Käsemann's words, justification and salvation history: is Paul's soteriology a subplot that finds its meaning within the story of God, Israel, and the nations, or is the gift of Jesus that calls sinners righteous the hermeneutical unveiling, the event in time that gives meaning and voice to all times?[3] To get at this question, however, I ask a more specific question: is Paul's revelation about the salvation of "all Israel" commensurable with the pattern of thought developed in Romans 9–10, or does it stand in irresolvable tension with the arguments that precede it? Proponents of the latter reading are not without evidence. If Paul's insistence that the "word of God has not failed" (9:6a) is not disqualified by the reduction of Israel to a remnant, is it not confused to assume, as Romans 11:11-32 seems to, that God's faithfulness will mean the erasing of the line between the remnant and the rest?[4] Does not the assertion that Israel is "loved on account of their fathers" (11:28) revert to precisely the genealogical

[2] E. Käsemann, *Commentary on Romans*, trans. G. W. Bromiley (Grand Rapids: Eerdmans, 1980), 314.

[3] E. Käsemann, "Justification and Salvation History in the Epistle to the Romans," in *Perspectives on Paul* (Philadelphia: Fortress, 1971), 60–78. For a discussion of this theme, and Käsemann's reading of justification more generally, see esp. P. F. M. Zahl, *Die Rechtfertigungslehre Ernst Käsemann* (Stuttgart: Calwer, 1996).

[4] See T. Donaldson, "'Riches for the Gentiles' (Romans 11:12): Israel's Rejection and Paul's Gentile Mission," *JBL* 12 (1993): 81–98: "while in Romans 9:1–11:10 the thrust of the argument is that the present situation is in no way inconsistent with God's promises to Israel, the argument from 11:11 proceeds on the assumption that the present situation has to be overcome if God is to be proved faithful" (89).

calculation of election that Romans 9:6-13 dismantled ("it is not the children of the flesh who are the children of God," says 9:8)?[5] Is it not the case that the juxtaposition of theses such as "there is no difference between Jew and Greek" (10:12) and "all Israel will be saved" (11:26) reflects a wrestling with the dual themes of God's impartiality and Israel's election that ends, not in a satisfying answer, but in an antimony?[6]

This chapter is a "no" to these questions. Unexpected though Paul's confidence about Israel's future feels in the wake of his grief and prayer, it is a confidence about the future forged in the history of God's word in the present and the past. At its core, the contention of Romans 9:6–11:10 is that the divine economy reflected in Israel's Scriptures is consonant with the habits of divine action that characterize Paul's present: as "the one who calls" (9:11), God is and has been "the one who has mercy" (9:16). Considered in conversation with the voices of Israel's historians and prophets, the surprising dealings of God in the present look less like an aberration than a modus operandi—a pattern that unites past and present and thereby reveals the rhyme scheme of history in all its tenses. And here, in the harmony of history present and past, is the ground of Paul's hope: God is the one who has mercy; God was the one who has mercy; God will be the one who has mercy. Because the present and the past it makes legible are connected by the operations of God's unconditioned and incongruous mercy, the witness of history in present and past tenses engender, to borrow a phrase from Johann Georg Hamann, "a like hope," a confidence that the future will rhyme with the present and the past as God's promise once again performs the miracle of mercy: "and this will be my covenant with them: I will take away their sins" (11:27).

[5] Cf. B. W. Longenecker, "Different Answers to Different Issues: Israel, the Gentiles and Salvation History in Romans 9–11," *JSNT* 36 (1989): 95–123.

[6] For this theme, see especially C. Cosgrove, *Elusive Israel: The Puzzle of Election in Romans* (Louisville, Ky.: Westminster John Knox, 1997), 27–38, 65–90. For variations of the thesis that Rom 11:11-32, or at least Rom 11:25-27, is ultimately incompatible with Rom 9:6–10:21 (or 9:6–11:10), see H. Räisänen, "Paul, God, and Israel: Romans 9–11 in Recent Research," in *The Social World of Formative Christianity and Judaism: Festschrift for H. C. Kee*, ed. J. Neusner et al. (Philadelphia: Fortress, 1988), 178–208; J. Lambrecht, "Israel's Future according to Romans 9–11: An Exegetical and Hermeneutical Approach," in *Pauline Studies* (Leuven: Peeters, 1994), 34–54; M. Wolter, "Das Israelproblem nach Gal 4:21-31 und Röm 9–11," *ZTK* 107 (2010): 1–30, 25–29. Do, however, see Wolter's chapter in this volume. I should note, too, that he said in our discussion of his paper that he would deny that Romans 9–10 and Romans 11 are in "contradiction" but would use the terms "tension" and "inconsistent."

My thesis then: Paul knows the future because he knows the present and the past. It is the pattern of divine action that is revealed in the present and read in the past that Paul promises as the future. Tracing this movement means standing with Paul in his present and, from that now of pain and grief, following his gaze, first backward as he rereads Israel's Scriptures, and then forward as he imagines Israel's salvation. Paul's promise, "all Israel will be saved" (11:26), is made at and as the end of this dynamic interplay between present, past, and future. Hope, you might say, is the child of history, and for Paul, in Romans 9–11, it is the union of history present and past that makes a promise: now is "not the end."

The Present

Strange reversals shape Paul's present: Israel has stumbled in their race to "the law of righteousness" (9:31; cf. 11:9, 11), while Gentiles, without running, find themselves at the finish line of the "righteousness of faith" (9:30; cf. 10:4, 20); whereas Israel is hardened (11:25), reduced to a remnant (9:27-29; 11:5; cf. 11:7-10), disobedient (10:21; 11:30-32), and disconnected from their life-giving root (11:17), the Gentiles, though not God's people and unloved, are called "my people," "loved," and "children of the living God" (9:25-26). Vis-à-vis the nations, this signals the success of Paul's Gentile mission (cf. 11:13); but it is, at the same time, a source of sorrow: "I am not lying," says Paul, "I have great pain and constant anguish" and "my heart's desire and prayer to God for them is that they may be saved" (9:2; 10:1).[7]

[7] The pathos here confirms Wolter's observation that "das Israelproblem" is about Israel qua Israel rather than Israel as representative of some more general theological question ("Das Israelproblem," 20–21). This resists the tendency to make Israel into a Pauline parable of either sin (e.g., Paul's critique of justification by works "strikes the hidden Jew in all of us") or salvation (e.g., Israel's redemption in Romans 11 is an illustration of the justification of the ungodly); see, respectively, E. Käsemann, "Paul and Israel," in *New Testament Questions of Today* (London: SCM Press, 1969), 183–87, 186 and *Commentary on Romans*, 260, 266, 317. This recalls the method of Moses Mendelssohn, who attempts to express Judaism as a natural, rational, and universal religion by filtering out the contextual and historical elements (the "temporal truths of history," in Lessing's phrase), leaving a religion that is supposedly identical to the "eternal truths" deducible through reason (*Jerusalem oder über religiöse Macht und Judentum* [Berlin: Friedrich Maurer, 1783]). This tendency to make Israel a representation or cipher rather than allow the concreteness of history to stand, together with all instances of reducing people (or better: persons) to a parable, are liable to Hamann's critique of Mendelssohn: he "severs . . . the temporal from the eternal"

Romans 9–11 is written from this open wound, but in this now of pain and prayer Paul also makes a promise: "The word of God has not failed."[8] As we will consider below, this means that the past history of God's word shares a shape with the surprises of Paul's present (9:6b-29; 11:1-10), but it also indicates that, for Paul, the paradoxes of what he calls "the now time" (11:5), far from disqualifying God's faithfulness, lay bare the grammar of God's word: God's word performs what it promises, both "carrying out" the divine "sentence" (9:27) and calling without condition (9:25-26). That Paul locates this double effect both in the present and as an effect of God's word is evident as he reapplies the voice of Hosea to describe the calling of the Gentiles—"her who was not loved I will call 'loved'" (9:25-26)—and as the reduction of Israel to a remnant is heard as the content of Isaiah's cry: "Though the number of the sons of Israel be as the sand of the sea, only a remnant of them will be saved" (9:27-29).[9] This suggests that, for Paul, as he reads his current and canonical history together, there is a twofold relation between past and present. First, the present is consistent with the scriptural past: as "Scripture says of Elijah . . . in the same way there is, at the present time, a remnant" (11:3, 5). Second, the present is the proper tense for the voice of Israel's prophets: Israel's stumble is occasioned by the placement of Isaiah's promised "rock of offense"

---

and leaves, where there was a living whole, "two dead halves" ("Golgotha and Scheblimini," in *Hamann: Writings on Philosophy and Language*, ed. K. Haynes [Cambridge: Cambridge University Press, 2007], 164–204, 179).

[8] For the programmatic significance of Rom 9:6a for Rom 9–11 as a whole, see C. E. B. Cranfield, *A Critical and Exegetical Commentary on the Epistle to the Romans*, 2 vols., ICC (Edinburgh: T&T Clark, 1979), 2:473; E. Lohse, *Der Brief an die Römer*, KEK 4 (Göttingen: Vandenhoek & Ruprecht, 2003), 270; cf. J. Flebbe's observation that Romans 9:6a indicates that, for Paul, the "Israelproblem" is also and more deeply a "Gottesfrage" (*Solus Deus: Untersuchungen zur Rede von Gott im Brief des Paulus an die Römer*, BZNW 158 [Berlin: Walter de Gruyter, 2008], 268–69).

[9] For Paul's appropriation of Hos 2:25 and 2:21 in Rom 9:25 and 9:26, respectively, see J. R. Wagner, "'Not from the Jews Only, but Also from the Gentiles': Mercy to the Nations in Romans 9–11," in *Between Gospel and Election*, ed. F. Wilk and J. R. Wagner, WUNT 257 (Tübingen: Mohr Siebeck, 2010), 417–31, 422. For the remnant motif indicating judgment in Romans 9:24-33, see F. Wilk, *Die Bedeutung des Jesajabuches für Paulus*, FRLANT 179 (Göttingen: Vandenhoeck & Ruprecht, 1998), 186; cf. U. Wilckens, *Der Brief an die Römer*, 3 vols., EKKNT (Zürich: Benziger Verlag and Neukirchener-Vluyn: Neukirchener Verlag, 1978–1982), 2:198; Lohse, *Der Brief an die Römer*, 276, 283.

(9:33, fusing Isa 8:14 to Isa 28:16),[10] and the Gentiles' reception of righteousness (9:30) is God's "yes and amen" to Hosea's prophecy: "in the very place where it was said of them, 'You are not my people,' there they will be called 'children of the living God'" (9:26; Hos 2:1).

As Paul listens to Israel's prophets, however, he hears more than a promised future that is his present; he hears an announcement that the future will be the aftermath of an event. The prophets, in other words, as Paul lets them speak in the present tense, say that salvation and stumbling are the double effect of a single cause. This is, perhaps, most evident as Paul invites Isaiah to provide the color commentary for the race to righteousness he announces in Romans 9:30-33. In a competition that Calvin describes as a "singular paradox,"[11] the "Gentiles, who did not pursue righteousness, attained righteousness," while "Israel, running after the law of righteousness, did not catch up with the law" (9:30-31). A bizarre result, to be sure; but as Paul reads Isaiah from the finish line, he discovers that this surprise is in Scripture. By adding the words "stumbling" and "rock" from Isaiah 8:14 to Isaiah 28:16, Paul, as Francis Watson notes, "creates a text that announces a forthcoming divine act with two contrasting outcomes":[12] "Behold, I am laying in Zion a stone of stumbling, and a rock of offense; and whoever believes in him will not be put to shame" (Rom 9:33). God, Paul hears Isaiah say, will place a stone that will simultaneously occasion stumbling and salvation.[13] Well . . . for Paul, what's promised is

[10] The lexemes that Paul lifts from Isa 8:14 are πρόσκομμα and πέτραν. For a full discussion of Paul's textual emendations to Isa 28:16 and an accompanying suggestion that Paul was writing from "a Septuagint text that had been reworked . . . to bring it closer to a Hebrew exemplar," see J. R. Wagner, *Heralds of the Good News: Isaiah and Paul in Concert in the Letter to the Romans*, NovTSup 101 (Leiden: Brill, 2002), 130.

[11] J. Calvin, "Acts 14–28 and Romans 1–6," in *Calvin's Commentaries*, trans. J. Owen (Grand Rapids: Baker, 2003), 19:377.

[12] F. Watson, *Paul, Judaism, and the Gentiles: Beyond the New Perspective* (Grand Rapids: Eerdmans, 2007), 323.

[13] For the future form of καταισχύνω as a reference to final judgment and thus as a reference to eschatological salvation when qualified by the negative particle (οὐ), see R. Bultmann, "αἰσχύνω κτλ," in *Theological Dictionary of the New Testament*, ed. G. Kittel, trans. G. W. Bromiley (Grand Rapids: Eerdmans, 1964), 1:189. For Israel's stumble as the result of intentional divine action, see M. Theobald, *Studien zum Römerbrief*, WUNT 136 (Tübingen: Mohr Siebeck, 2001), 374–78; F. Avemarie, "Israels rätselhafter Ungehorsam: Römer 10 als Anatomie eines von Gott provozierten Unglaubens," in Wilk and Wagner, *Between Gospel and Election*, 299–320.

present: the rock has reduced Israel to a remnant as it has, at the same time, created a "my people" out of the Gentiles.

Paul's diagnosis of his present does not stop here, however; it is more concrete—it is, in a word, more christological. While Romans 9–11 invites us to say, as Käsemann does, that "Salvation history is . . . the history of the word which . . . accomplishes election and rejection,"[14] Paul, in Romans 10, is more particular: the word that both calls and cuts short is, in Paul's phrases, "the word of faith that we proclaim" (10:8); it is "the word of Christ" (10:17). For Paul, the word of God that has not failed, the word spoken by the prophets and fulfilled in Paul's present, is active now as the apostolic announcement of Jesus Christ. Where Isaiah speaks of "those who proclaim good news" (Isa 52:7; Rom 10:15) and "the message" (Isa 53:1; Rom 10:16), Paul hears a reference to the preaching of "the gospel" (Rom 10:16). And it is this gospel, this "word of Christ," that is the agent of judgment and grace as rejection and election are concretely realized in and as unbelief and faith: "not all have obeyed the gospel" (10:16) and, conversely, "faith comes by hearing" (10:17).

This means, on the one hand, that Israel's stumble is the failure to "submit to the righteousness of God revealed in Christ" (10:3-4); the symptoms of Israel's "spirit of stupor" (11:8) are the pursuit of the law "as if by works" (9:32) and ignorance (10:2) of the "Christ" who "is the end of the law" (10:4); the "ears that would not hear" (11:8) can listen to Moses' words about "the righteousness of the law" as a summons to life via the law (10:5), but they are deaf to the presence of Christ in the promise spoken by the "righteousness of faith": "The word is near you" (10:6-8). However one reads the disputed references to "works," "law," and "their own righteousness," it is evident that Israel, according to Paul's diagnosis, assumes that God's calculation of righteousness will factor in their nomistic privileges and/or practices whereas Paul insists that in the divine economy the only currency is Christ.[15] This is, to the Jew, an offense, because in rendering their possession and observance of the law irrelevant for salvation, Paul effectively voids

[14] Käsemann, *Commentary on Romans*, 273.

[15] Käsemann, *Commentary on Romans*, 277, 281–82 and Cranfield, *Epistle to the Romans*, 2:515 articulate the view that Paul's critique is of a nomistic practice, which is problematic both because of transgression and, more deeply, because of the *ambitio divinitatis* that motives it. For the view that Paul's polemic targets a presumption rooted in Israel's privileges, especially election and the possession of the law, see, e.g., J. D. G. Dunn, *Romans*, 2 vols., WBC 38 (Dallas: Word, 1988), 2:595.

the soteriological value of what John Barclay calls "their pre-existing capital."[16] But this offense is, at the same time, an open door: "there is no distinction between Jew and Greek; for the same Lord is Lord of all, bestowing his riches on all who call on him" (10:12).

Here is the other side of the christological coin: though offensive in its unconditional distribution, the wealth of God given in Christ is, precisely because of its unconditional operations, given to all. This can be seen as much in the call that chooses the remnant as in the call that creates beloved children from the Gentiles. For Paul, Isaiah's promise that "a remnant will be saved" (Isa 10:22; Rom 9:27) is fulfilled in the present existence of "a remnant chosen according to grace" (Rom 11:5). This grace, defined negatively by the clause "not by works" (11:6), connects the call of the remnant both, as we will see below, to the "calling-into-being of Israel"[17] and to the current calling of the Gentiles. Like those who did "not bow the knee to Baal" in the time of Elijah because God acted, saying "I have kept for myself" (11:2-4),[18] like Jacob who was chosen "not because of works but because of him who calls" (9:11), and like the Gentiles who in contrast to Israel "did not pursue righteousness . . . as if by works" (9:30, 32), the remnant is constituted not "by works," but according to a grace that is active when works are absent and/or irrelevant (11:6).[19] This grace, as just noted, is the rock that causes those who race for righteousness "as if by works" to stumble (9:31-32), but it is also, in a world in which "none is righteous" (Rom 3:10) and God "has imprisoned all in disobedience" (11:32), the only rock on which to stand. Because Christ is present in the word without assistance or condition, because he is "near" without being brought either down from heaven or up from the abyss (10:6-8), God's grace can be defined in antithesis to works and as the gift of Christ to all (10:12; 11:6; cf. 9:11). The remnant exists, in other words, not because they, in distinction from the "rest," have

[16] J. M. G. Barclay, *Paul and the Gift* (Grand Rapids: Eerdmans, 2015). How this voiding relates to what appears to be its refunding in the references to election, the root, and the fathers in Romans 11 will be explored below.

[17] B. R. Gaventa, "On the Calling-into-Being of Israel: Romans 9:6-29," in Wilk and Wagner, *Between Gospel and Election*, 255–69.

[18] Paul adds the reflexive pronoun to the divine speech of 3 Kgdms 19:18, thereby signaling an emphasis on divine initiative that is sharpened to exclusivity by the antithesis that follows: "by grace, not by works" (11:4, 6).

[19] The contrast here between ἔργα and χάρις also echoes Paul's description of the justification of Abraham in Rom 4:4-5.

met mercy's conditions, but because God, as the one who has mercy, is the one who calls without condition.[20]

As with Israel, so with the Gentiles, though whereas the grace that calls the remnant can be described as a *creatio continua*—an ever-present act of creation that keeps that which mercy has already created—the calling of the Gentiles, as Paul depicts it, is a *creatio ex nihilo*. Paul's own image is that of the non-runners winning the race to righteousness, but it is his revoicing of the prophets that most pointedly captures the paradox of God's creative call. Isaiah: "I have been found by those who did not seek me; I have shown myself to those who did not ask for me" (Isa 65:1; Rom 10:20). Hosea: "I will call the not my people, my people, and the not loved I will call loved. And in the place where it was said to them, 'You are not my people,' there they will be called 'children of the living God'" (Hos 2:23 and 2:1; Rom 9:25). These dramatic mismatches—not seeking but finding, not loved but loved, not asking but seeing, not a people but a people—reveal both the power and the pattern of God's word: God's word is creative and unconditioned—that is, it performs the promise it speaks, creating from the nothingness of the Gentiles beloved sons and daughters of God.

So far Paul's present. The prophets announced an event and its impact, a divine act that would mean both stumbling and salvation. These promises are, as we have seen, Paul's present: the cutting short of Israel and the incongruous calling of the Gentiles are the double effect of the one "word of Christ." It is, in other words, the preached Christ that both occasions and makes sense of the paradoxes of Paul's present. But what of his past? If the word of God that has not failed is both the scriptural word and the word of faith, if it is, in other words, spoken in the past and the present, then the creative and unconditioned word operative in the present must cohere with the habits of God's word in Israel's canonical history. Paul thus becomes, in Walter Benjamin's sense, "a historian," one who "grasps the constellation which his own era has formed with a definite earlier one."[21] In returning to Israel's

[20] Cf. J. Barclay's discussion of the remnant as a sign of God's mercy on the ungodly rather than God's preservation of the godly in "Paul's Story: Theology as Testimony," in *Narrative Dynamics in Paul: A Critical Assessment*, ed. B. W. Longenecker (Louisville, Ky.: Westminster John Knox, 2002), 133–56, 151–52.

[21] W. Benjamin, "Theses on the Philosophy of History," in *Illuminations: Essays and Reflections*, ed. H. Arendt, trans. H. Eiland and K. McLaughlin (Cambridge, Mass.: Harvard University Press, 1999), 253–64, 263, Thesis A.

scriptural past, Paul does not so much construct as uncover a history written with the grammar revealed in the gospel. He is, in other words, more reader than writer. And thus, while it is the word of Christ that makes legible the words of Scripture,[22] this, for Paul, is not a reason to forget the canonical past; rather, the christological legibility of Scripture is an invitation to read—to remember.[23]

The Past

"To articulate the past historically," writes Walter Benjamin, "means to seize hold of a memory as it flashes up at a moment of danger."[24] This captures the pathos of Romans 9–11, the grief and pain that prompt Paul to remember. But it also describes Paul's response to his "moment of danger": he seizes hold of a memory by rereading Israel's Scriptures. The present moment of danger is occasioned and shaped by God's creative and unconditioned word, a word Paul defines as "the word of Christ," which both reduces Israel to a remnant and creates a people by calling those who are no-people. For Paul, however, the word of God that has not failed has a past as well as a present: it is the word spoken to Abraham, "In Isaac your seed will be called" (Rom 9:7; Gen 21:12), and "I will come and Sarah will have a son" (Rom 9:9; Gen 18:14); it is the word spoken to Rebekah, "The older will serve the younger" (Rom 9:12; Gen 25:23); it is the word spoken to Moses, "I will have mercy on whom I have mercy" (Rom 9:15; Exod 33:19); it is the word spoken to Pharaoh, "For this reason I raised you up, that I might demonstrate my power in you" (Rom 9:17; Exod 9:16).

22 See my *God, Grace, and Righteousness in Wisdom of Solomon and Paul's Letter to the Romans: Texts in Conversation*, NovTSup 152 (Leiden: Brill, 2013), 177–226.

23 For Paul, then, unlike G. E. Lessing, Israel's Scripture is not an "antiquated" "primer" or once helpful "hint" that can be "dispensed with" in the evolution of "the education of the human race" (*Lessing's Theological Writings*, trans. H. Chadwick [Stanford, Calif.: Stanford University Press, 1957], 82–98, 97, 91, 94). Hamann, riffing on Lessing, is closer to the Pauline suggestion that the time of the gospel, rather than rendering Israel's Scriptures outdated, opens the present as a new time of reading: "the entire history of the Jewish people [is] a living, mind- and heart-rousing primer of all historical literature in heaven, on and under the earth,—an adamantine hint forward to the Jubilee year" ("Golgotha and Scheblimini," 191–92). For Lessing, Christ comes to "tear the exhausted primer from the child's hand" (91); for Hamann, the scriptural scrolls are sealed until Christ comes and breaks them, but this breaking of seals is the opening of the scrolls and thus an invitation to read them—a point reflected in the allusive texture of the Pauline texts (not least Romans 9–11).

24 Benjamin, "Theses on the Philosophy of History," 255 Thesis VI.

These scriptural words, for Paul, are not just a record of the past; they are a promise. According to Romans 1:1-4, Paul reads the "holy Scriptures" as a pre-saying of the gospel (cf. Gal 3:8), but, as Romans 3:21 indicates, the hermeneutical transition from promise to witness occurs in the "now" of the revelation of God's righteousness in and as the event Paul calls "the redemption that is in Christ Jesus" (3:21-24). In the words of Romans 16:25-26, Scripture "now" (νῦν) speaks the mystery it long kept secret because the preaching of Jesus Christ unveils "the law and the prophets" (3:21) as witnesses to the gospel.[25] It is as the time of the preaching of Jesus Christ that Paul's present constitutes what Agamben calls Scripture's "now of legibility,"[26] the time at which the proclamation and impact of the gospel reveal, as if by retroactive echo, the "gospelness" of prior events.[27]

It is in this "now of legibility" that Paul rereads his canonical past, and what he hears is a history originated, ever newly created, and shaped by the same unconditioned and creative word at work in his present. Three antitheses structure Paul's interpretation of the material from Genesis and Exodus he considers. First, the ascription of sonship to Isaac by the words "through Isaac your seed will be called"

[25] For a similar account of Paul's hermeneutic, one that sees "Das Alte Testament als integraler Bestandteil des Evangelium" while insisting that the Old Testament is "ein integrales Element" of the gospel "in seiner *Interpretatio Christiana*," see F. Hahn, *Theologie des Neuen Testament*, 2 vols. (Tübingen: Mohr Siebeck, 2005), 1:195–201; cf. 2:38-142.

[26] G. Agamben, *The Time That Remains: A Commentary on the Letter to the Romans*, trans. P. Dailey (Stanford, Calif.: Stanford University Press, 2005), 145, uses the phrase "Das Jetzt der Lesbarkeit" to summarize and define the hermeneutic of Walter Benjamin. See W. Benjamin, "Theses on the Philosophy of History," in *Illuminations: Essays and Reflections*, trans. H. Zohn (New York: Schocken Books, 1968), 253–64; idem, *The Arcades*.

[27] J. D. Dawson, *Christian Figural Reading and the Fashioning of Identity* (Berkeley: University of California Press, 2002), 134. This relationship between scriptural past and christological present is adeptly described with the term typology as long as the "Innergeschichtlichkeit" of the *figura* and its fulfillment is maintained; so E. Auerbach, "Figura," *Istanbuler Schriften* 5, *Neue Dantestudien* (1944): 11–71, 54. Rather than dislocating a past event from its location in history and dissolving it into the antitype it anticipates, typology, as a description of Paul, is a description of the way the gospel unveils anticipations of itself in Israel's Scripture. For a different description of typology, see Agamben, who argues that the type/antitype conceptuality indicates "a caesura that divides the division between times . . . in which the past is dislocated into the present" and thus points to the "inseparable constellation" of types and antitypes (*Time That Remains*, 74).

means that "it is not the children of the flesh who are children of God, but the children of the promise are reckoned as his seed" (Rom 9:8). This curious notion of a promise giving birth recalls Paul's reading of the same narrative in Romans 4. There, the birth of Isaac is described as an act of resurrection in which the "God who gives life to the dead and calls into being that which does not exist" (4:17) creates life out of the deadness of Sarah's womb and Abraham's body (Rom 4:19). In Romans 9, Paul reads God's promise to Abraham as undercutting the assumption that being a child is determined by genealogy. In the case of Isaac, the status "son" is not constituted by parentage; it is called into being (καλέω, 9:7) by the "word of promise" (9:9). Isaac is a child of God because he is born as such by God's future-tense word: "I will come, and there will be . . ." (9:9). Read this way, the Isaac narrative underwrites Paul's thesis that "it is not the case that all who are descended from Israel are Israel" (9:6b) by demonstrating that, from their origins, Israelites are God's children, not on the basis of their genealogical relation to Abraham, but because they are, as the reformers liked to say, *creatura verbi Dei*.[28] Beverly Gaventa captures this: "the entity known as 'Israel' is not and never has been defined by birth but only by God's creation; it is not a biological but a theological category."[29] Just as Abraham was reckoned (λογίζομαι, 4:3, 5) righteous before and apart from works (4:1-13), so Isaac, irrespective of his parentage, is, by a promise, reckoned (λογίζομαι, 9:8) a child. The second generation of Israel, in other words, like the first, is called into being by the creative and unconditioned word of the one who both justifies the ungodly (4:5) and creates life out of death (4:17-19).

The third generation intensifies this. By recalling that Jacob and Esau are sons of the same sexual act (9:10), Paul emphasizes their similarity, thus accentuating his observation that the twins "are made dissimilar only by the divine words recorded in Scripture":[30] "The older

[28] Stephen Westerholm notes that Paul does not deny a relation between Abrahamic descent and divine election; he only insists that Abrahamic descent is not the basis for nor identical with being a child of God ("Paul and the Law in Romans 9–11," in *Paul and the Mosaic Law*, ed. J. D. G. Dunn (Grand Rapids: Eerdmans, 2001 [1996]), 215–37, 221–22.

[29] Gaventa, "On the Calling-into-Being of Israel," 259. Gaventa's broader argument in this section is that Paul is not apologizing for the current division within Israel but insisting that "the only Israel that exists is the one God brought into being through promise and call" (260).

[30] Watson, *Paul, Judaism, and the Gentiles*, 309–10.

will serve the younger" (Gen 25:23; Rom 9:12). Working from the scriptural word to Rebecca, "before the twins were born" and therefore before they "had done anything good or bad," Paul constructs his second antithesis: "not by works but by the one who calls" (9:11-12). For Paul, the timing of this promise as well as its content preclude any correlation between the divine decision and the worthiness of Jacob.[31] The emphasis here, as in the case of Isaac, is less on the "who" of election than the "how"—that is, Paul is tracing the pattern of election and interprets both the Isaac and the Jacob narratives as exemplifications of the unconditionality and initiative of God's word: God's choice does not respond to or recognize an antecedent human reality; it is, to quote Gaventa again, "an act of creation."[32] The purpose clause embedded in Romans 9:11 (ἵνα ἡ κατ' ἐκλογὴν πρόθεσις τοῦ θεοῦ μένῃ) accents this, concentrating the explanation for election exclusively in the pre-choice of God, the προ-prefix indicating that election precedes and therefore precludes any and all human criteria. Thus, as Paul reads the story of Jacob and Esau, he hears a word of election and rejection that neither corresponds to nor is contingent upon prior human difference. Jacob and Esau are the same; it is only God's choice that creates a difference. Rather than attempting to explain the rationale behind God's selection, Paul concludes with a ruthless restatement of God's pre-choice from Malachi: "Jacob I loved; Esau I hated" (Rom 9:13; Mal 1:2-3).

That this scriptural quotation is supposed to sting is confirmed by the question that follows: "What then shall we say, is there injustice

[31] Philo, alert to the destabilizing potential inherit in God's prenatal and unexplained choice of Jacob over Esau, appeals to divine foreknowledge and thus argues that while God's election of Jacob precedes his deeds, it is nevertheless proleptically based on them (*Leg. All.* 3.88–89). For this, see my "Rational or Radical: Origen on Romans 9:10-14," *Studia Patristica* 52 (2011), 63–69. Cf. Jub. 19 in which the antenatal choice is erased and the Jacob and Esau narrative is rewritten to highlight the correspondence between divine choice and human character.

[32] Gaventa, "On the Calling-into-Being of Israel," 260. As in the citation of Gen 21:21 in Rom 9:7, the use of καλέω here, especially as a divine predicate (ὁ καλῶν; 9:12), recalls the predication of God as ὁ καλῶν τὰ μὴ ὄντα ὡς ὄντα (Rom 4:17) and thereby evokes the creational connotations of the Pauline "calling" motif. For the creative connotations of καλέω in Paul, see S. J. Chester, *Conversion at Corinth: Perspectives on Conversion in Paul's Theology and the Corinthian Church*, SNTW (London: T&T Clark, 2003), 59–112.

with God?"[33] Paul's μὴ γένοιτο, however, is grounded not in an uncovering of the previously hidden criteria that distinguished Isaac from Ishmael and Jacob from Esau, but rather in God's words to Moses in the aftermath of the golden calf idolatry: "I will have mercy on whom I have mercy and I will have compassion on whom I have compassion" (Rom 9:15). As in the narrative of Exodus 32–34, for Paul, mercy is not the restoration of the righteous; it is the rebirth of the unrighteous, "the generative divine force that brings something into existence."[34] "Therefore," as Paul's third antithesis deduces from the Exodus quotation, "it is not of the one who wills, or of the one who runs, but of the God who has mercy" (9:16). The references to willing and running add human disposition and achievement to the list of excluded explanations for election, but the striking thing about this antithesis is not so much what is precluded as what is proposed. In tune with Paul's explanation of God's call solely in terms of God's identity as "the one who calls" (9:12), his accounting of the operations of mercy is reducible to a predication: God is "the one who has mercy."[35]

Mercy, however, is not the whole story. Scripture also speaks a word to Pharaoh: "For this reason I raised you up, so that I might demonstrate my power in you and so that my name might be proclaimed throughout the entire earth" (Rom 9:17; Exod 9:16).[36] Paul's silence about Pharaoh's role in the hardening of his own heart (see Exod 8:28; 9:34; 13:15; cf. 1 Sam 6:6) allows him to read God's word to Pharaoh as a counterpart to his word to Moses: "God has mercy on whom

[33] The history of interpretation of Rom 9:6-14 is, in part, a history of answering this question for Paul. Chrysostom, in his *Homiliae in epistulam ad Romanos*, Homily 16 on Rom 9, followed Philo and explained election in relation to divine foreknowledge. Origen, who, like Augustine after him (see, e.g., *De Spiritu et Littera*), read "not by works" as categorical rather than time-specific, still argued that the election of Jacob and rejection of Esau "did not happen without a reason" (*quomodo haec non extra rationem fiant*) Jacob was considered "worthy of God's love" before birth "according to the merits of his previous life" (*praecedentis videlicet vitae meritis*; *Princ.* 2.9.7).

[34] J. M. G. Barclay, "'I Will Have Mercy on Whom I Have Mercy': The Golden Calf and Divine Mercy in Romans 9–11 and Second Temple Judaism," *EC* 1 (2010): 82–106, 100. For Exodus 32–34 as an account of Israel's re-creation parallel to Genesis 6–10, see W. Moberly, *At the Mountain of God: Story and Theology in Exodus 32–34*, JSOTSup 22 (Sheffield: JSOT, 1983), 91–93.

[35] Cf. Wagner, *Heralds of the Good News*, 50–52.

[36] This is most likely an adapted quotation of Exodus 9:16 LXX, substituting ἐξεγείρω for διατηρέω and δύναμις for ἰσχύς; cf. Wagner, *Heralds of the Good News*, 55 n. 36.

he wills and hardens whom he wills" (9:18). Here, as in the contrast between love and hate in the Jacob and Esau narrative, the difference between mercy and hardening is reducible to the sheer fact that "God wills" (θέλει, 9:18). This duality is picked up in Paul's question about "vessels of wrath" and "vessels of mercy" in Romans 9:22-23. In this context, however, the two purpose clauses from God's word to Pharaoh (see the double ὅπως in Rom 9:17) seem to push the relationship between hardening and mercy "from symmetry to teleology."[37] God, as Paul insists by way of the image of the potter, is free to make different objects from the same lump of clay,[38] but his freedom is focused not on the destruction of "vessels of wrath"—an end that, notoriously, never occurs in the text—but on the revelation of "the riches of his glory upon the vessels of mercy." For Paul, the twofold effect of God's word is both asymmetrical, *enduring* vessels of wrath while *making known* his glory to vessels of mercy, and teleological: God "patiently endures the vessels of wrath . . . *in order to* (ἵνα) make known the wealth of his glory."

Mercy, then, while free and willed rather than natural and necessary as the potter motif recalls, is nevertheless, as Paul reads the canonical past, "the very fundament of history"[39]—that toward which the divine acts of hatred and hardening are directed. There is hope here. If Isaac and Jacob are called irrespective of their pedigree and performance (9:7-13), if Israel is reborn by mercy in the wake of idolatry (9:15-16), if God hardens in order to have mercy (9:17-23), then maybe the disobedient and hardened "rest" of Israel are not outside the range of God's unconditioned and re-creative grace. That the past and present grammar of God's word is one is evident as Paul connects the vessels of mercy with "us whom he calls, not only from the Jews but also from the Gentiles" (9:24). Like the present word of Christ that both reduces Israel to a remnant (9:27-29) and creates a people out of a no-people (9:25-26), the scriptural word both hardens and has mercy, both hates and loves. But if, as the call of the Gentiles reveals, "the word of Christ" says "loved" to those who not loved, then maybe there is hope on the far side of hatred and hardening. Maybe there is a future.

37 Watson, *Paul, Judaism, and the Gentiles*, 191.

38 For the potter motif as establishing divine freedom rather than denoting divine caprice, see R. Feldmeier, "Vater und Töpfer? Zur Identität Gottes im Römerbrief," in Wilk and Wagner, *Between Gospel and Election*, 377–90.

39 Barclay, "'I Will Have Mercy,'" 101.

The Future: "A Like Hope"

Romans 10 ends in crisis and in hope. Israel is still a "disobedient and contrary people," but Isaiah's image of God's outstretched arms leaves Paul's prayer for Israel unanswered yet open (10:21). Romans 11 makes a promise as an answer to this prayer: "all Israel will be saved" (11:26). This can feel jarring. The opening of Romans 11 says "no" to the question "has God rejected his people?" (11:1) by linking the current division within Israel between the remnant (11:1-6) and the rest (11:7-10) with, on the one hand, those God kept for himself in the time of Elijah and, on the other hand, imprecatory passages from Deuteronomy (29:4 LXX) and the Psalms (68:23-24 LXX). In Romans 11:11, however, Paul expresses a new hope—a horizon beyond the present division in which those who have stumbled are found to be within the sphere of God's mercy.

As noted in the introduction, it is here that some are inclined to call Paul's bluff, suggesting that the future he imagines for Israel is grounded either on nothing or the very premises he rejected to make sense of his present and past. Romans 9 is written to erase every "because" that could conceivably provide a human criterion that identifies or explains why God's mercy was attracted to an Isaac or Jacob rather than an Ishmael or Esau: not family, not social status, not works. In the void left by the denial of a rationale for election in terms of differentials in human worth, Paul names God: "the one who calls"; "the one who has mercy." Or again, in Romans 10, human action and initiative, whether it be ascending and descending, seeking and asking, or even observing the commandments, are excluded as explanations for the distribution of God's wealth. And again, where there is only nothingness in terms of the human canons of worth, Paul places one name: Jesus Christ (see 10:6, 7, 9; also vv. 11, 12, 13, 17).[40] But then there is Romans 11:28: Israel, as it concerns election, is loved on account of their ancestors. As Wagner remarks, this "appeal" to the patriarchs "has struck some interpreters as a *deus ex machina*,"[41] a wish

[40] For the christological references in Rom 10:11-13, see especially C. K. Rowe, "Romans 10:13: What Is the Name of the Lord?" *HBT* 22 (2000): 135–73; cf. my *God, Grace, and Righteousness*, 197–204.

[41] Wagner, "Mercy to the Nations," 429.

anchored in ancestry that forgets Paul's earlier insistence that "it is not the children of the flesh who are the children of God" (9:8).[42]

But the next verse tells a different story. Paul's argument does not run "all Israel will be saved because Israel is loved on account of their ancestors," but rather "Israel is loved on account of their ancestors *because* (γάϱ) the gifts and calling of God are irrevocable" (11:29).[43] Here, as in Romans 9, it is God's gifts and God's call, not Israel's ancestors, that ground election. As Barclay writes in relation to the identity of the "root" in the olive tree metaphor (11:17-24), "What matters about the patriarchs is that they were rendered significant by a grace and calling which bore no relation to their intrinsic worth." It is not the "patriarchs themselves" that sustain Israel or engender Paul's hope; it is "the calling or election of God," his "unconditioned favor."[44] By anchoring his hope for Israel in God's grace and call, Paul connects the future with the present, linking Israel with both the remnant chosen by grace and the Gentiles who are God's people and loved because of God's call. At the same time, this future-by-grace also evokes Israel's creation-by-grace, thereby uniting Israel's origin and destiny: as Israel was called into being by a word of unconditioned mercy, so Israel, though hardened and disobedient now, will be reborn by the unconditioned grace and creative call of God.

Hence my thesis: Paul's hope is anchored in history. But "history," as Hamann puts it, "is a sealed book, a concealed witness, a riddle that cannot be solved."[45] Paul's promise that "all Israel will be saved" is not

[42] One way to circumvent this apparent tension is to read "all Israel" in Romans 11:26 as a reference to the one people of God, Gentile as well as Jewish believers; so N. T. Wright, "The Letter to the Romans," in *The New Interpreter's Bible*, ed. L. E. Keck (Nashville: Abingdon, 2002), 10:620–99; Wright, *Paul and the Faithfulness of God*, 2 vols. (Minneapolis: Fortress, 2013), 1:1239–45. This interpretation is unlikely, however, as it leaves the division between the remnant and rest untouched, requires "Israel" to have two meanings in 11:25-26, is unable to account for the contrast between the "part" of Israel that is currently hardened and the "all" Israel that will be saved, and fails to make meaningful Paul's references to the "acceptance" and "fullness" of Israel (11:12, 15).

[43] On the grounding of Israel's elected belovedness in the call and grace of God, see Wagner's chapter in this volume. Note especially his translation of Rom 11:29: "For God does not repent of his calling and gifts."

[44] Barclay, *Paul and the Gift*, 550: "everywhere Paul discusses the patriarchs he is concerned to elucidate not *that* they were the origin of Israel, but *how* this was the case (Gal 3:6-19; 4:21-31; Rom 4:1-23; 9:6-13)."

[45] Hamann, "Socratic Memorabilia," in *Sämtliche Werke*, 2.65.

the obvious end to a story he's read from beginning to middle. Rather, for Paul, the past as much as the future is revealed. To borrow from Oswald Bayer, Paul's historiography works "from a key event that discloses the meaning of all events that come before and after it."[46] It is as God reveals himself in the gift of Jesus Christ as the one who gives irrespective of human prerequisites that Israel's scriptural past becomes legible as a history of *this* God and *this* grace. Israel's history, in other words, echoes Paul's christological present: as unveiled in the giving of Jesus, God is and has been the one whose grace is operative at the point of sin, nothingness, and death and as the gift that brings salvation, creation, and life (cf. Rom 4:5, 17). Jesus, to use the language of Romans 10, is the "word" (10:8, 17) that unearths the grammar of all God's words.[47] The present and the past, as revealed in Jesus and read in Scripture, is a history of the God who is speaking and has spoken in but one style: the grammar of grace. And it is here, in this history, that there is "a like hope": the word of mercy that now calls the Gentiles and has always created Israel will be the word that regrafts (11:23-24) and resurrects (11:15) "the rest" (11:7).

The history Paul promises as Israel's future, then, like the present and the past, is the history of God's word. As is the case with the Gentiles and the remnant, and as was the case in Israel's formation and history, the future is determined by God's call (11:29; 9:7, 12, 25-26), God's election (11:28; 9:11; 11:5, 7), God's mercy (11:30-32; 9:15-18), and God's grace (11:29; 11:5). The earlier uses of these words reveal particular definitions that Paul deduces from God's gift of Jesus: God calls without condition; his election precedes and precludes all human criteria; his mercy is not the restoration of the righteous but the re-creation of the sinful; and his grace is what he gives in giving Jesus (i.e., peace to enemies, salvation to sinners, justification to the ungodly, and life to the dead; cf. Romans 5:6-10, 17-18).

46 O. Bayer, *Theology the Lutheran Way*, ed. and trans. J. G. Silcock and M. C. Mattes, Lutheran Quarterly Books (Eerdmans: Grand Rapids, 2007), 200.

47 Cf. Hamann's reference to "the *stylus curiae* of the kingdom of heaven," "Cloverleaf of Hellenistic Letters, First Letter," in *Hamann: Writings on Philosophy and Language*, 35–42, 40. Cf. idem, "Gedanken über meinen Lebenslauf": "I found the unity of the divine will in the redemption of Jesus Christ, so that all history . . . and works of God flowed towards this center." See also U. Luz, *Das Geschichtsverständnis des Paulus* (Munich: Kaiser Verlag, 1968), 82: "Im Lichte der eschatologischen Gnade Gottes wird für Paulus die Einheit des Heilshandelns Gottes durch die Geschichte hindurch sichtbar" (I was directed to this reference by John Barclay).

The recurrence of this vocabulary as Paul imagines Israel's future is an indication that the salvation of Israel will share this shape. Israel is now an enemy (11:28), disobedient (11:31-32), guilty of transgression (11:12), sinful (11:27), ungodly (11:26), lost (11:15), and in need of nothing less than life (11:15). And it is this Israel—disobedient, hardened, stumbling, excluded, and broken off—that Paul promises God will accept (11:15), include (11:12), forgive (11:27), save (11:26; cf. 11:14), have mercy upon (11:31-32), and resurrect (11:15).

That the future Paul promises is patterned by the same unconditioned grace revealed in the christological present and thereby made legible in Israel's Scripture indicates that the salvation of Israel is not, for Paul, a soteriological sleight of hand, some dream that will not die even if Paul's own arguments have killed it. Rather, the gospel of Jesus Christ uncovers the grammar of God's word and thus illuminates the "gospelness" not just of the past but of the future. The God who is and has been the one who, in mercy, raises the dead and justifies the ungodly (cf. Rom 4:5, 17) will be the one who resurrects and redeems Israel (Rom 11:15, 26). And in fact, for Paul, this is easier to imagine than the current miracle of grace at work in the calling of the Gentiles. Through the repeated use of "greater to lesser" rhetoric, Paul asks if the Gentiles, though wild branches, are grafted onto the cultivated olive tree, "how much more" (πόσῳ μᾶλλον) will the God who is able to regraft natural branches (11:23) do exactly that (11:24). Or again: if Israel's trespass and loss mean wealth and reconciliation for the world, "how much more" (πόσῳ μᾶλλον) will their "fullness" and "acceptance" mean (11:12, 15)?[48]

More important for our purposes than *that* Paul knows Israel's future, however, is *how* he knows it. The "greater to lesser" logic suggests not just that Paul has always assumed the story ends with Israel's salvation, but that the nature of grace seen in the unconditioned call of the Gentiles reveals the grammar of God's word and thus engenders the assurance that the ever unexpected yet ever spoken word of mercy will again be addressed to Israel. In this sense, the histories of Israel and the Gentiles are deeply interwoven. Israel's trespass occasions the Gentiles' salvation, which in turn has the potential to provoke Israel to jealousy (11:11).[49] There is one root and one olive tree, but God,

[48] Cf. Wagner, "'Not from the Jews Only,'" 429.

[49] For the jealousy motif, see R. H. Bell, *Provoked to Jealousy: The Origin and Purpose of the Jealousy Motif in Romans 9–11*, WUNT 63 (Tübingen: Mohr Siebeck, 1994).

with an arboricultural approach as unnerving and hopeful as his grace, breaks off the natural branches (Israel) to make room for the wild branches (the Gentiles), and yet is both able and intending to regraft those branches he has broken off (11:17-24). Israel's disobedience has led to the reception of mercy by the disobedient Gentiles, and somehow this mercy generates a "momentum"[50] that will also mean mercy for Israel (11:30-31). It is notable that in these interwoven histories, neither Israel nor the Gentiles become the subject of salvific verbs: "salvation belongs to the Lord," suggests Paul's grammar.[51] In the case of the Gentiles it is, as Wagner writes, "not as active agents, but . . . as recipients of blessings promised to Israel that these Gentiles provoke God's people."[52] Similarly, while Gentiles are shown mercy because of Israel's disobedience, it is God who has mercy (11:30; cf. 9:16).

Here, however, it is necessary to remember what Paul has already said: the event that renders Israel disobedient, even as it is mercy for the Gentiles, is specific and concrete; it is the advent and announcement of Israel's Christ (9:30–10:17). That Paul has not forgotten this is evident both as he describes Israel's instrumentality vis-à-vis the salvation of the Gentiles and as he imagines the future salvation of Israel. To say that Israel's rejection or loss (ἀποβολή) occasions the reconciliation (καταλλαγή) of the world (11:15) is to interpret the scriptural ordering of rejection and election (cf. the use of Exod 9:16 in Rom 9:16-24) through the crucified and risen Christ. That sin or transgression can lead to salvation (11:11-12) is an unheard-of idea that Paul brings to his present from the saving history of Jesus: "where sin increased, grace super-abounded" (Rom 5:20). Just as the death of God's son means the reconciliation of God's enemies (Rom 5:10), so the loss of God's people means the reconciliation of the world. Similarly, Israel's salvation is described in terms that suggest a christological imagination. According to Paul's diagnosis, Israel is lost (11:15) and imprisoned in disobedience (11:32), and therefore salvation must

[50] I borrow this word from Barclay's discussion of Rom 11:11-32 in *Paul and the Gift*.

[51] The verbs of salvation that have God as the (implied) subject include ἐγκεντρίζω (11:17, 19, 23, 24), σῴζω (11:26), ἀφαιρέω (11:27), ἐλεέω (11:30, 31, 32). The one exception is that Paul is the subject of σῴζω in 11:14, but, as Wagner suggests, this is an exception that proves the rule: "[Paul] portrays himself as the *sole* active *intermediary*" ("'Not from the Jews Only,'" 426; italics added). The nouns that name Israel's salvation also point to God as the acting subject: πλήρωμα, 11:12; πρόσλημψις, 11:15.

[52] Wagner, "'Not from the Jews Only,'" 426.

mean "life from the dead" (11:15) and mercy (11:31-32). Because it is God who both breaks off and regrafts, who both loses and resurrects—because grace operates on the other side and out of divine judgment—this saving history is always hidden under the sign of its opposite. But for Paul, the life, death, and life again of Jesus, God's unconditioned gift to the ungodly, while itself foolish, scandalous, and *sub contrario* (cf. 1 Cor 1:18-25), is the one history according to which, as Bayer puts it, "one learns to spell history."[53] Rejection and resurrection, in others words, are descriptive of Israel's current situation and coming salvation only as Israel's present and future are reimagined around the rejected and resurrected Jesus. Just as Paul brings God's christological acts of justification and resurrection to the Abraham narrative in Romans 4, interpreting Abraham's reckoning of righteousness as the justification of the ungodly (4:3-5) and Abraham's age and Sarah's barrenness as conditions of deadness that require resurrection (4:17-21), so in Romans 11 Paul tells Israel's ongoing story in the shape of the crucified and risen Christ.

This suggests that while Jesus, in Romans more than in, say, Galatians, is integrated into the history of Israel as "the seed of David" (Rom 1:3), "the root of Jesse" (15:12), and the "Messiah from [Israel] according to the flesh" (9:5), the hermeneutical direction is not, in the first instance, from Israel's story to Israel's Christ; it is, rather, from Israel's Christ to Israel's story.[54] Jesus, to return to Agamben's suggestive phrase, is history's "now of legibility," the time in which the mysteries contained but kept secret in Israel's Scriptures are unveiled and given voice (cf. Rom 16:25-26). Hence, the mystery Paul discloses in Romans 11:25-27.[55] The salvation of "all Israel" will occur "as it is written" (11:26a). But as Paul's conflation of two texts from Isaiah

[53] O. Bayer, *A Contemporary in Dissent: Johann Georg Hamann as a Radical Enlightener*, trans. R. A. Harrisville and M. C. Mattes (Grand Rapids: Eerdmans, 2012), 219.

[54] For a fuller discussion of what I regard as the reciprocal yet asymmetrical relationship between Christ and Scripture, see *God, Grace, and Righteousness*, 177–226. As I say on page 178 n. 3: "Paul's 'hermeneutic,'" as J. L. Martyn remarks, "works from the previously unknown and foolish gospel of the cross to the previously known and previously misunderstood Scripture" and, as Martyn does not say, back again ("John and Paul on the Subject of Gospel and Scripture," in *Theological Issues in the Letters of Paul* [Edinburgh: T&T Clark, 1997], 221)."

[55] For the modal interpretation of καὶ οὕτως (11:26a), together with the proposal that μυστήριον refers "to one particular . . . aspect of God's plan of salvation" (i.e., Israel's salvific instrumentality), see M. Bockmuehl, *Revelation and Mystery in Ancient Judaism and Pauline Christianity*, WUNT 36 (Tübingen: J.C.B. Mohr, 1990),

indicates (59:20-21 and 29:7a LXX), the ability to read requires revelation. While Paul lifts the words "he will remove ungodliness from Jacob" (ἀποστρέψει ἀσεβείας ἀπὸ Ἰακώβ) verbatim from Isaiah as he describes the work of the "the redeemer" (ὁ ῥυόμενος; cf. 1 Thess 1:10), the context of the Isaiah text (especially 59:16-21 LXX) suggests that the coming of the redeemer "on account of Zion" (ἕνεκεν Σιων) will mean the salvation of Israel from their ungodly enemies. Paul's context by contrast, has the redeemer coming "from Zion" (ἐκ Σιων)[56] to a hardened, lost, stumbling, cut off, and disobedient Israel not in order to save them from the ungodly but to save Israel as the ungodly. The addition of Isaiah 27 confirms this. Paul, by adding Isaiah 27 to Isaiah 59, lets the prophet interpret his own promise: "this will be the covenant from me to them" (59:21a), "when I take away their sins" (27:9a).

This future echoes Israel's origin. Just as Abraham, according to Paul's reading of Genesis, was called without condition (Rom 4:10), justified though ungodly (4:5), and blessed by the forgiveness of sins (4:7-8), so Israel has a future because God's covenant is unconditioned (it is "a covenant from me" and "for them"), and because God will banish Israel's ungodliness and forgive Israel's sin. Or again: the God who called Isaac and Jacob before and irrespective of their lives and who remade Israel by mercy after the golden calf idolatry (9:7-16) will again come and re-create Israel through an unconditioned word: "I forgive you."

For Paul, however, while his reading of the past and his promise about the future rhyme, it is the present that reveals the rhyme scheme. The end will be like the beginning, but both beginning and end are legible from the middle. It is Paul's "now" that finally grounds his hope: "just as (ὥσπερ) you [Gentiles] were once disobedient to God but *now* (νῦν) receive mercy, in the same way also (οὕτως καί) [Israel] is *now* (νῦν) disobedient . . . so that they might receive mercy" (11:30-31). It is God's present-tense word of mercy to Gentiles, what Paul calls "the word of Christ," that reveals the pattern according to which God is, has been, and therefore will be "the God who has mercy"

170–75, 226. When read with the phrase ἄχρι οὗ (11:25), καὶ οὕτως unveils the divinely appointed means and the redemptive historical order of Israel's salvation.

[56] For the significance of the change from ἕνεκεν Σιων to ἐκ Σιων, see my *God, Grace, and Righteousness*, 221; cf. Wilk, *Die Bedeutung des Jesajabuches für Paulus*, 39–40; H. Hübner, *Gottes Ich und Israel: Zum Schriftgebrauch des Paulus in Römer 9–11*, FRLANT 126 (Göttingen: Vandenhoeck & Ruprecht, 1984), 115–16.

on Israel. What the call of the once disobedient Gentiles tells Paul is that Israel's current disobedience, rather than disqualifying them from God's grace, puts them in the one and only meeting place of mercy. It is at the site of sin and death that God creates righteousness and life. "Grace," in Marilynne Robinson's phrase, is an "ecstatic fire,"[57] at once reducing to ashes all hopes anchored in human worth as it kindles a hope that even disobedience and death cannot burn. As Käsemann writes, "there is hope always only for those who have no more hope."[58] And so: there is hope for Israel.

It is, then, to answer the question that opened this chapter, the history of God's creative and unconditioned mercy, revealed to Paul in the gift of Jesus and thus legible in Israel's Scriptures, that engenders "a like hope" for the future: "all Israel," disobedient though they now are, "will be saved." Naming this ground of hope, however, also hints at the answers to the implicit question about the relationship between the history of Jesus and the history of Israel and the nations that precede and follow it. As Paul's conclusion indicates, the grace revealed in the giving of Jesus underwrites Paul's hope for Israel's future because it unveils the grammar of God's history-writing word: now, then, and always—"God shut up all in disobedience in order that he might have mercy on all" (11:32).[59] History may be, to return to Hamann, "a riddle that cannot be solved"[60]—hidden under the opposite and ever beyond calculation because mercy is always unconditioned. But, to add Paul's voice to Hamann's words, "the entire riddle of [history], the impenetrable night of its terminus a quo and terminus ad quem, are dissolved by the charter of the Word [of Christ]."[61]

57 M. Robinson, *Gilead* (London: Virago, 2005), 224

58 Käsemann, *Commentary on Romans*, 303.

59 See Peter Stuhlmacher's description of Romans 11:32 as "the quintessential structural law of God's gracious work" and "history's fundamental principle" (*Revisiting Paul's Doctrine of Justification: A Challenge to the New Perspective*, trans. D. P. Bailey [Downers Grove, Ill.: IVP Academic, 2001]), 30, 71; cf. Käsemann, "Justification and Salvation History," 70, 75–76.

60 Hamann, "Socratic Memorabilia," in *Sämtliche Werke*, 2.65.

61 J. G. Hamann, "Zweifel und Einfälle" (1776), in *J. G. Hamann 1730–1788: A Study in Christian Existence*, ed. and trans. Ronald Gregor Smith (New York: Harper, 1960), 59 (my translation).

Bibliography

Abasciano, Brian J. *Paul's Use of the Old Testament in Romans 9.1-9: An Intertextual and Theological Exegesis*. LNTS 301. London: T&T Clark, 2005.

Agamben, Giorgio. *The Time That Remains: A Commentary on the Letter to the Romans*. Translated by Patricia Dailey. Stanford, Calif.: Stanford University Press, 2005.

Andersen, Wayne. *The Ara Pacis of Augustus and Mussolini*. New York: Editions Fabriart, 2005.

Arthurs, Joshua. *Excavating Modernity: The Roman Past in Fascist Italy*. Ithaca, N.Y.: Cornell University Press, 2012.

Auerbach, E. "Figura." *Istanbuler Schriften* 5, *Neue Dantestudien* (1944): 11–71.

Avemarie, F. "Israels rätselhafter Ungehorsam: Römer 10 als Anatomie eines von Gott provozierten Unglaubens." Pages 299–320 in Wilk and Wagner, *Between Gospel and Election*.

———. *Neues Testament und frührabbinisches Judentum*. WUNT 316. Tübingen: Mohr Siebeck, 2013.

Badenas, R. *Christ the End of the Law: Romans 10.4 in Pauline Perspective*. Sheffield: JSOT, 1985.

Barclay, John M. G. "Grace within and beyond Reason: Philo and Paul in Dialogue." Pages 9–21 in *Paul, Grace and Freedom: Essays in Honour of John K. Riches*. Edited by P. Middleton, A. Paddison, and K. Wenell. London: T&T Clark, 2009.

———. "'I Will Have Mercy on Whom I Have Mercy': The Golden Calf and Divine Mercy in Romans 9–11 and Second Temple Judaism." *EC* 1 (2010): 82–106.

———. *Paul and the Gift*. Grand Rapids: Eerdmans, 2015.

———. "Paul's Story: Theology as Testimony." Pages 133–56 in *Narrative Dynamics in Paul: A Critical Assessment*. Edited by Bruce W. Longenecker. Louisville, Ky.: Westminster John Knox, 2002.

———. "Unnerving Grace: Approaching Romans 9–11 from the Wisdom of Solomon." Pages 91–109 in Wilk and Wagner, *Between Gospel and Election*.

Barr, James. *Biblical Words for Time*. 2nd rev. ed. London: SCM Press, 1969.

Barrett, Charles Kingsley. *The Epistle to the Romans*. BNTC 6. Grand Rapids: Baker, 2011.

Barth, Karl. *Church Dogmatics*. Vol. 2: *The Doctrine of God, Part 2*. Edited by G. W. Bromiley and T. F. Torrance. Edinburgh: T&T Clark, 1957.

Barth, Karl. *The Epistle to the Romans*. Translated from the 6th edition by E. C. Hoskyns. Oxford: Oxford University Press, 1933.

Bauckham, Richard J. *Jesus and the God of Israel: God Crucified and Other Studies on the New Testament's Christology of Divine Identity*. Grand Rapids: Eerdmans, 2008.

Bayer, O. *A Contemporary in Dissent: Johann Georg Hamann as a Radical Enlightener*. Translated by R. A. Harrisville and M. C. Mattes. Grand Rapids: Eerdmans, 2012.

———. *Theology the Lutheran Way*. Edited and translated by Jeffrey G. Silcock and Mark C. Mattes. Lutheran Quarterly Books. Grand Rapids: Eerdmans, 2007.

Bell, Richard. *The Irrevocable Call of God: An Inquiry into Paul's Theology of Israel*. WUNT 184. Tübingen: Mohr Siebeck, 2005.

———. *Provoked to Jealousy: The Origin and Purpose of the Jealousy Motif in Romans 9–11*. WUNT 63. Tübingen: Mohr Siebeck, 1994.

Belli, Filippo. *Argumentation and the Use of Scripture in Romans 9–11*. AnBib 183. Rome: Gregorian and Biblical Press, 2010.

Benjamin, Walter. "Theses on the Philosophy of History." Pages 253–64 in *Illuminations: Essays and Reflections*. Edited by H. Arendt. Translated by H. Eiland and K. McLaughlin. Cambridge, Mass.: Harvard University Press, 1999. Original edition: Translated by H. Zohn. New York: Schocken Books, 1968.

Bockmuehl, Markus. *Revelation and Mystery in Ancient Judaism and Pauline Christianity*. WUNT 236. Tübingen: J.C.B. Mohr, 1990.

Brandenburger, E. "Paulinische Schriftauslegung in der Kontroverse um das Verheißungswort Gottes (Röm 9)." *ZTK* 82 (1985): 1–47.

Bultmann, Rudolf. "αἰσχύνω κτλ." Page 189 in vol. 1 of *Theological Dictionary of the New Testament*. Edited by G. Kittel. Translated by G. W. Bromiley. Grand Rapids: Eerdmans, 1964.

Burkitt, F. C. "On Romans ix 5 and Mark xiv 61." *JTS* 5 (1904): 451–55.

Byrne, Brendan. *"Sons of God"—"Seeds of Abraham": A Study of the Idea of the Sonship of God of All Christians in Paul against the Jewish Background*. AnBib 83. Rome: Editrice Pontificio Istituto Biblico, 1979.

Caird, G. B. *Principalities and Powers: A Study in Pauline Theology*. Chancellor's Lectures for 1954 at Queen's University, Kingston, Ontario. Oxford: Clarendon, 1956.

Calvin, John. "Acts 14–28 and Romans 1–6." Page 377 in vol. 19 of *Calvin's Commentaries*. Translated by J. Owen. Grand Rapids: Baker, 2003.

Campbell, William S. "The Freedom and Faithfulness of God in Relation to Israel." *JSNT* 13 (1981): 27–45.

Capes, David B. *Old Testament Yahweh Texts in Paul's Christology*. Tübingen: Mohr, 1992.

Carraway, George. *Christ Is God over All: Romans 9:5 in the Context of Romans 9–11*. LNTS 489. New York: Bloomsbury, 2013.

Castriota, David. *The Ara Pacis Augustae and the Imagery of Abundance in Later Greek and Early Roman Imperial Art*. Princeton, N.J.: Princeton University Press, 1995.

Chester, S. J. *Conversion at Corinth: Perspectives on Conversion in Paul's Theology and the Corinthian Church*. SNTW. London: T&T Clark, 2003.

Clarke, John. *Art in the Lives of Ordinary Romans: Visual Representation and Non-elite Viewers in Italy, 100 B.C.–A.D. 315*. Joan Palevsky Books in Classical Studies. Berkeley: University of California Press, 2006.

Conlin, Diane Atnally. *The Artists of the Ara Pacis: The Process of Hellenization in Roman Relief Sculpture*. Chapel Hill: University of North Carolina Press, 1997.

Cosgrove, Charles. *Elusive Israel: The Puzzle of Election in Romans*. Louisville, Ky.: Westminster John Knox, 1997.

Cranfield, C. E. B. *A Critical and Exegetical Commentary on the Epistle to the Romans*. 2 vols. ICC. Edinburgh: T&T Clark, 1979.

———. "Some Comments on Professor J. D. G. Dunn's *Christology in the Making* with Special Reference to the Evidence of the Epistle to the Romans." Pages 267–80 in *The Glory of Christ in the New Testament: Studies in Christology in Memory of George Bradford Caird*. Edited by L. D. Hurst and N. T. Wright. Oxford: Clarendon, 1987.

Cranford, Michael. "Election and Ethnicity: Paul's View of Israel in Romans 9.1-13." *JSNT* 50 (1993): 27–41.

Crossan, John Dominic, and Jonathan Reed. *In Search of Paul: How Jesus's Apostle Opposed Rome's Empire with God's Kingdom. A New Vision of Paul's Words & World*. San Francisco: Harper, 2004.

Cullmann, Oscar. *Christ and Time: The Primitive Christian Conception of Time and History*. Translated by F. V. Filson. Philadelphia: Westminster, 1950.

———. *Salvation in History*. Translated by S. G. Sowers. New York: Harper & Row, 1967.

Dahl, N. A. *Studies in Paul: Theology for the Early Christian Mission*. Minneapolis: Augsburg, 1977.

Dawson, J. D. *Christian Figural Reading and the Fashioning of Identity*. Berkeley: University of California Press, 2002.

de Boer, Martinus. *Galatians: A Commentary*. Louisville, Ky.: Westminster John Knox, 2011.

———. "Paul and Jewish Apocalyptic Eschatology." Pages 169–90 in *Apocalyptic and the New Testament: Essays in Honor of J. Louis Martyn*. Edited by J. Marcus and M. L. Soards. Sheffield: JSOT, 1989.

Deissmann, Adolf. *Paul, A Study in Social and Religious History*. Translated by William E. Wilson. London: Hodder & Stoughton, 1926.

Donaldson, Terence. *Paul and the Gentiles: Remapping the Apostle's Convictional World*. Minneapolis: Fortress, 1997.

———. "'Riches for the Gentiles' (Romans 11:12): Israel's Rejection and Paul's Gentile Mission." *JBL* 112 (1993): 81–98.

Dunn, J. D. G. *Christology in the Making: An Inquiry into the Origins of the Doctrine of Incarnation*. London: SCM Press, 1980.

———. *Romans*. 2 vols. WBC 38. Dallas: Word, 1988.

———. *The Theology of Paul the Apostle*. Grand Rapids: Eerdmans, 1998.

Eastman, Susan Grove. "Israel and the Mercy of God: A Re-reading of Galatians 6:16 and Romans 9–11." *NTS* 56 (2010): 367–95.

Elliott, Neil. *The Arrogance of Nations: Reading Romans in the Shadow of Empire*. Paul in Critical Contexts. Minneapolis: Fortress, 2008.

Esler, Philip F. "Ancient Oleiculture and Ethnic Differentiation: The Meaning of the Olive-Tree Image in Romans 11." *JSNT* 26 (2003): 103–24.

Fee, Gordon. *The First Epistle to the Corinthians*. NICNT. Grand Rapids: Eerdmans, 1987.

———. *Pauline Christology: An Exegetical-Theological Study*. Peabody, Mass.: Hendrickson, 2007.

Feldmeier, R. "Vater und Töpfer? Zur Identität Gottes im Römerbrief." Pages 377–90 in Wilk and Wagner, *Between Gospel and Election*.

Fitzmyer, Joseph A. *Romans*. AB 33. New York: Doubleday, 1993.

Flebbe, Jochen. *Solus Deus: Untersuchungen zur Rede von Gott im Brief des Paulus an die Römer*. BZNW 158. Berlin: Walter de Gruyter, 2008.

Flower, Harriet I. *Ancestral Masks and Aristocratic Power in Roman Culture*. Oxford: Clarendon, 1996.

Furnish, Victor. *II Corinthians*. AB 32A. New York: Doubleday, 1984.

Gager, John G. *The Origins of Anti-Semitism: Attitudes towards Judaism in Pagan and Christian Antiquity*. New York: Oxford University Press, 1983.

———. *Who Made Christianity? The Jewish Lives of the Apostle Paul*. American Lectures on the History of Religions. New York: Columbia University Press, 2015.

Gaston, Lloyd. "Israel's Enemies in Pauline Theology." *NTS* 28 (1982): 400–423.

———. *Paul and the Torah*. Vancouver: University of British Columbia Press, 1987.

Gathercole, Simon J. *Defending Substitution: An Essay on Atonement in Paul*. Grand Rapids: Baker, 2015.

———. "Pauline Christology." Pages 172–87 in *The Blackwell Companion to Paul*. Edited by S. Westerholm. Oxford: Blackwell, 2011.

———. "Torah, Life and Salvation: Leviticus 18:5 in Early Judaism and the New Testament." Pages 131–50 in *From Prophecy to Testament: The Function of the Old Testament in the New*. Edited by C. A. Evans and J. A. Sanders. Peabody, Mass.: Hendrickson, 2004.

Gaventa, Beverly Roberts. "The Cosmic Power of Sin in Paul's Letter to the Romans: Toward a Widescreen Version." *Int* 58, no. 3 (2004): 229–40.

———. "Interpreting the Death of Jesus Apocalyptically." Pages 125–45 in *Jesus and Paul Reconnected: Fresh Pathways in an Old Debate*. Edited by Todd D. Still. Grand Rapids: Eerdmans, 2007.

———. "On the Calling-Into-Being of Israel: Romans 9:6-29." Pages 255–69 in Wilk and Wagner, *Between Gospel and Election*.

Georgi, Dieter. *Theocracy in Paul's Praxis and Theology*. Translated by David E. Green. Minneapolis: Fortress, 1991.

Given, Mark. *Paul's True Rhetoric: Ambiguity, Cunning, and Deception in Greece and Rome*. Emory Studies in Early Christianity 7. Harrisburg, Pa.: Trinity International, 2001.

Güttgemanns, Erhard. *Studia Linguistica Neotestamentica*. BEvT 60. Munich: Chr. Kaiser Verlag, 1973.

Haacker, Klaus. *Der Brief des Paulus an die Römer*. 4th ed. THKNT 6. Leipzig: Evangelische Verlagsanstalt, 2012.

Hahn, F. *Theologie des Neuen Testament*. 2 vols. Tübingen: Mohr Siebeck, 2005.

Hamann, Johann. *Hamann: Writings on Philosophy and Language*. Edited by K. Haynes. Cambridge: Cambridge University Press, 2007.

———. *J. G. Hamann 1730–1788: A Study in Christian Existence*. Edited and translated by Ronald Gregor Smith. New York: Harper, 1960.

———. *Sämtliche Werke*. 6 vols. Edited by J. Nadler. Vienna: Herder, 1949–1957.

Harink, Douglas. "Time and Politics in Four Commentaries on Romans." Pages 282–312 in *Paul, Philosophy and the Theopolitical Vision*. Edited by Douglas Harink. Eugene, Ore.: Cascade, 2010.

Harrill, J. Albert. *Paul the Apostle: His Life and Legacy in their Roman Context*. New York: Cambridge University Press, 2012.

Hays, Richard B. "Christ Prays the Psalms: Paul's Use of an Early Christian Exegetical Convention." Pages 122–36 in *The Future of Christology: Essays in Honor of Leander E. Keck*. Edited by A. J. Malherbe and W. A. Meeks. Minneapolis: Fortress, 1993.

———. *Echoes of Scripture in the Letters of Paul*. New Haven, Conn.: Yale University Press, 1989.

———. "Justification." Pages 1129–33 in vol. 3 of *The Anchor Bible Dictionary*. Edited by David Noel Freedman. New York: Doubleday, 1992.

Heil, John Paul. "From Remnant to Seed of Hope for Israel: Romans 9:27-29." *CBQ* 64 (2002): 703–20.

Hekster, Olivier. *Emperors and Ancestors: Roman Rulers and the Constraints of Tradition*. Oxford Studies in Ancient Culture and Representation. New York: Oxford University Press, 2015.

Hodge, Caroline Johnson. *If Sons, Then Heirs: A Study of Kinship and Ethnicity in the Letters of Paul*. New York: Oxford University Press, 2007.

———. "Olive Trees and Ethnicities, Judeans and Gentiles in Rom 11.17-24," Pages 77–89 in *Christians as a Religious Minority in a Multicultural City: Modes of Interaction and Identity-Formation in Early Imperial Rome*. Edited by Jürgen Zangenberg and Michael Labahn. JSNTSup 243. New York: T&T Clark, 2004.

Hofius, Otfried. *Paulusstudien*. WUNT 51. Tübingen: J.C.B. Mohr, 1989.

Horsley, Richard A., ed. *Paul and Empire: Religion and Power in Roman Imperial Society*. Harrisburg, Pa.: Trinity International, 1998.

Hübner, Hans. *Gottes Ich und Israel: Zum Schriftgebrauch des Paulus in Römer 9–11*. FRLANT 136. Göttingen: Vandenhoeck & Ruprecht, 1984.

Jewett, Robert. *Romans*. Hermeneia. Minneapolis: Fortress, 2007.

Johnson, E. E. "Romans 9–11: The Faithfulness and Impartiality of God." Pages 211–39 in *Romans*. Vol. 3 of *Pauline Theology*. Edited by D. M. Hay and E. E. Johnson. Minneapolis: Fortress, 1995.

Kampen, Natalie Boymel. *Family Fictions in Roman Art*. New York: Cambridge University Press, 2009.

Käsemann, Ernst. *Commentary on Romans*. Translated by G. W. Bromiley. Grand Rapids: Eerdmans, 1980.

———. *New Testament Questions of Today*. London: SCM Press, 1969.

———. *Perspectives on Paul*. Philadelphia: Fortress, 1971.

Keck, Leander. "Christology, Soteriology, and the Praise of God." Pages 85–97 in *The Conversation Continues: Studies in Paul and John in Honor of J. Louis Martyn*. Edited by R. T. Fortna and Beverly Roberts Gaventa. Nashville: Abingdon, 1990.

———. *Romans*. ANTC. Nashville: Abingdon, 2005.

Kennedy, George. *A New History of Classical Rhetoric*. Princeton, N.J.: Princeton University Press, 1994.

Khalil, Jack. "Translating Rom 9:7a: For an Accurate Understanding of a Difficult Verse." Pages 691–97 in Schnelle, *Letter to the Romans*.

Kirk, J. R. D. "Why Does the Deliverer Come ἐκ Σιών (Rom 11.26)?" *JSNT* 33 (2010): 81–99.

Klumbies, Paul-Gerhard. "Israels Vorzüge und das Evangelium von der Gottesgerechtigkeit in Römer 9–11." *WuD.NF* 18 (1985): 135–57.

Kotansky, Roy D. "A Note on Romans 9:6: *ho logos tou theou* as the Proclamation of the Gospel." *StBT* 7 (1977): 24–30.

Kraus, Wolfgang. *Das Volk Gottes: Zur Grundlegung der Ekklesiologie bei Paulus*. WUNT 85. Tübingen: Mohr Siebeck, 1996.

Kuttner, Ann L. *Dynasty and Empire in the Age of Augustus: The Case of the Boscoreale Cups*. Berkeley: University of California Press, 1995.

Lambrecht, Jan. *Pauline Studies*. Leuven: Peeters, 1994.

Lamp, Kathleen S. *A City of Marble: The Rhetoric of Augustan Rome*. Studies in Rhetoric/Communication. Columbia: University of South Carolina Press, 2013.

Lattey, C. "The Codex Ephraemi Rescriptus on Romans ix 5." *ExpTim* 35, no. 1 (1923): 42–43.

———. "The Codex Vaticanus on Romans ix 5." *ExpTim* 34, no. 7 (1923): 331.

Lazzaro, Claudia. "Forging a Visible Fascist Nation: Strategies for Fusing Past and Present." Pages 13–31 in *Donatello among the Blackshirts: History and Modernity in the Visual Culture of Fascist Italy*. Edited by Claudia Lazzaro and Roger J. Crum. Ithaca, N.Y.: Cornell University Press, 2005.

Lessing, G. E. *Lessing's Theological Writings*. Translated by H. Chadwick. Stanford, Calif.: Stanford University Press, 1957.

Levenson, Jon. *The Death and Resurrection of the Beloved Son*. New Haven, Conn.: Yale University Press, 1993.

Lietzmann, Hans. *An die Römer*. 3rd ed. HNT 8. Tübingen: Mohr Siebeck, 1928.

Lincoln, Bruce. *Between History and Myth: Stories of Harold Fairhair and the Founding of the State*. Chicago: University of Chicago Press, 2014.

Linebaugh, Jonathan. *God, Grace, and Righteousness in Wisdom of Solomon and Paul's Letter to the Romans: Texts in Conversation*. NovTSup 152. Leiden: Brill, 2013.

———. "Rational or Radical: Origen on Romans 9:10-14." *Studia Patristica* 52 (2011): 63–69.

Lohse, E. *Der Brief an die Römer*. KEK 4. Göttingen: Vandenhoek & Ruprecht, 2003.

Longenecker, Bruce W. "Different Answers to Different Issues: Israel, the Gentiles and Salvation History in Romans 9–11." *JSNT* 36 (1989): 95–123.

Lopez, Davina C. *Apostle to the Conquered: Reimagining Paul's Mission*. Paul in Critical Contexts. Minneapolis: Fortress, 2008.

Lopez, Davina C., and Todd Penner. "Paul and Politics." In *The Oxford Handbook of Pauline Studies*. Edited by R. Barry Matlock. New York: Oxford University Press, forthcoming.

L'Orange, Hans Peter. *The Roman Empire: Art Forms and Civic Life*. New York: Rizzoli, 1985.

Lowe, Dunstan. "The Symbolic Value of Grafting in Ancient Rome." *TAPA* 140 (2010): 461–88.

Lüdemann, Gerd. "The Relationship of Biblical Studies to the History of Religions School, with Reference to the Scientific Study of Religion." *Toronto Journal of Theology* 24, no. 2 (2008): 171–81.

Marchal, Joseph A. *The Politics of Heaven: Women, Gender, and Empire in the Study of Paul*. Paul in Critical Contexts. Minneapolis: Fortress, 2008.

Marshall, I. H. *The Pastoral Epistles*. ICC. London: T&T Clark, 1999.

Martyn, J. Louis. *Galatians*. New York: Doubleday, 1997.

———. *Theological Issues in the Letters of Paul*. Edinburgh: T&T Clark, 1997.

Mellor, Ronald. *Thea Rhōmē: The Worship of the Goddess Roma in the Greek World*. Göttingen: Vanderhoeck & Ruprecht, 1975.

Mendelssohn, Moses. *Jerusalem oder über religiöse Macht und Judentum*. Berlin: Friedrich Maurer, 1783.

Metzger, Bruce M. "The Punctuation of Romans 9:5." Pages 95–112 in *Christ and Spirit in the New Testament: Studies in Honour of Charles Francis Digby Moule*. Edited by B. Lindars and S. S. Smalley. Cambridge: Cambridge University Press, 1973.

Michel, Otto. *Der Brief an die Römer*. 5th ed. KEK 4. Göttingen: Vandenhoeck & Ruprecht, 1978.

Moberly, W. *At the Mountain of God: Story and Theology in Exodus 32–34*. JSOTSup 22. Sheffield: JSOT, 1983.

Moo, Douglas J. *The Epistle to the Romans*. NICNT. Grand Rapids: Eerdmans, 1996.

Morris, Leon. *The Epistle to the Romans*. Grand Rapids: Eerdmans, 1988.

Munck, Johannes. *Christ and Israel*. Philadelphia: Fortress, 1967.

Mussner, F. *Traktat über die Juden*. Göttingen: Vandenhoeck & Ruprecht, 2009 (1979).

Nanos, Mark D. "'Broken Branches': A Pauline Metaphor Gone Awry? (Romans 11:11-24)." Pages 339–76 in Wilk and Wagner, *Between Gospel and Election*.

———. *The Mystery of Romans: The Jewish Context of Paul's Letter*. Minneapolis: Fortress, 1996.

Nicolet, Claude. *Space, Geography, and Politics in the Early Roman Empire*. Jerome Lectures 19. Ann Arbor: University of Michigan Press, 1991.

Noreña, Carlos. *Imperial Ideals in the Roman West: Representation, Circulation, Power*. New York: Cambridge University Press, 2011.

Oropeza, Brisio J. "Paul and Theodicy: Intertextual Thoughts on God's Justice and Faithfulness to Israel in Romans 9–11." *NTS* 53 (2007): 57–80.

Painter, Borden W. *Mussolini's Rome: Rebuilding the Eternal City*. Italian and Italian-American Studies. New York: Palgrave Macmillan, 2007.

Penner, Todd, and Davina C. Lopez. *De-introducing the New Testament: Texts, Worlds, Methods, Stories*. Hoboken, N.J.: Wiley-Blackwell, 2015.

———. "Rhetorical Approaches: Introducing the Art of Persuasion in Paul and Pauline Studies." Pages 33–52 in *Studying Paul's Letters: Contemporary Perspectives and Approaches*. Edited by Joseph A. Marchal. Minneapolis: Fortress, 2012.

Piper, John. *The Justification of God: An Exegetical Study of Romans 9:1-23*. Grand Rapids: Baker, 1983.

Pollini, John. *From Republic to Empire: Rhetoric, Religion, and Power in the Visual Culture of Ancient Rome*. Oklahoma Series in Classical Culture 48. Norman: University of Oklahoma Press, 2012.

———. "The Gemma Augustea: Ideology, Rhetorical Imagery, and the Creation of a Dynastic Narrative." Pages 258–98 in *Narrative and Event in Ancient Art*. Edited by Peter Holliday. New York: Cambridge University Press, 1993.

Räisänen, Heikki. "Paul, God, and Israel: Romans 9–11 in Recent Research." Pages 178–206 in *The Social World of Formative Christianity and Judaism: Festschrift for H. C. Kee*. Edited by J. Neusner et al. Philadelphia: Fortress, 1988.

———. "Römer 9–11: Analysc eines geistigen Ringens." *ANRW* 2.25.4 (1987): 2891–939.

———. "Torn between Two Loyalties: Romans 9–11 and Paul's Conflicting Convictions." Pages 19–39 in *The Nordic Paul: Finnish Approaches to Pauline Theology*. Edited by L. Aejmelaeus and A. Mustakalio. LNTS 374. London: T&T Clark, 2008.

Ramsay, Sir William Mitchell. *Pauline and Other Studies in Early Christian History*. New York: A.C. Armstrong, 1906.

Rowe, C. Kavin. "Romans 10:13: What Is the Name of the Lord?" *HBT* 22 (2000): 135–73.

Sanday, W., and A. C. Headlam. *A Critical and Exegetical Commentary on the Epistle to the Romans*. 5th ed. ICC. Edinburgh: T&T Clark, 1902.

Sanders, E. P. "Comparing Christianity and Judaism: An Academic Autobiography." Pages 11–41 in *Redefining First-Century Jewish and Christian Identities: Essays in Honor of Ed Parish Sanders*. Edited by Fabian E. Udoh, with Susannah Heschel, Mark Chancey, and Gregory Tatum. Christianity and Judaism in Antiquity. South Bend, Ind.: University of Notre Dame Press, 2008.

———. *Paul, the Law and the Jewish People*. Philadelphia: Fortress, 1983.

———. *Paul and Palestinian Judaism: A Comparison of Patterns of Religion*. Philadelphia: Fortress, 1977.

Sänger, Dieter. *Die Verkündigung des Gekreuzigten und Israel*. WUNT 75. Tübingen: Mohr Siebeck, 1994.

Sass, Gerhard. *Leben aus den Verheißungen: Traditionsgeschichtliche und biblisch-theologische Untersuchungen zur Rede von Gottes Verheißungen im Frühjudentum und beim Apostel Paulus*. FRLANT 165. Göttingen: Vandenhoeck & Ruprecht, 1995.

Schlatter, Adolf. *Gottes Gerechtigkeit: Ein Kommentar zum Römerbrief*. Stuttgart: Calwer Vereinsbuchhandlung, 1935.

Schlier, Heinrich. *Der Römerbrief*. 2nd ed. HThKNT 6. Freiburg: Herder, 1977.

Schnelle, Udo. *Apostle Paul: His Life and Theology*. Translated by M. E. Boring. Grand Rapids: Baker, 2005.

———, ed. *The Letter to the Romans*. BETL 226. Leuven: Uitgeverij Peeters, 2009.

Schreiner, Thomas R. *Romans*. BECNT. Grand Rapids: Baker, 1998.

Siegert, Folker. *Argumentation bei Paulus, gezeigt an Röm 9–11*. WUNT 34. Tübingen: Mohr Siebeck, 1985.

Simon, Erika. *Ara Pacis Augustae*. Greenwich, Conn.: Graphic Society, 1968.

Smith, R. R. R. *The Marble Reliefs from the Julio-Claudian Sebasteion*. Aphrodisias 6. Mainz: Verlag Philipp von Zabern, 2013.

Spieckermann, Hermann. *Gottes Liebe zu Israel*. FAT 33. Tübingen: Mohr Siebeck, 2004.

Sprinkle, P. M. *Law and Life: The Interpretation of Leviticus 18:5 in Early Judaism and Paul*. WUNT 241. Tübingen: Mohr Siebeck, 2008.

Stählin, G. "Zum Gebrauch von Beteuerungsformeln im Neuen Testament." *NovT* 5 (1962): 115–43.

Stanley, C. D. "'The Redeemer Will Come ἐκ Σιών': Romans 11:26-27 Revisited." Pages 118–42 in *Paul and the Scriptures of Israel*. Edited by Craig A. Evans and J. A. Sanders. JSNTSup. Sheffield: Sheffield Academic, 1993.

Stendahl, Krister. *Final Account: Paul's Letter to the Romans*. Minneapolis: Fortress, 1995.

Stowers, S. *A Rereading of Romans: Justice, Jews, and Gentiles*. New Haven, Conn.: Yale University Press, 1994.

Stuhlmacher, Peter. *Revisiting Paul's Doctrine of Justification: A Challenge to the New Perspective*. Translated by D. P. Bailey. Downers Grove, Ill.: IVP Academic, 2001.

Theobald, Michael. *Studien zum Römerbrief*. WUNT 136. Tübingen: Mohr Siebeck, 2001.

———. "Unterschiedliche Gottesbilder in Röm 9–11?" Pages 135–77 in Schnelle, *Letter to the Romans*.

Torelli, Mario. *Typology and Structure of Roman Historical Reliefs*. Jerome Lectures 14. Ann Arbor: University of Michigan Press, 1982.

Wagner, J. Ross. "The Christ, Servant of Jew and Gentile: A Fresh Approach to Romans 15:8-9." *JBL* 116, no. 3 (1997): 473–85.

———. *Heralds of the Good News: Isaiah and Paul in Concert in the Letter to the Romans*. NovTSup 101. Leiden: Brill, 2002.

———. "'Not from the Jews Only, but Also from the Gentiles': Mercy to the Nations in Romans 9–11." Pages 417–31 in Wilk and Wagner, *Between Gospel and Election*.

Watson, Francis. *Paul and the Hermeneutics of Faith*. London: T&T Clark, 2004.

———. *Paul, Judaism, and the Gentiles: Beyond the New Perspective*. Grand Rapids: Eerdmans, 2007.

Westerholm, Stephen. "Paul and the Law in Romans 9–11." Pages 215–37 in *Paul and the Mosaic Law*. Edited by J. D. G. Dunn. Grand Rapids: Eerdmans, 2001 (1996).

———. *Perspectives Old and New on Paul: The "Lutheran" Paul and His Critics*. Grand Rapids: Eerdmans, 2003.

Wilckens, Ulrich. *Der Brief an die Römer*. 3 vols. EKKNT 6. Zürich: Benziger Verlag, 1978–1982.

Wilk, Florian. *Die Bedeutung des Jesajabuches für Paulus*. FRLANT 179. Göttingen: Vandenhoeck & Ruprecht, 1998.

———. "Rahmen und Aufbau von Römer 9–11." Pages 227–53 in Wilk and Wagner, *Between Gospel and Election*.

Wilk, Florian, and J. Ross Wagner, eds. *Between Gospel and Election: Explorations in the Interpretation of Romans 9–11*. WUNT 257. Tübingen: Mohr Siebeck, 2010.

Wolter, Michael. "Das Israelproblem nach Gal 4:21-31 und Röm 9–11." *ZTK* 107 (2010): 1–30.

———. *Paul: An Outline of His Theology*. Waco, Tex.: Baylor University Press, 2015.

———. *Paulus: Ein Grundriss seiner Theologie*. Neukirchen: Neukirchener Verlag, 2011.

Wolterstorff, Nicholas. *Divine Discourse: Philosophical Reflections on the Claim That God Speaks*. Cambridge: Cambridge University Press, 1995.

Wright, N. T. *The Climax of the Covenant: Christ and the Law in Pauline Theology*. Edinburgh: T&T Clark, 1991.

———. "The Letter to the Romans." Pages 620–99 in vol. 2 of *The New Interpreter's Bible*. Edited by Leander E. Keck. Nashville: Abingdon, 2002.

———. *Paul and the Faithfulness of God*. 2 vols. Minneapolis: Fortress, 2013.

———. *Paul: In Fresh Perspective*. Minneapolis: Fortress, 2005.

Yinger, Kent. *The New Perspective on Paul: An Introduction*. Eugene, Ore.: Wipf & Stock, 2011.

Zahl, P. F. M. *Die Rechtfertigungslehre Ernst Käsemann*. Stuttgart: Calwer, 1996.

Zeller, Dieter. *Der Brief an die Römer*. RNT. Regensburg: Friedrich Pustet, 1985.

———. *Juden und Heiden in der Mission des Paulus: Studien zum Römerbrief*. Stuttgart: Verlag Katholisches Bibelwerk, 1976 (1973).

Zetterholm, Magnus. *Approaches to Paul: A Student's Guide*. Minneapolis: Fortress, 2008.

Contributors

SIMON GATHERCOLE is Reader in New Testament at the University of Cambridge, and Fellow and Director of Studies in Theology at Fitzwilliam College.

L. ANN JERVIS is Professor of New Testament at Wycliffe College, University of Toronto.

JONATHAN A. LINEBAUGH is Lecturer in New Testament Studies at the Faculty of Divinity, University of Cambridge.

DAVINA C. LOPEZ is Professor of Religious Studies at Eckerd College in St. Petersburg, Florida.

J. ROSS WAGNER is Associate Professor of New Testament and Director of the Th.D. Program at Duke Divinity School.

MICHAEL WOLTER is Professor Emeritus of New Testament at the Faculty of Protestant Theology at the University of Bonn, and Honorary Professor at the Theological Faculty, University of Pretoria.

Index of Scripture and Ancient Sources

II. Jewish Sources

III. Non-Canonical Early Christian Writings